Praise for Books by Douglas A. Gray

The Complete Canadian Small Business Guide (with Diana L. Gray)

"This guide is truly a gold mine . . . taps into the authors' extensive expertise . . . an encyclopedia compendium . . . the bible of Canadian small business."

Profit Magazine

"I can say with absolute certainty that this guide is *the best*. . . . It is well organized, written in a very informative way and at the right level of detail. . . . The samples, checklists, glossary, and sources of other information can best be described as exemplary. Just a great piece of work . . . recommended to everyone I deal with."

Steve Guerin, Former Project Manager
Office of Research and Innovation
Ryerson Polytechnical University, Toronto

"Thorough and wide-ranging . . . bursts with practical tips and explanations."

Vancouver Sun

"Excellent . . . geared especially to Canadians, unlike most available small business guides . . . and fills the vacuum."

Financial Times

"If you're thinking of launching your own business, or if you want to pick up invaluable tips on running the one you already own, this Canadian book on small business is a terrific resource tool."

This Week in Business, Montreal

"The strength of the book is its attention to the practical needs of small business . . . provides a board overview of 18 major topic areas. . . . Full of numerous "street-smart" tips on how to successfully open and operate a business. . . . Contains a plethora of "how-to" features and useful resource information."

Ottawa Citizen

"Detailed, very informative, scrupulously objective as well as being written in a style that is refreshingly clear of jargon. . . . This one is a 'must buy.' "

B.C. Business

Home Inc.: The Canadian Home-Based Business Guide (with Diana L. Gray)

"Outstanding . . . peppered with practical no-nonsense tips . . . invaluable information throughout."
Calgary Herald

"Should be required reading for all potential home-basers . . . authoritative, current and comprehensive."

Edmonton Journal

"An absolute necessity for your bookshelf . . . crammed with useful information . . . will pay for itself in short order."

Victoria Times-Colonist

Making Money in Real Estate: The Canadian Residential Investment Guide

Mortgages Made Easy: The Canadian Guide to Home Financing

Home Buying Made Easy: The Canadian Guide to Purchasing a Newly-Built or Pre-Owned Home

Condo Buying Made Easy: The Canadian Guide to Apartment and Townhouse Condos, Co-ops and Timeshares

"Gray delivers the goods. It is all-Canadian, and not a retread book full of tips that are worthless north of the U.S. border. It's chock full of practical streetsmart strategies and advice, pitfalls to avoid, samples, what-to-look-out-for checklists and information sources. . . . the information that Gray passes along is invaluable, thorough and eminently usable. . . . the book has an easy style to it that is almost conversational."

Business In Vancouver

"Gray's latest endeavour is a good educational tool . . . no legalese here, just some good ol' street level English that explains—mostly for the benefit of novices—all the real and perceived complexities of mortgages."

Calgary Herald

"The prolific output of real-estate and financial books establishes Gray as a Canadian voice . . . provides consumer insights into securing the best deal and avoiding the pitfalls. Gray's legal background has given him valuable insights."

Edmonton Journal

"Author knows what he is talking about . . . full of street-smarts and practical advice."

Halifax Chronicle-Herald

Risk-Free Retirement: The Complete Canadian Planning Guide (with Tom Delaney, Graham Cunningham, Les Solomon, and Dr. Des Dwyer)

"This book is a classic . . . will be invaluable for years to come. . . . it is arguably the most comprehensive guide to retirement planning in Canada today."

Vancouver Sun

Raising Money: The Canadian Guide to Successful Business Financing (with Brian Nattrass)

"The authors have combined their formidable talents to produce what may be *the* definitive work on raising money in the Canadian marketplace . . . written in plain language, with a user-friendly question and answer format, and contains invaluable checklists, appendices and information sources . . . a definite keeper for potential and practising entrepreneurs alike . . . "

Canadian Business Franchise

The Complete Canadian Franchise Guide (with Norma Friend)

"This book tells it like it is, a realistic look at franchising and what it takes to be successful. The information provided is clear, concise, practical and easy to apply. . . ."

Richard B. Cunningham
President, Canadian Franchise Association and
Co-Chair, World Franchise Council

The Canadian Snowbird Guide

The Canadian Snowbird Guide

Everything you need to know about living part-time in the U.S.A.

Douglas A. Gray

McGRAW-HILL RYERSON LIMITED

Toronto   New York   London   Sydney   Mexico
Johannesburg   Panama   Düsseldorf   Singapore   Sao Paulo
Kuala Lumpur   New Delhi

The Canadian Snowbird Guide

Copyright © 1995 Douglas A. Gray. All rights reserved. No part of this publication may be reproduced, stored in a data base or retrieval system, or transmitted, in any form or by any means, electronic, mechanical, photocopying, recording, or otherwise, without the prior written permission of the publisher.

The material in this publication is provided for information purposes only. Laws, regulations, and procedures are constantly changing, and the examples given are intended to be general guidelines only. This book is sold with the understanding that neither the author nor the publisher is engaged in rendering professional advice. It is recommended that legal, accounting, tax, and other advice or assistance be obtained before acting on any information contained in this book. Personal services of a competent professional should be sought.

The author, publisher, and all others directly or indirectly involved with this publication do not assume any responsibility or liability, direct or indirect, to any party for any loss or damage by errors or omissions, regardless of the cause, as a consequence of using this publication, nor accept any contractual, tortious, or other form of liability for the publication's contents or any consequences arising from its use.

First published in 1995 by
McGraw-Hill Ryerson Ltd.
300 Water Street
Whitby, Ontario
L1N 9B6

Canadian Cataloguing in Publication Data

Gray, Douglas A.
    The Canadian snowbird guide

ISBN 0-07-551737-X

1. Retirees – Canada – Finance, Personal.
2. Canadians – United States – Finance. Personal.
3. Retirement, Places of – United States – Handbooks, manuals, etc.   4. Retirement – Canada – Handbooks, manuals, etc.   5. Retirement – United States – Handbooks, manuals, etc.   I. Title.

HG179.G73 1995   332.024'0696   C95-931501-2

Publisher: Joan Homewood
Production Coordinator: Yolanda Pigden
Cover Design: Steve Eby
Page Makeup: McGraphics Desktop Publishing
Copy Editor: Nancy Flight

Contents

Acknowledgements

I am indebted to many individuals, too numerous to mention, who have given generously of their time and expertise in the preparation of this book. I am also grateful for the helpful assistance given to me by various federal, provincial, and state governments, medical insurance companies, financial planning and seniors' associations, and tax experts and authorities. I would like to thank John Budd, chartered accountant and tax and estate planning expert with Deloitte and Touche in Toronto, for his kind assistance in reviewing key parts of Chapter 6, "Tax Issues and Options."

In particular, I would like to thank the Go Camping America Committee and Christine Morrison for their permission to use material from their excellent publications, including the camping vacation planner, as briefly discussed in parts of Chapter 4 and shown in Appendix A, items 32–43. I would also like to express my appreciation to the International Association for Financial Planning for permission to use some of the information from their customer brochure "Selecting a Financial Planner" in Chapter 8.

I would also like to thank Leo and Arlene Hevey, of Belleville, Ontario, for their enthusiastic example of how rewarding the Snowbird lifestyle can be. They have been most helpful with feedback and suggestions on the issues and concerns of being a part-time resident in the United States. As their guest on numerous visits to the United States over the years, I have shared first-hand their activities, pleasures, friendships, and rejuvenating experiences as Canadian Snowbirds.

Last, but not least, I would like to thank my publisher, Joan Homewood, my editor, Nancy Flight, Christine Langone, editorial co-ordinator and the staff of McGraw-Hill Ryerson for their support and insightful and constructive suggestions.

Preface

There are many matters to deal with when you are spending up to six months in the United States as a Canadian Snowbird. You must consider issues such as family, friends, finances, fluctuations in currency exchange rates, investments, taxes, immigration, customs, housing, travel, safety and security, and medical and other types of insurance. You also need to give thought to such important matters as money management, financial planning, wills, estate planning, and the need for reliable professionals and other advisors. You might even be tempted to consider becoming a full-time U.S. resident. All of these issues are discussed in this book or referenced in the Appendices.

The eight chapters in this book are designed to provide practical and helpful information about the main issues of importance to Snowbirds. Although each chapter has a separate topic, the topics of the chapters are interrelated.

All the chapters have a similar format. For example, each chapter includes an introduction and overview, a section on tips before leaving Canada, and a quick reference guide to relevant sections of the appendices.

The appendices are very comprehensive and provide a ready reference source of further information to assist you and save you time, money, and hassle. They also include suggested additional reading and retirement, financial, and estate planning checklists.

I hope you enjoy this book and find it practical and helpful. Best wishes for a healthy and enjoyable Snowbird retirement.

Douglas A. Gray
July 1995

CHAPTER

1

The Snowbird Lifestyle

A. INTRODUCTION

The thought of spending up to six months in a warm and sunny U.S. Sunbelt state during Canada's cold winter season is becoming increasingly appealing and popular for millions of Canadian retirees. This trend is increasing every year, as Canada's population ages. Because Canadians are living longer and staying healthy longer, retirement could last 30 years. With proper planning, the Snowbird lifestyle can provide the most active, stimulating, satisfying, and enjoyable experience of your retirement years. Many Snowbirds leave Canada for the United States in early November and return at the end of April. This way they can have the best of both worlds, enjoying the benefits of both countries.

This chapter covers preliminary issues such as where to stay, how to get there, what to do once you get there, tips on saving money, and safety and security.

B. KEY FACTORS TO CONSIDER

Planning is very important. With research and preparation, you will maximize your enjoyment of your U.S. stay and minimize unexpected and unwanted surprises. This guide is designed to help you meet these objectives.

Here is an overview of some of the important preliminary issues you need to consider:

1. Where to Stay

There are many possibilities. The most popular U.S. Sunbelt states are Florida, Arizona, Texas, and California. You might want to be based in one area and just take side trips for a day or several days to sightsee. Or you might want to use a recreational vehicle (RV) and travel through various states. There are many factors to consider in choosing where to stay, depending on your interests and needs. For example, do you prefer varied terrain, spectacular scenery, or hot weather? Do you prefer a dry climate or a humid climate? Maybe you prefer the ocean, the mountains, or the desert. Do you like the proximity of city life or a rural ambience? Friends could also be a factor drawing you to one place or another. Refer to Appendices A and B for information about places to stay, as well as for where to obtain free state tourism booklets and information. Contact the local Chamber of Commerce for more information. Check with your local library for videos of the state and specific city you are considering. Also speak with other people you know who are Snowbirds from that location. Before making a decision to buy a condo, house, or mobile home, you may wish to rent one for the first season to see if you like it. Alternatively, if you have an RV, you can check out many places.

2. How to Get There

You have lots of options. You could fly down to your Sunbelt home, drive your car, or have someone else drive it for you. There are companies who will do that for a fee. Or perhaps you have an RV.

There are many sources of free and low-cost information to make your trip more enjoyable. Refer to Appendix A for contact numbers of provincial and state tourism departments. Contact your local automobile club to obtain travel guides and detailed trip-planning schedules. Look at travel books for the specific areas or states you are travelling through. These can be found in libraries or your local bookstore.

If you are driving, remember that there are many discounts for seniors for accommodation, restaurants, and so on. Ask. If you are a member of a seniors' association, find out if it offers travel-related discounts. There are also seniors' discounts available if you are flying, so make enquiries.

If you are planning to fly, long hours of physical inactivity or crossing time zones can contribute to jet lag or fatigue, and it can take several days for your natural body cycle to adjust. Heeding the following advice while you are on the plane will aid the process:

- Walk around whenever it is convenient.
- Change the position of your body at least every hour, even when you are dozing.
- Wear a sweater or jacket to deal with fluctuating temperatures.
- Drink plenty of nonalcoholic fluids, since they prevent dehydration. The air-conditioning in the cabin tends to have a dehydrating effect.
- Wear loose-fitting clothing with an expandable waistband to make movement more comfortable.

- Leave your shoes on. Since your feet tend to swell during flight, you may have trouble getting your shoes back on if you take them off.
- Avoid a heavy intake of alcohol, since a drink has a greater impact during flight because of the effects of air pressurization.
- Avoid carbonated beverages and heavy meals, since they tend to cause discomfort.
- If you are going through time changes, attempt to lessen the impact by changing your sleeping schedule two or three days before you leave.

3. What to Do When You Get There

One of the many reasons the Snowbird lifestyle is so attractive is the wide range of activities available. You are bound to meet many kindred spirits and form new friendships. Some of the activities that may interest you include:

- Participating in regularly scheduled social activities at the mobile home park, RV park, or other retirement community.
- Participating in social activities through local social clubs that have regular events and members who are part-time or full-time Canadians in the U.S.
- Participating in recreational activities such as golfing, swimming, tennis, shuffleboard, cards, bingo, dancing, and keep-fit exercises.
- Travelling to explore new sights and scenery as part of a tour group or in your own car or RV, or in a convoy with others. Possibly taking a cruise.
- Taking continuing education courses through local university, college, or school board adult education programs for retirees. Courses are offered on almost every subject you can imagine and can be taken for credit, noncredit, or just to expand your knowledge. Also consider the many excellent programs available through Elderhostel. Refer to item 31 in Appendix A for more detail and contact numbers.
- Pursuing a hobby. There are many different types of hobbies or crafts that are inexpensive and creative or challenging.
- Keeping informed through subscribing to newspapers written specifically for Canadian Snowbirds, such as *Canada News* and the *Sun Times of Canada*. Refer to Appendix A, item 23. Also subscribe to local newspapers to find out what is happening in your community.

4. Tips on Saving Money

There are many ways of saving money as a senior. Get into the habit of asking if there is a seniors' discount, and comparison-shop. Here are some other ways to save money:

- *National seniors' associations*
  Various Canadian and U.S. associations for Snowbirds or seniors have membership benefits such as discounts on travel packages, cruises, accommodation, meals, tourist attractions, and currency exchange. Refer to Appendix A, item 21, to obtain further information.

- *Long-distance discount rates*
  You can save a lot of money with various programs set up by the major long-distance companies such as AT&T, Sprint, and MCI in the United States, and your provincial telephone company, Sprint, or Unitel in Canada. Comparison-shop to see who has the best rate package for your needs in each country. Check to see if rates are further reduced during the normal telephone company long-distance discount time periods, such as between 6:00 P.M. and 8:00 A.M. and on weekends. Different companies can have different policies. Before you commit yourself to a particular company, make sure you have the program's details clearly spelled out in writing.

- *State tourism catalogues*
  Most states have incentive packages or special seasonal promotions to spend tourist dollars in their respective states. These could include discounts, dollar-at-par offers, and coupon books for use for attractions, entertainment, accommodations, meals, RV rentals, and so on. Contact the specific state tourism departments and ask for the tourist information package. See item 18 in Appendix A.

- *Transportation discounts*
  Almost every company offering bus, train, or plane transportation has seniors' discounts.

- *Discount shopping malls*
  There are many of these malls throughout the United States and especially the Sunbelt states. They offer discount prices on a wide range of name-brand products. Find out why particular items are discounted—whether they are seconds, inventory overruns or surplus, off-season items, low-demand items, and so on. Refer to Appendix B, item 7.

- *Seniors' guides*
  Contact Health Canada (see Appendix A, item 4) for a directory of money-saving discounts and free services for seniors in Canada for government-related amenities such as museums, parks, and trains. Many provinces also have similar discount policies for seniors for provincially owned attractions such as museums and parks.

- *Local Chamber of Commerce*
  One of the main purposes of a local Chamber of Commerce is to stimulate economic activity in the community. One way of doing this is to offer a special tourist discount package for the services and products of chamber

members. Contact the Chamber of Commerce in areas where you are visiting or will be staying. Refer to item 26 in Appendix A.

- *Local newspapers*
Many local newspapers in key Sunbelt areas have special Snowbird discount subscription packages for seasonal residents. In addition, there are frequently visitor discount package coupons for local products or services given to seasonal subscribers by the newspaper's advertisers.

- *Banks, trust companies, credit unions, and savings and loans institutions*
Almost all of these institutions have discounts on services to seniors. In addition, many major Canadian financial institutions, as well as several U.S. ones in Sunbelt states, have developed additional discount or other unique programs especially for the needs of Canadian Snowbirds. These could include U.S.-dollar credit cards, Canadian-dollar accounts, lack of holding period on Canadian cheques deposited in your U.S. bank account, currency exchange rate commission discounts, and mortgages for U.S. real estate.

- *Advance supply of medication*
If you are on medication, you can probably project your needs for a future period of up to six months while you are in the United States. Have your doctor prescribe enough medication to cover your needs before you leave Canada so that you don't have to buy medication in the United States.

- *Annual discount books*
Several companies sell books listing a wide variety of discounts on restaurants, attractions, and events. The books are published annually and are generally valid from November 1 through October 31 or December 1 through November 30. If you are residing for up to six months in an area close to a major city—for example, Phoenix, Tucson (Arizona), San Diego, Los Angeles (California), or St. Petersburg, Fort Meyers, or West Palm Beach (Florida), you may want to check into these types of books. The books generally cost about U.S. $25. If you go out a lot, or frequently entertain visiting relatives or friends, you may find that you can save a lot of money with these books. One of the major companies is Entertainment Publications. Their toll-free number for information and ordering is 1-800-374-4464.

5. Safety and Security

One of the main concerns of any Snowbird is safety and security. To ensure that you do not have a bad experience, you need to find out about how to safety-proof your home before you leave, travelling precautions, city travel, and special areas of risk. Here is where you can obtain free information to assist you:

- *Travel Information Service of the Department of Foreign Affairs and International Trade (Canada).* This service continually monitors and assesses potential risks to Canadians in all countries outside Canada. For example, a travel information report is available on Florida, including specific precautions to avoid being a victim of crime. Contact the Travel Information Service before your departure date. They can be reached twenty-four hours a day, seven days a week, at 1-800-267-6788. If you want the free report faxed to you immediately, call 1-800-575-2500.

- *Local police department.* You could contact the police in the place you are planning to stay to obtain crime statistics in the area and cautions to follow.

- *State tourism offices.* These offices can provide you with travel safety tips and cautions in specific areas (e.g., Florida).

- *Travel agencies.* Various travel agencies have free booklets and pamphlets giving general safety tips and tips specific to certain areas. For example, Grand Circle Travel in Boston has a free booklet entitled *Going Abroad: 101 Tips for Mature Travelers.* Contact them at 1-800-221-2610. Tel: (617) 350-7500.

- *Seniors' Guidebook to Safety and Security.* This book is published by the RCMP Crime Prevention Branch, 1200 Vanier Parkway, Ottawa, ON K1H 0R2. Tel: (613) 993-8435.

- *Travel guides.* Your auto club (CAA or AAA affiliate offices) produces travel guides that include travel safety tips and cautions.

C. TIPS BEFORE LEAVING CANADA

- Thoroughly plan your Snowbird vacation before you leave by taking the time to do your research. The more preparation time, the more the enjoyment. The appendices provide a wealth of helpful information.

- If you are planning to stay in an area you have not stayed in before, find out how safe it is before you go. Obtain information from the local police, the local automobile club, and the state tourist bureau.

- Compare various discount plans with seniors' associations and decide which ones will save you the most money in your travels and on your stay. Also check into seniors' and other discounts you can use in the United States— for example, entertainment books or discounts offered through government agencies. Refer to Appendix A for associations.

- If you are considering staying at a retirement community or in an RV park or mobile home park, contact the management and get names of others who reside there as references. Contact several of them and ask questions to ensure that the place is compatible with your needs.

- Arrange with Canada Post to have your mail forwarded to your address in the United States.
- If you are trying the Snowbird lifestyle for the first time, consider renting for the first year rather than buying.
- Subscribe to one or both of the weekly newspapers for Canadians to keep aware of issues and information of interest. Refer to Appendix A, item 23. When you are living in the United States, many popular Snowbird destinations have regular radio news reports specifically for Canadians. Refer to item 24 in Appendix A.
- Consider subscribing to newsletters with expert information for Canadian Snowbirds, such as the *Canadian Snowbird Advisor.* See item 22 in Appendix A.

D. QUICK REFERENCE GUIDE TO RELEVANT PARTS OF THE APPENDICES

To help you obtain further information and contact numbers, here are the parts of the Appendices that are relevant to the contents of this chapter.

Appendix A: Items 9, 18, 19, 21, 22, 23, 24, 25, 27, 29, 31, and 32-43

Appendix B: Items 1, 2, 3, 5, 6, 7, and 8

CHAPTER

2

Financial Planning
and Money Management

A. INTRODUCTION

In order to achieve and maintain the Snowbird lifestyle, you need to have a
realistic understanding of your present and future financial resources so that
you can plan and budget accordingly. This chapter covers the typical risk
areas you should be aware of, the financial planning process, types of federal
and provincial government pensions, employer-funded pension plans, your
own tax-sheltered plans, the safety of your retirement plans and deposits, and
your home as a source of additional income.

Numerous Canadian books are available on financial planning and money
management issues and options. Books on these topics are becoming a Canadian growth industry. Many of these books are objective, balanced, informative, and relevant. Others are written to market the writer or his or her company
or services and products and thus may be biased. It therefore pays to read
selectively and carefully and to assess the credentials, credibility, and motivation of the writer. It also helps to read several books to get different perspectives
and become familiar with the concepts involved. Some suggested reading is
found in Appendix B. This is a partial list only.

Various educational seminars are available to further inform you about
topical matters relating to retirement and Snowbird issues. The same cautions
noted above relating to books apply to seminars.

In any event, you should obtain objective professional advice before you em-
bark on any particular course of action. How to select professional and other
advisors is covered in Chapter 8. The quality of the advice you rely on will
profoundly affect your financial well-being, peace of mind, and quality of lifestyle.

B. POTENTIAL FINANCIAL AND OTHER RISK AREAS

There are 15 risk areas that could affect your financial net worth, cash flow,
and lifestyle. In many cases, you can eliminate, minimize, or control each of

these risk areas by knowing about them, doing research, and making prudent decisions. If you are retired, are planning retirement, or wish to become a Snowbird, these 15 key risk areas are particularly important to know. Statistically, if you retire at 55 years of age, you can expect to live to 85 and have 30 years of retirement—almost as long as your working life. Planning to have enough funds to meet your lifestyle needs is obviously critically important. Some of the potential risk areas are interrelated, but they are considered separately because they should be specifically identified as risk. They all have financial implications, directly or indirectly. By obtaining customized financial planning advice relevant to your own situation, you should be able to anticipate and neutralize many of the key financial risks.

1. Currency Risk

This is a particularly important issue for Canadian Snowbirds. If the Canadian dollar drops in value relative to the U.S. dollar, you will obviously notice an increase in the cost of living due to the reduced purchasing power of your Canadian money when you convert it to U.S. currency. The value of the Canadian dollar is dependent on many variables, both national and international. If it goes down 5 percent, you have lost 5 percent of purchasing power in the United States.

2. Inflation Risk

This is one of the most serious financial risks to those in retirement. Although both Canada and the United States currently enjoy very low inflation rates, that can quickly change. As you are probably aware, inflation eats away at your purchasing power. Inflation at 5 percent will reduce your purchasing power by 50 percent in less than 15 years. If you have investments that have interest rates or value that is keeping up with the rate of inflation, or if you have annuities or RRIFs indexed for inflation, then your purchasing power would at least remain constant. If you have a fixed income, the inflation issue is especially critical.

For example, with Canada Savings Bonds, inflation would erode the purchasing power of the bond as well as the interest. You also have to look at the real rate of return on your money, after tax and inflation is factored in. If you were earning 10 percent interest and were taxed at 35 percent, your net return would be 6.5 percent. If inflation were 7 percent, you would actually be losing purchasing power with your money, in real terms.

3. Deflation Risk

If there is a severe or prolonged economic downturn or recession, the value of your assets could drop accordingly.

4. Interest Rate Risk

Interest rates in Canada and the United States have been very volatile over the past 15 to 20 years on any type of interest-sensitive financial investment. In the early 1980s the prime rate was in the double digits, up to 22 percent. This was of course attractive for people with interest income from term deposits, mortgages, or bonds. By the mid-1990s, rates had plunged to the low single digits, down to 5 percent. Interest rate risk can cut both ways, however. For example, if you set your lifestyle needs based on high interest rate returns, your lifestyle will be negatively affected when rates fall. Or if you lock yourself into a fixed-rate bond when rates are low and then interest rates increase, the value of the bond investment will go down when you try to sell it. Another example is if you have a locked-in annuity bought at a low interest rate. If rates go up and there is inflation along with it, your purchasing power and lifestyle will be affected.

5. Government Policy Risk

The Canadian and U.S. governments are constantly changing the tax or pension laws, depending on the political philosophy of the party in power and on economic pressures. For example, Old Age Security pension payments are reduced if the recipient's income exceeds a certain amount. This amount could become lower and lower over time. The Guaranteed Income Supplement could be reduced or the eligibility criteria tightened up. Federal and/or provincial income taxes could be increased. The $100,000 personal capital gains deduction was removed over the past few years. Provincial governments could reduce out-of-country medical coverage, resulting in increased out-of-country supplemental insurance premiums. The U.S. government could bring in legislation to increase taxes paid by non-U.S. residents, or a state could increase an estate tax on death on real estate or U.S. assets that you own.

6. Repayment Risk

This type of risk comes in several forms. One form of risk is not being repaid what you are owed when it is due or when you want your money. For example, if you buy a bond, the issuer's ability to repay you determines whether you are going to get your money back. Although bonds issued by municipalities, corporations, or governments rarely default, several levels of credit risk are normally involved. Agencies such as Standard & Poor, Moody's Investors Service, and Dominion Bond Rating Service rate the credit risk of various bonds, which generally ranges from AAA to D. These ratings indicate the repayment risk you are taking with a particular bond issue.

Insurance companies are also rated by different agencies, including one in Canada called TRAC. Considering that some insurance companies go under from time to time, you don't want to risk losing money you might be expecting from insurance proceeds, cash surrender value funds, disability insurance payments, or annuities.

If you place money in an institution by means of a term deposit, for example, you want to feel confident that you will get your money back, including all principal plus interest, if the institution fails.

A discussion of certain types of money protection you should be aware of is covered in Section G in this chapter.

Another form of repayment risk is receiving your invested money back sooner than you expect or want it. For example, if you lock in a bond with a 12 percent yield and the rate falls 7 percent, you will not be able to replace that bond with a new one at the same yield if the bond issuer redeems or calls the bond earlier than anticipated. Many corporate bond issuers have this right after a certain number of years after the bond was issued. Most government bonds cannot be called.

7. Market Cycle Risk

Many markets, such as the real estate market, stock market, and bond market, are cyclic. Depending on where your investment is at any point in the cycle, it could slowly or rapidly diminish in value. If you wanted or needed to sell it, you could lose money. Being aware of the market and the direction of the cycle is obviously important. Generally, the longer you hold an investment, the less the risk. The shorter the term you intend to keep the investment, the higher the risk that a market correction could impair your investment return.

8. Economic Risk

The economy obviously has an effect on such assets or investments as real estate or stocks. The more buoyant the economy, the more buoyant the price of real estate and stocks, and vice versa.

9. Lack of Diversification Risk

The risk here is having all your assets in one specific kind of investment, like real estate or bonds or stocks. You are not protected if that asset drops in value and you do not have alternative assets to buffer the loss. If you spread the risk, you lower the risk. To spread the risk, you could have different types of assets as well as different kinds of investments within each type of asset.

10. Lack of Liquidity Risk

Liquidity means the speed at which you can sell your asset, either at all, or at a fair price. For example, if you need to sell your home or stocks and the market has dropped, you could still sell, but it could take much longer and you will obtain a lower price. Negative publicity about stocks and real estate can have a dramatic short-term effect on the market, as potential buyers become nervous. Less demand means lower prices.

11. Taxation Risk

This risk affects your lifestyle if increased taxation reduces your anticipated retirement income. This form of risk could come from higher levels of income tax, the taxing of part or all of your income currently exempt from taxation (e.g., Guaranteed Income Supplement), or the taxing of RRSPs or RRIFs in some fashion, other than when you take the money out. Naturally, all the above possible initiatives would result in a strong public demand to rescind them. Economic pressure on federal or provincial governments to reduce their respective debts, however, could result in all areas of personal income being subject to review for additional tax.

12. Pension Risk

This type of risk takes various forms. One form is for federal or provincial governments to reduce the net amount of pension you receive through Old Age Security (OAS), Canada Pension Plan (CPP), or Guaranteed Income Supplement (GIS), through taxation, increased taxation, clawbacks based on your other income, reduction in amount of money, or more restrictive eligibility criteria. As you may know, if your taxable income is over $53,000, your OAS is "clawed back," or reduced by the amount of your income over $53,000. Another form of risk is that a pension fund manager may not invest money prudently and the return to the pension fund is less than expected. Or an employer may not make any profit in a particular year and therefore does not contribute anything to the pension fund. Or possibly an employer reduces or eliminates some pension plan collateral benefits such as life insurance or health and dental plan coverage for cost-saving reasons. Types of employer-funded pension plans are covered in this chapter in Section E.

13. Acts of God Risk

When selecting your Sunbelt retirement location, it is important to assess the risk from natural disasters or "acts of God." These could include hurricanes, floods, fires, or earthquakes. For example, certain parts of California are prone to brush fires and earthquakes. Parts of Florida are prone to hurricanes or floods. Not only do these disasters pose a risk for your home or health and for the resale potential or value of your home, many insurance policies exclude any coverage of acts of God or specifically exclude potential risks of that nature that may be endemic to the area you are considering. Make sure you know what risks are partially or fully excluded. If you make a claim, an insurance company may require you to pay a deductible amount you cannot afford. Check with local insurance companies, real estate agents, and the local, state, or federal weather bureaus for seasonal statistics and risks in the geographic area you are considering.

14. Weather Risk

Apart from acts of God risks, when selecting your Sunbelt or retirement home consider such weather issues as average snowfall (if applicable, in Canada), rainfall, and temperature at various times of the year. A very hot climate may hinder your comfort and outdoor activities and increase your air-conditioning costs. Conversely, a cold, rainy climate could reduce your physical comfort and safety, as well as increasing your heating bills, increasing the amount of home maintenance required, and reducing outside activity. Check with the weather bureau for seasonal statistics in the area you are considering. If the weather conditions are not attractive, the resale value of a home there could be affected.

15. Crime Risk

Certain Sunbelt states have areas of higher crime than others. Clearly this is an important area to clarify. Apart from your own peace of mind and health, local crime could result in break-ins, theft, vandalism, muggings, or other criminal activities that could affect you. It would also affect the insurance premiums you pay (based on risk and claims experience) or increase the deductibles you might have to pay on any claim. The resale value of your home would obviously be affected. Check with the local police department for crime statistics in the area you are considering.

C. THE FINANCIAL PLANNING PROCESS

Financial planning is very individual and personal. It should take into account all the psychological and financial factors that may have an impact on your financial goals and objectives. In short, comprehensive financial planning provides you with a long-term strategy for your financial future, taking into consideration every aspect of your financial situation and how each one affects your ability to achieve your goals and objectives. A financial plan can help you construct the foundation on which to build a secure financial future.

1. How a Financial Advisor Helps You

Through six distinct steps in the comprehensive financial planning process, a financial advisor helps you:

- Clarify your present situation
- Decide where you want to be by identifying both financial and personal goals and objectives
- Identify financial problem areas
- Provide a written financial plan with recommendations
- Implement the agreed-upon recommendations
- Periodically review and revise your plan

2. What a Comprehensive Financial Plan Contains

Your financial plan is the strategy for achieving your goals and objectives. A comprehensive financial plan should address all pertinent areas relating to your situation. Those areas that the planner does not personally address in the development of the plan should be coordinated by the planner.

You may want your plan to cover only a specific area, such as estate or investment planning. Although a plan for such a goal or objective may be appropriate for the areas covered, you should be aware that it is not a comprehensive plan.

Your financial plan document should contain not only the plan strategies but also all pertinent data relating to the development of the plan. Although the order and style of presentation may vary, the plan document should include at least the 13 essential elements described below. This does not necessarily mean that your plan will be long, since each area should be addressed so that it suits your personal situation. As mentioned earlier, completing Appendix C will provide a lot of the background data for dealing with the following areas:

- Personal data
- Your goals and objectives
- Identification of issues and problems
- Assumptions used in plan preparation
- Balance sheet/net worth
- Cash flow management (e.g., income and expenses)
- Income tax strategies
- Risk management (e.g., different types of insurance)
- Investments
- Special needs, such as retirement planning
- Estate planning
- Recommendations
- Implementation

If any area of the financial plan is not within the range of the financial planner's expertise, the planner has the responsibility to coordinate with other professionals and document such coordination in the financial plan report. Documentation of such areas can include the professional's name and when the review will be completed.

The analysis that is called for in all the elements of the plan should consist of a review of pertinent facts, a consideration of the advantage(s) and/or disadvantage(s) of the current situation, and a determination of what, if any, further action is required. The plan should include a summary statement providing the planner's comments on the analysis and his or her recommendations, where appropriate, for each element of the plan.

Once you have a plan in place, you should have it reviewed and revised from time to time to make sure you are on track and the current strategies are still appropriate for your needs.

As noted earlier, how to select a professional financial planner is covered in Chapter 8.

D. GOVERNMENT PENSION PLANS

There are many forms of federal and provincial government pension or financial assistance programs. Following is a brief overview of the key programs and guidelines that you should be familiar with. They are periodically modified, of course, so obtain a current update of regulations and criteria relevant to your circumstances. In addition, there could be exceptions in your case to the general guidelines outlined. For more information and assistance, including eligibility benefits, indexing, and payment outside of Canada, contact the Income Security Programs Branch of the Human Resources Development Canada (HRDC) office closest to you. Look in the Blue Pages of the phone book under "Government of Canada." The HRDC covers all the programs described below, except for number 4 (covered by provincial governments) and number 10 (covered by Veterans Affairs Canada). Also contact your closest Health Canada office, found in the same "Government of Canada" section of the phone book (Blue Pages). Ask for their free publications, including the *Seniors Guide to Federal Programs and Services,* which will provide you with information about other government subsidized services for seniors.

Keep in mind that the OAS, GIS, SPA, and CPP benefits are *not* paid automatically. You have to apply for them. You can arrange to have these funds automatically deposited into your bank account, a convenient option for Snowbirds.

1. Old Age Security Pension (OAS)

The OAS pension is a monthly benefit available, if applied for, to anyone 65 years of age or over. OAS residence requirements must also be met. An applicant's employment history is not a factor in determining eligibility, nor does the applicant need to be retired. You have to pay federal and provincial income tax on your OAS pension. Higher-income pensioners also repay part or all of their benefit through the tax system, referred to as a clawback. Contact your local HRDC office or Health Canada for the current amount of the clawback. This amount could be increased by the government over time.

To receive an OAS pension outside the country, a person must have lived a minimum of 20 years in Canada.

All benefits payable under the Old Age Security Act are increased in January, April, July, and October of each year based on increases in the cost of living as measured by the Consumer Price Index (CPI).

Once a full or partial OAS pension has been approved, it may be paid indefinitely outside Canada, if the pensioner has lived in Canada for at least 20 years after reaching 18 years of age. Otherwise, payment may be made only for the month of a pensioner's departure from Canada and for six additional months, after which payment is suspended. The benefit may be reinstated if the pensioner returns to live in Canada.

2. Guaranteed Income Supplement (GIS)

The GIS is a monthly benefit paid to residents of Canada who receive a basic, full, or partial OAS pension and who have little or no other income. GIS payments may begin in the same month as OAS pension payments. Recipients must reapply annually for the GIS benefit. Thus, the amount of monthly payments may increase or decrease according to reported changes in a recipient's yearly income. Unlike the basic OAS pension, the GIS is *not* subject to income tax.

The GIS may be paid outside Canada for only six months following the month of departure from Canada, regardless of how long the person lived in Canada.

3. Spouse's Allowance/Widowed Spouse's Allowance (SPA)

The SPA is paid monthly. It is designed to recognize the difficult circumstances faced by many widowed persons and by couples living on the pension of only one spouse. Recipients must reapply annually. Benefits are *not* considered as income for income tax purposes.

The SPA is not payable outside Canada beyond a period of six months following the month of departure, regardless of how long the person lived in Canada.

4. Provincial Social Security Supplement Programs

Some provinces have guaranteed annual income systems. If you are 65 years of age or older and you receive the federal Guaranteed Income Supplement, you might qualify for additional benefits from your province. These benefits will ensure that your incomes does not fall below the province's guaranteed income level.

To apply for provincial assistance, contact your provincial government. For a list of addresses and telephone numbers of provincial offices for seniors, refer to item 8 in Appendix A.

5. Canada Pension Plan (CPP)/Quebec Pension Plan (QPP)

The CPP is a contributory, earnings-related social insurance program. It ensures a measure of protection to a contributor and his or her family against the loss of income due to retirement, disability, or death. The plan operates throughout Canada. Quebec has its own similar program, the Quebec Pension Plan (QPP), which is closely associated with the CPP. The operation of the two plans is coordinated through a series of agreements between the federal and Quebec governments. Benefits from either plan are based on pension credits accumulated under both, as if only one plan existed.

Benefits paid by the CPP are considered income for federal and provincial income tax purposes. You must apply for all CPP benefits, and you should apply for your retirement pension at least six months before you want to receive it.

A CPP retirement pension may be paid at age 60. The contributor must have wholly or substantially ceased pensionable employment, however. Contributors are considered to have substantially ceased pensionable employment if their annual earnings from employment or self-employment do not exceed the maximum retirement pension payable at age 65 for the year the pension is claimed. After turning 65, a pensioner is not required to stop work to receive a retirement pension.

All CPP benefits are adjusted in January each year to reflect increases in the cost of living as measured by the Consumer Price Index.

All benefits under the CPP are payable no matter where the beneficiary lives, whether in Canada, in the United States, or abroad.

6. CPP Disability Pension

To receive a disability pension, a contributor must have been disabled according to the terms of the CPP legislation, must have made sufficient contributions to the plan, must be under the age of 65, and must apply in writing.

A contributor is considered to be disabled under CPP if he or she has a physical or mental disability that is both severe and prolonged. "Severe" means that the person cannot regularly pursue any substantially gainful occupation. "Prolonged" means that the disability is likely to be long continued and of indefinite duration or is likely to result in death.

A disability pension begins in the fourth month after the month a person is considered disabled. It is payable until the beneficiary turns 65 or recovers from the disability (if this occurs before age 65), or until the beneficiary dies. When the recipient of a disability pension reaches age 65, the pension is automatically converted to a retirement pension.

7. CPP Surviving Spouse's Pension

A spouse of a deceased contributor or a person of the opposite sex who lived in a marital relationship with a contributor before his or her death may be eligible for a survivor's pension. To qualify, the deceased must have contributed to the CPP during at least one-third of the number of calendar years in his or her contributory period. If the deceased's contributory period was less than 9 years, then at least 3 years' worth of CPP contributions are needed. If the contributory period was more than 30 years, at least 10 years' worth of contributions are required.

To qualify for a benefit, the surviving spouse must be 45 or more years of age. There are some exceptions for those younger than 45 years of age.

8. CPP Death Benefit

A death benefit may be paid to the estate of a deceased contributor, if contributions to the CPP were made for the minimum qualifying period. This minimum period is the same as for a surviving spouse's pension. The death benefit is also paid if there is no will or estate. In this case, the benefit is usually paid to the person or agency responsible for funeral costs.

The death benefit is a lump-sum payment equal to six times the monthly retirement pension of the deceased contributor or roughly 10 percent of the year's maximum pensionable earnings, whichever is less.

9. Reciprocal Social Security Agreements with the United States

Reciprocal social security agreements allow for the coordination of two countries' social security programs and make social security benefits portable between countries. The United States is party to this agreement with Canada on the items discussed below.

a) Old Age Security

The OAS program is included in reciprocal social security agreements. Such agreements enable people who live or who have lived in the other contracting country—for example, the United States—to add those periods of residence abroad to periods of residence in Canada to satisfy the minimum eligibility requirements for the basic OAS pension and the SPA. For example, someone who has lived in Canada for less than the 10 years required to receive a partial

OAS pension in Canada would be able to use periods of residence in the other country to meet the 10-year requirement. A similar provision would apply for someone who has lived in Canada for less than the 20 years needed to receive a partial OAS pension outside the country.

Under some agreements, benefits may be based only on periods of residence or contributions after specific dates. Residents who have little or no other income may receive the GIS. As noted earlier, the GIS is not payable outside Canada beyond a period of six months, regardless of how long the person lived in Canada.

b) Canada Pension Plan

Agreements are designed to avoid duplicate coverage—that is, the need to contribute to both the CPP and the comparable program of the other country for the same work.

Agreements may help people to qualify for disability, survivor's, and death benefits under the CPP. Each of the benefits has minimum qualifying conditions. An agreement may allow periods of contribution to the other country's social security system (or in some cases periods of residence abroad) to be added to periods of contribution to the CPP in order to meet these conditions. Once eligibility has been established, the amount of benefits is based on actual contributions to the CPP.

The CPP retirement pension is not included in agreements, since it is payable to anyone who has made at least one valid contribution. It is not necessary, therefore, to use periods of contribution in the other country to establish eligibility for the retirement benefit.

c) Provincial Social Security Programs

Canada's reciprocal social security agreements contain a provision that allows provinces to conclude understandings with other countries concerning social security programs under their jurisdiction—for example, the workers' compensation plans.

d) U.S. Social Security Programs

In many countries, nationality is an important criterion in determining eligibility for social security benefits. Noncitizens may be required to meet special conditions before they can receive a pension, and the payment of benefits to noncitizens living abroad may be severely restricted or even prohibited. Through the social security agreement between Canada and selected countries, including the United States, citizens and noncitizens become entitled to those benefits on the same conditions as the citizens of the other country. Most important, Canadian residents may start to receive benefits from the other country.

Most social security programs require contributions during a minimum number of years before a benefit can be paid. There may also be requirements for contributions in the period just before application for a benefit. People who have contributed to the programs of another country may not have enough periods of contributions to meet such requirements. Under the Canada-U.S. agreement, periods of residence in Canada and/or periods of contributions to the CPP may be used to satisfy the eligibility conditions of the other country's social security system.

10. Veterans' Pension

Veterans Affairs Canada provides a wide range of services and benefits to war veterans and former members of the Canadian Armed Forces in the form of disability pensions, survivors' pensions, and help with funeral and burial expenses. For more information, contact the nearest Veterans Affairs district office, listed in the Blue Pages of your telephone directory under "Government of Canada." You must apply for all pensions or services provided by Veterans Affairs Canada. They do not start automatically.

E. EMPLOYER-FUNDED PENSION PLANS

You should be aware of the types of retirement plans sponsored by employers. You can make enquiries as to what exact benefits you will receive, how they will be structured, and how soon you could receive them. Some employers have more than one plan. Some employers will also include extended health and dental plan coverage as well as life insurance coverage after you retire.

1. Registered Pension Plans (RPPs)

These are the most heavily regulated by the government. The two main types of plans are defined benefit and defined contribution. The plan could be "contributory," in which you and the employer contribute payments, or "non-contributory," in which the employer pays the full amount due each year.

a) Defined Benefit Plan

This type of plan promises you a pension of a specific amount of money, based on your years of service and/or salary. There is no risk that your pension funding could be affected by economic or market fluctuations, since the employer must set aside, by law, enough money, separate from other employer funds, to capitalize the specific pension that has been promised to you. The pension fund will therefore exist even if the employer ceases to operate, though future benefits could then be restricted. If the pension fund investments do poorly, the employer must compensate by putting extra money into the fund.

There are two forms of defined benefit plans:

- *Accruing benefits plan.* This plan can vary considerably, depending on the employer. Some offer a pension based on a percentage (e.g., 2 percent) of your average salary over your final three or five years of employment. This amount is then multiplied by your years of employment with the company. Other plans average all your earnings during your employment with the firm. This is not as attractive an arrangement as the previous one, which is based on your tax-earning years.

  Some employers offer a supplemental pension plan to extend the amount of pension from the RPP pension ceiling set by Revenue Canada.

- *Flat benefit plan.* This type of plan bases the calculation of the pension on a flat amount per month for each year of employment—for example, $30 per month.

Some of these two types of plans include partial or full indexing for inflation. If this is your situation, you should verify that this provision is guaranteed, or possibly required by provincial legislation, rather than optional on the part of the company.

b) Defined Contribution Plan
These plans are sometimes referred to as "money purchase plans." The employer promises to contribute a certain amount to your pension account annually—for example, 3 to 6 percent of your annual salary. The amount of the pension, however, is not specified. You may be able to make your own contributions. In this type of plan, your employer invests the contribution on your behalf. The amount of your pension will vary, depending on the value of your pension account on retirement. If your employer invests well, you will receive a greater retirement income benefit. If not, you will get a lower amount. Your risk is related to the success of the pension fund manager and the level of interest rates when you retire.

c) Vesting
Vesting means that the pension credits you have earned are locked in, so you won't lose these benefits if you change your job. Ask your employer or the federal or provincial pension authorities responsible for your plan. Depending on the regulations, you might have to participate in the plan for two to five years or more before it can be vested.

If you quit your job, you can let your vested credits remain with your employer, rather than taking out the amount you are entitled to in a lump sum, which would be taxable income, of course. If the vested credits remain, you could receive a retirement pension that could net you more than you otherwise could have earned. It all depends on your needs and circumstances and what you want to do with the money. Alternatively, you could transfer the money into a locked-in RRSP. Although you can't withdraw it until your normal retirement age, you would control how it is invested. You must use the funds to provide retirement income, which would normally require you to buy a life annuity or a Life Income Fund (LIF). An LIF could allow you to wait until the age of 80, if you want, before buying a life annuity. Check what regulations and options apply in your case.

2. Deferred Profit Sharing Plans (DPSPs)

These plans are also regulated by government but are less restrictive than RPPs. They are similar to a defined contribution RPP in the sense that the amount you receive relates to the amount of the employer contribution and how effectively the money was invested.

There are some significant differences, however, from RPPs. The employer is only permitted to contribute half the amount of a defined contribution plan. If there is an annual profit, the employer is obligated to make a minimum contribution. No contribution is required if the company shows a loss that year. Another difference is that you may not have to wait until retirement to withdraw money from the plan.

3. Group RRSPs

Some employers prefer not to have the regulatory controls of an RPP or DPSP but still provide an employer-sponsored pension plan. A common approach is for the employer to contract with a professional money manager to establish an RRSP for each employee, with the administration fee normally borne by the employer. The employer could then increase your salary and deduct the increase from your salary to put into the individual RRSP. The benefit to you is that you have a form of forced savings plan, and you will receive more net pay each month, since the employer can withhold less for tax deductions as a result of the RRSP off-set. The disadvantage is that you do not normally have the freedom to select your RRSP investments. The phrase "group RRSP" is a misnomer; although it is set up for a group of employees, each RRSP is individual.

F. YOUR OWN TAX-SHELTERED PENSION PLANS

1. Registered Retirement Savings Plans (RRSPs)

a) Types of RRSPs
There are three main types of RRSPs:

- *Deposit plans.* These are offered by banks, trust companies, credit unions, and life insurance companies, and they include term deposits or Guaranteed Investment Certificates (GICs). Terms generally range from one to five years. It is prudent to vary the dates that your money comes due to average out changes in interest rates.

- *Managed plans.* In this type of plan, which includes mutual funds, your money is pooled with that of others in a diversified portfolio of stocks, bonds, real estate, and other assets. Alternatively, you may have a singular plan managed just for your investments. The value of the assets can vary, of course, depending on the market.

- *Self-directed plans.* With these plans, you are responsible for managing your own portfolio, subject to various restrictions. The funds are held by a trust company. You can buy and place in your plan a wide variety of assets, such as stocks, bonds, or mortgages.

Many retired people prefer to opt for the deposit plan or managed plan in conservative investments so that preservation of capital is foremost.

b) Types of RRSP Withdrawal Options

At some point you will have to decide what to do with the money you have built up in an RRSP—in other words, turn retirement savings into retirement income. If you have RRSP funds transferred from a pension plan, you may be subject to pension legislation. For example, you may be required to purchase only life annuities with your funds. Some provinces have approved various alternatives to life annuities. They are called Life Income Funds (LIFs) and/or Locked-in Retirement Income Funds (LRIFs). You basically have three RRSP withdrawal options:

- *Lump-sum withdrawal.* Since all the money you withdraw is taxable in the year you receive it, most people don't choose this option unless there is an urgent need. Depending on the amount you take out, the tax liability could be high. Conversely, you may prefer to take out smaller amounts with low taxable consequences for specific purposes. Keep in mind that the more you take out, the less money is available for future retirement income and future potential growth in your retirement plan.

- *Registered Retirement Income Fund (RRIF).* This option is covered in more detail below. It means you can keep deferring tax on your money, as with an RRSP.

- *Annuities.* Annuities provide regular income for life or for a specific period. This option is covered in more detail in section 3.

2. Registered Retirement Income Funds (RRIFs)

An RRIF has become a very popular retirement income option because it provides the flexibility to control your retirement income and investments. It is like an RRSP in that you can select the investments you want, adjust your income payments, or take lump-sum withdrawals at your pleasure. You can have a self-directed RRIF if you want. Like an RRSP, an RRIF can grow tax-free, if you have income or growth types of investments. An RRIF is like an

RRSP in reverse. Instead of putting in a certain amount of money each year, you withdraw money that is taxable income. You have to draw a minimum mandatory amount, but there is no maximum amount. Obviously, the higher the payments you make to yourself, the sooner your funds will be depleted. RRIFs can continue for the lifetime of the holder or their spouse. You have to make a conversion from an RRSP to RRIF by the end of your 71st year, although you can do it at age 65 if you prefer—for example, if you need to qualify for the Pension Income Credit.

Your choice of RRIF will have an important impact on meeting your retirement needs. The key factors to consider include the amount of income you anticipate you will require in the short term and long term, and how long your savings will last.

a) Types of RRIF Withdrawal Options

There are various options for withdrawing your RRIF. Since you are permitted to have more than one RRIF, you might want to combine your withdrawal options to suit your needs. Not all institutions provide the options listed below. Obtain professional advice in advance.

- *Level payout.* Payments are the same each month, for example, over a 25-year period. Although it is similar in some aspects to an annuity, you have control at all times.

- *Fixed-term payout.* Used by people who want to use up the funds in a shorter period of time—for example, 10 to 15 years—frequently because of ill health.

- *Minimum payout.* This option maximizes your investment by allowing the funds to grow in a compounding tax-free environment. You can set up your RRIF at the end of your 71st year, but, for example, with payments to commence at the end of your 72nd year. You don't have to take any payments in the calendar year it is funded. If your spouse is younger, you can set the formula based on his or her age, since there are advantages to this. Obtain further information for your situation.

- *Interest-only payout.* In this case, you would receive interest only until the deadline arrives for minimum withdrawals. At this point your capital will start eroding, and therefore growth will not occur. In the meantime, though, you would have preserved your capital.

- *Indexed payout.* Payments are increased annually based on a projected inflation rate—for example, 5 percent.

- *Smoothed payout.* Payments are adjusted so that you receive higher payments in the early years and lower payments in the later years. The schedule of payments is calculated according to actuarial projections.

b) Factors to Consider When Making Your RRSP or RRIF Selection
You can continue making RRSP payments up to your 71st year if you want, when you have to convert to an RRIF or an annuity or to take a lump-sum withdrawal. With both RRSPs and RRIFs, you can place your funds in different types of investments, from no risk to high risk. In choosing the type of investment you want, you should take into account the following considerations:

- *Safety.* Since you are retired or nearing retirement, preservation of capital is a primary consideration, followed by income or growth strategies that will at least neutralize inflation. You don't want to speculate. You want to spread any risk by diversifying your portfolio, unless you simply want to have money market funds such as GICs, Canada Savings Bonds, or term deposits. You don't want to invest in any product that could result in your losing money you can ill afford. Such an occurrence would negatively affect your retirement lifestyle or impair your peace of mind.

- *Diversification.* As you mature, you want to move into more stable and secure investments. Equity-based mutual funds or actual stocks tend to be too risky for most people. Either they don't understand the market or feel anxious about the potential risk of eroding their capital, with little time for recovery. Conversely, if you have some "extra" money, you may wish to place some of it in more growth-oriented investments. There are many issues to consider, however.

- *Rate of return.* There is a direct correlation between risk and potential return. The lower the risk, the lower the return; the higher the risk, the higher the potential return. Since you want to preserve your capital, you will probably opt for safety and certainty. By actively considering your options and thoroughly checking out the competition, however, you could still get 1 to 4 percent more money without any risk of impairing your capital. Over time, this extra percentage could make a considerable difference as it is compounded tax-free in your RRSP or RRIF.

- *Liquidity.* This refers to how quickly you can access your money. You want to have access to a certain amount of money when you need it, or if interest rates start increasing considerably, you want to take advantage of that opportunity.

- *Fees.* Normally fees are not an issue for people with deposit funds, such as GICs and term deposits. If you have a self-directed RRSP or RRIF, however, or a managed plan such as a mutual fund, or if you have a personally managed portfolio, the issue of fees for management is a consideration.

3. Annuities

An annuity involves putting a lump sum of money into a plan that provides a regular income for life or for a specified period. There are some limitations to be aware of related to RRIFs. With an annuity, you have no income payment flexibility or opportunity to manage investment options so that you might increase your retirement income. You may also have little or no inflation protection unless the annuity is indexed for inflation. Some policies permit this. The amount an annuity pays is determined by your age and the interest rates at the time of purchase. For some people, however, annuities are a viable option if they cannot or prefer not to manage their own money, as you can with an RRIF. There are other considerations and potential benefits as well.

Term certain annuities are sold by various institutions, including banks, trust companies, credit unions, and insurance companies. Life annuities are sold only by life insurance companies. Make sure you ask about deposit insurance protection, estate preservation, and fees on any RRIF or annuity before you invest. Make sure you comparison shop.

Here are the two main types of annuities:

- **Term Certain Annuity to Age 90 (TCA90)**
  This annuity provides regular periodic payments, which can continue until your 90th year. Payments are normally level but can usually be indexed for inflation. If your spouse is younger than you are, you can purchase the TCA90 to continue after your death until your spouse's 90th year. If you die before 90 and do not have a spouse, you can make arrangements for the payments to go to your estate. Some issuers offer a TCA90 with an alternative to a fixed rate of return. In this option, the yield and payments are adjusted periodically to interest rates.

- **Life Annuity**
  A life annuity provides regular payments that will continue for the rest of your life, no matter how long you live. When you die, however, any money left in the annuity goes to the issuer, not your estate. The exception is if you arrange an annuity that has a guaranteed payment period.

  There are various types of life annuities:

  - *Straight life annuity.* This type of annuity is for an individual only and provides you with the highest amount of income for each dollar of premium in monthly or annual payments. However, it only lasts for your lifetime, when the annuity payments stop, unless you have a guaranteed period. This type of plan might be suitable for people who have no dependents.

  - *Life annuity with a guaranteed period.* This provides a guarantee that you or your beneficiary will receive back all of your investments, plus full interest if you wish, even if you only live for a short time. Alternatively, you may have the guarantee period set up to provide income payments for a fixed time frame, such as 5, 10, or 15 years from the start of payments to you, or until you or your spouse reach a certain age, such as 90. The longer the guaranteed period, the lower the payments.

– *Joint and last survivor annuity.* This annuity provides a regular income as long as either spouse is living. Payments can continue at the full amount to the surviving spouse, or they can be reduced by any stipulated percentage on the death of either spouse or specifically at your death. If you select the reduction option, this will result in higher payments while both spouses are alive, since a higher income stream is necessary as the cost of living is higher for two people than one. Although this type of plan results in less income for each dollar invested in the annuity, to many people the additional benefits are worth it.

– *Instalment refund annuity.* If you die before you have received as much money as you paid for the annuity, this annuity will continue income payments to your beneficiary until they equal the amount you originally paid.

– *Cash refund annuity.* With this plan, instead of receiving continued income payments, as in the above example, your beneficiary receives a lump-sum payout.

– *Indexed life annuity.* This provides for annuity payments that automatically increase each year, from 1 to 5 percent, for example, based on the return of a specified group of assets. Although this plan provides you with some protection against rising living costs due to inflation, it will also reduce your payments in the early years.

– *Integrated life annuity.* If you wish, you can integrate your Old Age Security (OAS) payments with your annuity. With this plan, you would receive substantially increased annuity payments until age 65, at which time the payments would be reduced by the maximum OAS entitlement at the time you purchased the annuity.

G. ARE YOUR DEPOSIT MONIES, RRSPS, RRIFS, AND ANNUITIES PROTECTED AGAINST DEFAULT?

Depending on how and where you invest your money, it may or may not be partially or fully protected. Making sure your retirement investments and insurance benefits are protected is naturally a matter of concern. Some banks, trust companies, credit unions, and savings and loans institutions in the United States, and insurance companies in Canada and the United States have ceased to operate from time to time. Here is a brief overview of your protection. Make sure you verify all the information in this section to ensure that it is current, accurate, and relevant to your situation.

1. Protection of Deposit Monies, RRSPs, RRIFs, and Annuities in Canada

- *Deposits in a bank or trust company.* These are protected by the Canada Deposit Insurance Corp. (CDIC) up to a certain amount. In Quebec, the plans are protected by the Quebec Deposit Insurance Board. Your RRSP deposit or RRIF, regular savings or chequing funds on deposit, or term deposits are automatically insured for up to $60,000 for each separate account. Each deposit (in the form of an RRSP or otherwise) must mature in five years or less. If you have more than $60,000, you can divide your funds among several CDIC members who are separate financial institutions. Some banks and trust companies have subsidiaries that are separate CDIC members, resulting in a ceiling of $60,000 each. For information and confirmation, contact CDIC at 1-800-461-2342.

- *Deposits in a credit union.* These are protected by a provincial deposit insurance plan. Each province varies in its protection for deposits—savings, chequing, or term deposit, or RRSP or RRIF with term deposits or GICs less than five years. Depending on the province, the protection can range from $60,000 to unlimited protection—that is, 100 percent. Contact a credit union in your province to enquire, or phone the CDIC number noted in the previous point to obtain contact numbers for the credit union deposit insurance head office in your province.

- *Deposits in a life insurance company.* These are covered by an industry-operated protection plan called CompCorp up to certain limits and in certain situations, depending on the nature of the investment. The limit for policies registered under the Income Tax Act, such as RRSPs, RRIFs, and pension policies, is $60,000. The limit is also $60,000 for nonregistered policies, such as cash value of a life insurance policy. For information and confirmation, contact CompCorp directly at 1-800-268-8099.

- *Managed funds.* Generally, these funds are protected if they are in an RRSP in the form of deposit funds—for example, term deposits or GICs under five years. Mutual funds have no protection as such, because of the nature of the pooled investment. The funds' investments are segregated from the assets of the fund manager, however, in case the fund manager ceases to operate.

- *Self-directed plans.* These plans are not protected as such against the default of the institution holding them. Certain investments in the plan, however, such as term deposits or GICs under five years, could be protected. The amount of the protection depends on whether the institution is a bank, trust company, credit union, or brokerage firm. Refer to the deposit ceilings discussed earlier for these types of institutions.

If a brokerage firm ceases to operate, there could be protection for certain investments in your self-directed plan up to $500,000 under an industry plan called the Canadian Investor Protection Fund. Only members, such as a Canadian stock exchange (Vancouver, Alberta, Toronto, and Montreal), the Toronto Futures Exchange, and members of the Investment Dealers Association of Canada, are covered by this fund. No mutual fund companies or investment advisors not associated with a member broker are covered by this particular fund.

For further information and confirmation, contact your broker or the CIPF office in Toronto at (416) 866-8366.

- *Life insurance companies.* If a company that is a member of the CompCorp protection plan makes promises in a life insurance, health insurance, money-accumulation, or annuity policy to pay either a fixed or a minimum amount of money to a person or on a person's death, and that company goes under, you could be protected up to a certain amount. If you have life insurance protection, the limit is $200,000; for life annuity and disability income policies with no options of a lump-sum withdrawal, the limit is $2,000 a month; and for health benefits other than disability income annuities, the limit is $60,000 in total payments.

  For further information and confirmation, contact CompCorp at 1-800-268-8099.

- *Creditor-proofing.* If you have personally guaranteed loans for an incorporated company, or if you operate an unincorporated business, you could be exposed to claims from potential creditors. Funds placed with certain types of products from life insurance companies or with trust companies in Quebec could be protected from creditors. Obtain advice from the institution involved and verify it with your lawyer.

2. Protection for Deposit Monies in the United States

- *Deposits in U.S. federal or state banks, trust companies, and savings and loans institutions.* These are covered by the Federal Deposit Insurance Corporation (FDIC) up to $100,000 for each individual account.

  If you want further information, consumer brochures on deposit insurance, or confirmation that the institution is covered by FDIC, contact FDIC at 1-800-934-3342 (Canada and the U.S.), or call (202) 393-8400.

- *Deposits in U.S. credit unions.* These are covered up to $100,000 by the National Credit Union Share Insurance Fund (NCUSIF) for each individual account.

  For further information, a consumer brochure on deposit insurance, or confirmation that the credit union is covered by NCUSIF, contact the fund at 1-800-755-5999 (U.S. only), or call (703) 518-6300.

H. USING YOUR HOME AS A SOURCE OF ADDITIONAL INCOME

Many Canadian seniors prefer to remain in their own homes as long as possible for a variety of reasons, including the support network they have built up over the years, through neighbours, friends, church, or other regular social activities. Many seniors are unable to pay to remain at home, however. It is not uncommon for seniors to be house-rich and cash-poor.

There are many reasons why a senior may need extra cash or income to supplement existing financial resources. Even if contributions have been made to several savings programs, such as private pension plans, government pensions, or RRSPs, there could still be insufficient financial resources for the senior's needs or wants. Being a Snowbird and living in the U.S. Sunbelt states for up to six months a year could be one reason for lack of financial resources. Other seniors may not have the savings income mentioned and may rely only on federal Old Age Security (OAS) income, perhaps along with a federal Guaranteed Income Supplement (GIS). Some of these federal or provincial programs involve a means test. This means the government sets a maximum income level to be eligible. If you exceed this income, you do not get the funding, since you are not deemed financially needy. Many seniors who have fixed savings have had their purchasing power eroded by inflation. The home is the single largest form of "savings" for seniors, especially if they can tap into the equity that has accumulated, for lump-sum and/or continuous income, without having to make monthly payments.

Many seniors think that a home cannot readily be converted into a source of income unless the home is sold. This can be a very stressful scenario to some. In contrast, there are seniors who, by circumstance or choice, sell their homes, buy a condominium, in many cases in a retirement area, and have a considerable amount of cash left over, which they might decide to spend on being a Snowbird, for example. For information about housing and real estate for Snowbirds, see Chapter 4.

There are options for seniors who want to stay in their own homes but need or wish to supplement their income. One option is to rent out a self-contained basement suite to provide income. Another option is to rent out spare rooms in the house, taking in boarders who share common kitchen facilities and washrooms. In many cases the income is not taxable, either because the income can be offset against a percentage of the house expenses or because of the low amount of income involved. Some seniors find these options attractive because they may provide additional benefits in the form of companionship and the feeling of security. This latter benefit could be particularly attractive, especially if the owner is a Snowbird, or away often on trips. For other seniors, these options may not be attractive because of the loss of privacy. There could also be municipal bylaw regulations that could technically restrict having tenants. In many cases these regulations are flexible, depending on various factors, current municipal policy regarding enforcement, and extenuating circumstances of the owner.

There are many reasons why a senior may wish to have extra money or income, such as to meet daily living expenses, to pay increasing property taxes, to travel, to live as a Snowbird in the United States for up to six months, to undertake home renovation or maintenance and repairs, to make a major purchase such as a car or RV, to hire help, to purchase luxuries to enhance the quality of life, to deal with an unexpected emergency, or to provide financial help to children or grandchildren.

1. Deferred Payment Plans

Keep in mind that the following plans vary from province to province and are constantly changing. Obtain a current update. Also contact your local Canada Mortgage and Housing Corporation (CMHC) office for information about their wide range of programs and publications for seniors.

This type of plan involves the postponement of certain expenses until a fixed time in the future or until the house is sold. Generally, the expenses, along with any interest applicable, constitute a debt, with the equity in the home as security. This is the simplest form of equity conversion. Under these plans, you maintain ownership and possession of the home, as well as any equity appreciation. Here are some examples of deferred payment plans:

a) Deferment of Property Taxes

There are many people who are mortgage-free but who spend a significant amount of their net income on property taxes, even after a provincial homeowners' property tax grant is deducted. In addition to property taxes, there are other recurring expenses that further erode disposable income, including costs of maintenance, lighting, heating, water, or garbage removal.

Although property taxes are collected by and for the municipality, in most cases some provincial governments have established property tax deferment plans. Under this arrangement, a senior is entitled to delay payment of property taxes and accrued interest until the home is sold or the senior's estate is settled. Check with your local property tax department to see if such a program is available or is being considered.

b) Deferment or Subsidy of Home Rehabilitation Expenses

This arrangement is similar to the previous example in that any loans approved for improvement or rehabilitation of the home may be deferred until your home is sold, until your estate is settled, or until a fixed date in the future. In some cases, there is an outright subsidy that does not have to be repaid. There are several variations of this type of program, depending on whether funds are obtained through a federal CMHC or provincial government program. Find out what current programs are available. The advantage of this type of home rehabilitation expense deferment is that it allows you to improve your standard of living without eroding your income.

If you are considering either of the above deferred payment plan programs, there are several key questions that you should ask:

- Is there a limit on the income of applicants to be eligible?
- Is there a subsidy of the deferral plan?
- Is there a limit on the amount of payment due (e.g., property taxes) that can be deferred?
- Is there a limitation on the time that an amount will be deferred?
- What is the interest charge on the amount deferred?
- How often is the interest rate adjusted, if at all, on the deferred payment?
- What is the formula used for determining the interest rate and how frequently is it compounded?
- If the amount of payment deferred and accrued interest eventually exceeds the value of the home, will you be obligated to sell the home?

Keep in mind that although property taxes can increase every year, for example, and that interest rates over time, especially compounded rates, can eat away the equity in the home, these effects should be partially offset by an increase in the value of the home as a result of inflation and market demand.

2. Reverse Mortgages

Reverse mortgages, reverse annuity mortgages (RAMs), and home equity plans are similar concepts that are becoming increasingly popular among seniors or early retirees across Canada. Over the years, many people can build up considerable equity in their houses, townhouses, or condominiums. Many Canadians have decided to turn their largest asset into immediate cash and/or regular revenue and still remain in the home.

The basic concept behind these various plans is simple. You take out a mortgage on part of the equity of your home (the debt-free portion of your home), and in exchange receive a lump-sum amount of money and/or a monthly income for a fixed period or for your life and, if you are married, for the life of the surviving spouse. When you sell the home, or when you die, or if you are married, when your surviving spouse dies, the mortgage and accrued interest must be repaid. You do not have to make any payments in the meantime. If there is any balance left in residual equity in the home after the sale, it belongs to the senior or his or her estate.

The various reverse mortgage options have different features. Here are some of the main ones:

- Reverse mortgages, RAMs, and other home equity programs are readily available through a variety of agents and brokers. This permits you to compare and contrast in a competitive marketplace and end up with a plan that has features customized for your specific needs. Look in the Yellow Pages under "Financial Planning Consultants" and "Mortgages" for companies that offer these home equity plans.

- The main home equity type of plans that are available have obtained an opinion from Revenue Canada that the lump-sum payment and monthly annuity payments are tax free, as long as you live in your home. If you have selected a monthly income annuity that continues after you have moved out of your home, the income from the sale may be subject to favourable prescribed annuity taxation rules. The current ruling on the various means-tested programs, such as the federal Guaranteed Income Supplement (GIS), is that receiving the annuity will not interfere with your eligibility for, or cause a reduction in, the GIS. As tax laws and regulations change, make sure you obtain current independent advice from a tax accountant and Revenue Canada on this issue.

- Since you retain ownership, you benefit from an appreciation in the value of your home over time—that is, you get an increase in equity. For example, if your property goes up 10 percent a year in value, and you locked in the mortgage on your property for the reverse mortgage or RAM at 8 percent, then you are technically ahead in the interest differential. In reality, because you are not making regular payments on your mortgage, the interest on it is being compounded and therefore, in practical terms, is ultimately eroding the increasing equity. The reduction could be substantially offset by an attractive average annual appreciation in property value.

Although many of the reverse mortgages, RAMs and related plans operate in similar ways among various companies, there are variables among the plans in interest rates and other specific conditions. Here are some of the points to consider in choosing a plan:

- What are the age requirements to be eligible for the lump-sum or annuity plan?

- Do you need to have clear title on your home?

- Can you transfer the mortgage to another property if you move?

- What percentage of your home equity is used to determine the reverse mortgage or RAM, and what percentage of that is available for a lump-sum payment and annuity?

- Is the interest rate on the mortgage fixed for your lifetime or duration of the annuity, or is it adjusted, and if so, how regularly and using what criteria?

- If the reverse mortgage and lump sum is for a term period, what are the various terms available?
- What if the equity of the home on sale is insufficient to pay the mortgage and accrued interest? Are you or your estate liable for the shortfall?
- Can the agreement of the term be extended if the home has appreciated in value?
- Can you move out of the house, rent it, and still maintain the home equity plan?
- What if you already have a mortgage on the house?
- If the annuity is for life, is there a minimum guaranteed period of payment, or will payments stop immediately upon the death of the recipient and/or the surviving spouse?
- How will the income received under the proposed plan be taxed, if at all?
- Will the income received affect your eligibility under any federal or provincial housing or social programs?

The process of obtaining a reverse mortgage or RAM takes about four to six weeks on average, including home appraisal, annuity calculations, and other matters. Since these plans are fairly complex, it is essential that you obtain independent legal and tax advice in advance and thoroughly compare the features and benefits.

3. Renting Out Part of Your Home in Canada or the United States

If you choose to rent out a basement suite, you are entitled to offset the rental income you receive against a portion of your house-related expenses. For example, if you received rent of $300/month ($3,600 a year) from the rented area, and the total house-related expenses were $14,400 a year, and the rented area comprised 25 percent of the total square footage of the home, or $3,600 of the total expenses ($14,400 x 25 percent), then the income would be offset by expense, leaving a zero taxable income. In all instances you should obtain tax advice from a professional accountant to make sure you are doing the calculations correctly.

If you are renting out part of your home, check with your provincial government to obtain information about your obligations and rights as a landlord; you will be governed and regulated by that legislation. For example, some provinces have rent control, and others do not. Ideally, you want to have a tenancy agreement that supplements the provincial legislation and deals with such issues as your policy on smoking, pets, noise, and the number of people living in the suite.

Your municipality has the authority to regulate zoning and determines whether a residence is zoned for single families. Technically, therefore, you could contravene a municipal zoning bylaw by renting out a part of your home to a nonrelative. In effect, you would be operating as if your home were multi-family, which it wouldn't be zoned for. If you hear the term "illegal suite," then, it simply means it technically contravenes the existing municipal bylaw on the issue. The contravention has nothing to do with provincial legislation (dealing with landlord-tenant matters) or federal legislation (dealing with income tax). Each level of government is independent of the other.

Check with your local municipality. It could be that certain areas in the municipality are encouraged to have rental suites. Alternatively, the municipality may have the technical restriction but does not actively enforce it unless there is a complaint by a neighbour. If a municipal inspector does investigate, you normally have a right to appeal. One of the grounds of appeal is economic hardship for you, the owner, and serious inconvenience for the tenant. Some municipalities have a moratorium (temporary freeze) on enforcing the bylaw because of a shortage of rental accommodation and/or general recessionary hardship of property owners, who need a "mortgage helper" to meet payments.

Some provincial governments have programs to encourage home renovation in order to create rental suites. In addition, the CMHC has some programs for renovation to accommodate handicapped or elderly people.

Make enquiries. The tax aspects of renting your U.S. Sunbelt home are covered in Chapter 6.

4. Operating a Business Out of Your Home

Many people, at some point, intend to start part-time or full-time businesses out of their homes. There is a growing trend to do this for various reasons, including eliminating daily commuting to work, fulfilling a lifestyle choice, creating retirement opportunity, supplementing salaried income, testing a business idea, or saving on business overhead and thereby reducing financial risk by writing off house-related expenses. There are many different types of home-based businesses. If you are interested in operating out of the home, read *Home Inc.: The Canadian Home-Based Business Guide,* second edition, by Douglas A. Gray and Diana L. Gray, published by McGraw-Hill Ryerson, which covers in detail the various issues you should know about, including tax tips to save money. Refer to Appendix B for other publications on operating a small business. It is important to keep in mind that you need competent tax and legal advice before you start up. The last thing you want is potential risk, since that could deplete your retirement funds and hamper your lifestyle. You need to obtain a GST number if you have over $30,000 in income in your business or are paying GST on items you purchase and want to offset it against GST you are charging. Check with your accountant and closest GST office (Revenue Canada).

Expenses may be claimed for the business use of a work space in your home if either

- the work space is your principal place of business for the part-time or full-time self-employed aspect of your career (you could have a salaried job elsewhere; it is not required that you meet people at your home) or
- you only use the work space to earn income from your business and it is used regularly for meeting clients, customers, or patients. In this case, you could also deduct expenses from an office outside the home.

You may be able to claim 100 percent of the cost of business purchases or a depreciated amount over time, depending on the item. To clarify what you can deduct and how to do it, as well as other home business tax issues, speak to your accountant. It is also important that you speak with your lawyer about the various types of legal issues when starting a business. See Chapter 8 for information about selecting advisors.

The tax and legal aspects of working in the United States are covered in the chapters on tax and immigration.

5. Keeping Records

If you are going to be renting out part of your principal residence or Sunbelt condo to a tenant, or if you intend to have a home-based business, make sure that you keep detailed records of all money collected and paid out. Purchases and operating expenses must be supported by invoices, receipts, contracts, or other supporting documents.

You do not need to submit these records when you file your return, but you need to have them in case you are ever audited.

I. TIPS BEFORE LEAVING CANADA

- Investigate and evaluate the various potential financial and other risks discussed in Section B in this chapter and make the appropriate decisions before your departure.
- Review your government, employer, or personal pension plans and make arrangements to have your pension or other income (e.g., dividends, tax refunds) deposited directly into your bank account during your absence.
- Make sure that your funds will receive the best interest rate, depending on your liquidity and safety of principal needs. For example, if your direct deposit goes into a low interest or chequing account, arrange to have a regular transfer of the funds (e.g., monthly) into an investment that provides you with a higher return (e.g., GIC, term deposit, Treasury bill). Always make sure your Canadian account funds are receiving interest.

- If you foresee that you will need some of your Canadian funds during your absence, have your financial institution forward the desired funds directly to your Sunbelt bank. Always confirm your instructions in writing and keep a copy.

- Keep an accurate record of when any GICs, term deposits, or Treasury bills come due during your absence so that appropriate arrangements can be made.

- Estimate how much money you will need while you are in the United States and how to readily access it. Check your credit card and line of credit limits. If they are not high enough for possible emergencies, arrange to have them increased.

- With Automated Banking Machines (ABMs), you do not need to carry a lot of cash. But check on your bank cash card withdrawal limit. For example, you may be limited to $100 a week, so arrange to have that increased before you leave, if you want to access a higher amount.

- You can arrange to have your monthly bank statements forwarded to your Sunbelt address.

- You can pay your Canadian bills personally, on your Canadian chequing account, by having your mail forwarded to your Sunbelt address. It can be more convenient and efficient, however, to arrange for automatic debiting of your Canadian bank account. Alternatively, you can arrange to have the bills sent to your financial institution to pay on your behalf. If you choose this alternative, put your instructions in writing. Bills that can be paid this way include utility bills, cable, house taxes, condominium maintenance fees, and quarterly income tax instalments.

- You may have other investments your financial institution can deal with in your absence—for example, reinvestment of income, deposit of coupons, rollover of maturing deposits, or purchase and sale of securities. Make sure your instructions are in writing and any required documentation is signed in advance. Ask for copies of all transactions dealt with on your behalf to be sent to you at your Sunbelt address.

- If you plan to purchase real estate in the United States, many American financial institutions and some Canadian ones will not lend money to you for a mortgage. Find out whether your Canadian financial institution will lend money for a Sunbelt property based on your Canadian or U.S. assets.

- It is a good idea to take enough money in traveller's cheques to meet your needs for the first month. Many American financial institutions put a hold on a cheque from a Canadian account until it has cleared. This could take over three weeks. After you have established a relationship, however, many U.S. financial institutions will credit your U.S. account the same day you deposit your Canadian cheque.

- If you do not already have an existing U.S. bank account, you can facilitate "no hold" chequing privileges by planning before you leave Canada. For example, you could ask the manager of your Canadian financial institution whether it has a correspondent banking relationship with a U.S. financial institution. If so, this will facilitate a "no hold" policy. Refer to Appendix A, items 29 and 30.

- Ask your bank manager to provide you with a letter of introduction to give to a U.S. bank. Such a letter confirms your good banking track record and creditworthiness and personalizes you. Once you have opened an account in a Sunbelt state, advise the manager you want regular cheque-writing privileges without a 21-day hold for clearing. In other words, you want an immediate deposit. If you have any hassles, there are many other financial institutions that would be delighted to have your business.

- Before you leave Canada, check to see what special Snowbird features are available from Canadian and American financial institutions. Refer to Appendix A, items 29 and 30.

- Consider the benefits of having a U.S. dollar chequing and/or savings account at a Canadian financial institution. These cheques are generally designed to clear through the U.S. clearing system. Also, consider a U.S. dollar credit card from a Canadian financial institution.

- Several major Canadian financial institutions have a special toll-free telephone access for you to pay bills in Canada or the United States in Canadian dollars or U.S. dollar funds, as well as to make balance enquiries.

- Always arrange to have a trusted friend or relative know how to contact you quickly in case of an emergency or to advise you of economic conditions that could affect your investments during your absence.

- Subscribe to one or both of the weekly newspapers for Canadian Snowbirds so that you can be kept aware of news, information, or issues in the United States or Canada relevant to Snowbirds. You can have the publications sent to your Canadian or U.S. address or both, depending on the duration of your Snowbird stay. Refer to item 23 in Appendix A. Also refer to item 22 for a newsletter for Snowbirds.

J. QUICK REFERENCE GUIDE TO RELEVANT PARTS OF THE APPENDICES

To help you obtain further information and contact numbers, here are the parts of the Appendices that are relevant to the contents of this chapter.

Appendix A: Items 1, 4, 8, 13, 22, 23, 29, and 30

Appendix B: Items 3 and 4

Appendix C

CHAPTER

3

Immigration and Customs

A. INTRODUCTION

Many people don't know what regulations apply when they are living in the United States for an extended stay each year. Each country has different regulations that will affect you, and you need to know what they are. Under the Canada-U.S. Free Trade Agreement (FTA), there is reciprocity of goods that are exempt from duty or have reduced duty when crossing the border, if the goods were made in the United States or Canada. The FTA also permits Canadians to stay in the United States longer for business or employment reasons.

This chapter provides an overview of the information about immigration and customs that you need to know.

B. IMMIGRATION REGULATIONS

The following is a summary of the immigration regulations for people travelling or living in the United States.

1. Moving to the United States Part-Time

Many Canadian Snowbirds live in the U.S. Sunbelt states for up to six months a year, during Canada's coldest months. There are tax and other considerations if you wish to stay longer. If you intend to stay only up to six months and you are a Canadian citizen, you will have no difficulty with U.S. immigration regulations. The process is very simple. You simply declare your intention at a U.S. point of entry. Remember to bring your passport, of course.

As a separate issue, you could be considered a U.S. resident for tax purposes only, even though you are still a Canadian citizen, if you stay in the United States for more than a set number of days a year over several years. This topic is discussed in Chapter 6.

2. Moving to the United States Full-Time

There are many implications of moving to the United States full-time. You have to consider issues such as tax, estate planning, financial planning, pensions, housing and health costs, and cost of living, as well as possibly leaving friends and family. There are different tax, pension, and other implications, depending on whether you are living full-time in the United States, permanently or temporarily, and the nature of your stay—for example, whether you are retired, working, or investing in the country. There are also distinct societal and governmental differences between Canada and the United States that become more apparent if you are living in the United States full-time.

Here are the steps to take if you want to explore the process of emigrating to the United States, remaining there over six months, working as a business visitor or professional, or entering under a trader or investor category:

- Contact the closest U.S. Immigration and Naturalization Service (INS) to get information and find out if you are eligible and the procedures to follow. Refer to item 15 in Appendix A.

- Contact the closest U.S. Consulate or U.S. Embassy if you wish to enter the United States under a trader or investor category. They will advise you as to your eligibility. Refer to item 12 in Appendix A for U.S. Consulates in Canada.

- Contact the U.S. Internal Revenue Service (IRS) to determine the tax implications of living full-time in the United States. The IRS is equivalent to Revenue Canada and has an office in Ottawa. Refer to item 13 in Appendix A.

- Contact Revenue Canada to determine the tax implications if you are leaving Canada to live full-time in the United States. Refer to item 1 in Appendix A.

- Contact Health Canada (item 4 in Appendix A) and your provincial office for seniors (item 8) to determine the implications for federal pensions or federal and provincial Medicare coverage.

- Contact your employer/union/association retirement benefit plan to determine the implications of living full-time in the United States.

- Contact a lawyer in Canada who specializes in immigration law relating to emigrating to the United States or living there full-time. Contact your local lawyer referral service or look in the Yellow Pages of your phone book under "Lawyers." You may also want to obtain a second opinion from a U.S. immigration lawyer. Ask your lawyer to give you a referral for U.S. lawyers who are experts on wills and estate issues, real estate, and so on so that you can have your interests looked after for continuity before departure and after your arrival in the United States. Refer to Chapter 8 for information about selecting professional and other advisors in both Canada and the United States.

- Contact a professional accountant in Canada who specializes in tax to obtain customized advice for your situation. Most major international chartered accountancy firms have experts on the tax issues of Canadians living part-time or full-time in the United States. You may also want to have a second opinion from a U.S. Certified Public Accountant (CPA) who is an expert on cross-border tax issues. Arrange to have a referral to a U.S. accountant in the area where you will be living who is a tax expert. You want to have continuity of advice before leaving Canada. Refer to Chapter 8 for further information.

- Contact an objective, professional financial planner to give you customized assessment and advice after you move to the United States full-time. Again, refer to Chapter 8 for further information about selecting a financial planner. If you are staying in the United States full-time on a temporary basis—in other words, if you still have a cross-border connection with Canada—you will want to maintain a relationship with a professional financial planner in Canada.

- Read *Immigrating to the U.S.A.*, written by two U.S. immigration lawyers, Dan Danilov and Howard Deutsch, and published by Self-Counsel Press. Make sure you have the most current edition. This book will give you a good overview of the key concepts and regulations.

- Read the booklets on the tax aspects for Canadians working or doing business in the United States that are available free from international accountancy firms. Refer to item 4 in Appendix B.

3. Different U.S. Immigration Categories

You can become a citizen or lawful permanent resident of the United States through derivative citizenship, family, employment, investment, or business. Immigration procedures are highly technical, so you should retain an immigration lawyer experienced in U.S. immigration to assist you.

a) Derivative U.S. Citizenship
This concept means that you are entitled to obtain U.S. citizenship through ancestry. Perhaps you have ancestors or distant relatives who were U.S. citizens before their death. If you think you do, research your family tree and archival documents and records. You can hire professionals who do this type of research. After you have all the documentation and facts available, speak to a U.S. immigration lawyer.

b) Family-Based Immigration
There are various ways that U.S. citizens or lawful permanent residents can bring their relatives into the United States under the family category. Some of the categories have an annual numerical limit and others don't.

- *Immediate relative.* There is no limit on the number of people who can be sponsored under this category. It includes the children, spouse, and parents of a U.S. citizen. The U.S. citizen must be at least 21 years of age. Children are defined as unmarried persons under 21 years of age who are legitimate or legally legitimized children, adopted, or stepchildren.
- *Non-immediate relative.* This category has annual quotas, and members of this category are ranked in order of preference. There are four preference levels. First is an unmarried son or daughter over the age of 21 of a U.S. citizen. Second is a spouse of a lawful permanent resident alien or an unmarried son or daughter of a lawful permanent resident alien. Third is a married son or daughter of a U.S. citizen. The fourth preference level is a brother or sister of a U.S. citizen who is over 21 years of age.

c) Employment-Based Immigration

This form of immigrant visa has four levels of preference. There are annual quotas in each category except for returning U.S. legal permanent residents or former U.S. citizens seeking reinstatement of citizenship.

The first preference is for priority workers, that is, people of extraordinary ability, outstanding professors and researchers, and multinational executives and managers. The second preference is for a professional with an advanced degree or exceptional ability. The third preference is for a professional without an advanced degree, a skilled worker, or an unskilled worker. The last and fourth preference is for what is called special immigrants, including religious workers and returning U.S. legal permanent residents or former U.S. citizens seeking reinstatement of citizenship.

d) Investor Immigration

The U.S. government wants to attract investors from other countries and, if the conditions are met, will give them an immigrant visa. The reason is to stimulate economic activity and employment. Canada has the same type of foreign investor interest, as do most other countries. Canadians wishing to make a business investment in the United States may qualify for this immigrant visa. It is referred to as a fifth preference category (E-5) and has an annual limit. In addition, the Canada-U.S. Free Trade Agreement (FTA) gives Treaty Trader (E-1) and Treaty Investor (E-2) status to Canadian nonimmigrant investors.

A Canadian may qualify under the E-5 category of immigrant visa if certain criteria are met. These could include establishing and investing in a business and employing at least 10 U.S. workers full-time. Depending on the location and need, the financial investment required could range from $500,000 to $1 million.

e) Business Travellers under the Canada-U.S. Free Trade Agreement (FTA)

The FTA became effective on January 1, 1989, and was designed to facilitate trade and travel between the two countries. The agreement respecting various categories of business travellers is designed for nonimmigrants who could be living full-time in the United States. The FTA affects only temporary entrants into the United States. It is possible, however, that a history of operating under one of these categories could facilitate a subsequent application for an immigrant visa under another category. Spouses and children accompanying business travellers must satisfy normal admission requirements and cannot work or study (as full-time students) in the United States without prior authorization.

There are several categories, the four main ones being:

- *Business visitor (B-1 status).* Canadian citizens who visit the United States on business for their Canadian company and receive remuneration from their Canadian employer.

- *Intra-company transfer (L-1 status).* A person who has been employed continuously for at least one year by a Canadian firm, as executive, manager, or specialist. This person can render services temporarily to the same firm (or its subsidiary or affiliate) in the United States. The position has to be in an executive or managerial capacity, or in a position of special knowledge.

- *Professionals (TC-1 status).* A Canadian professional, with an approved occupation, travelling to the United States to work temporarily in the profession for which they are qualified.

- *Traders and Investors (E-1 and E-2 visas).* A trader who works in a Canadian-owned or -controlled firm in the United States that carries on substantial trade in goods or services, principally between Canada and the United States. The position must be supervisory or executive, or involve skill essential to the operation of the U.S. firm.

  An investor who has invested, or is in the process of investing, a substantial amount of capital in the United States. The investor must develop and direct the operation of the business in the United States.

C. CUSTOMS REGULATIONS

1. Travelling to the United States

If you are a resident of Canada on a visit to the United States as a Snowbird for up to six months, your U.S. customs status is that of a nonresident. There are various regulations involved, exemptions permitted, and privileges allowed.

If you are arriving in the United States by land, air, or sea, a simple oral declaration that the allowed exemptions from duty apply to you is generally sufficient. In certain situations you might be requested to fill out a written declaration. Make sure you bring your passport with you.

The following is a discussion of the main areas you need to know. Contact the U.S. Customs Service for further information and free explanatory brochures. Refer to item 14 in Appendix A, as well as items 16 and 17. Since regulations can change, make sure you have current information from the U.S. Customs Service.

a) Exemptions

Here are some of the main federal exemptions for nonresidents of the United States:

- *Personal effects* are exempt from duty if they are for your personal use, are owned by you, and accompany you to the United States.
- *Alcoholic beverages* are free of duty and internal revenue tax if they are for personal use and do not exceed one litre. Some state alcoholic beverage laws may be more restrictive than federal liquor laws.
- *Vehicles* can be temporarily imported to the United States for one year or less if they are used for transportation for you, your family, or your guests.
- *Household effects* are free from duty if they are for your personal use and not for another person or for sale.

b) Gifts

There are several exemptions under this category:

- *Gifts you bring with you* are free of duty or tax if you are remaining in the United States for at least 72 hours and if the gifts do not exceed U.S. $100 in retail value. This $100 exemption can be claimed once every six months. Alcoholic beverages are not included. Articles bought in so-called duty-free shops are subject to U.S. Customs duty and restrictions if they exceed your exemption.
- *Gifts sent by mail* are free of duty if they are mailed from Canada to the United States, and do not exceed U.S. $50 in retail value. You may send as many gifts as you wish, but if they are all sent to the same U.S. addressee, there will be duty payable if the daily receipt of gifts exceeds $50. Packages should be marked "unsolicited gift" with the name of donor, nature of the gift, and fair retail value of the gift clearly written on the outside of the package.

c) Items Subject to Duty

If you import items to the United States that cannot be claimed under the allowed exemptions, they will be subject to applicable duty and tax. After deducting your exemptions and the value of any duty-free articles, a flat rate of duty of 10 percent will be applied to the next U.S. $1,000 worth (fair retail value) of merchandise. If you exceed $1,000 worth, you will be charged duty at various rates, depending on the item. The flat rate of duty applies only if the items are for personal use or for gifts.

d) Shipping Goods

You do not need to accompany personal and household effects to the United States that are entitled to free entry. You can have them shipped to your United States address at a later time if it is more convenient. You do not need to use a customs broker to clear your shipment through Customs. You may do this yourself after you arrive in the United States or designate a friend or relative to represent you in Customs matters. If you take the latter route, you must give your representative a letter addressed to the Officer in Charge of Customs authorizing that person to represent you as your agent on a one-time basis in clearing your shipment through Customs. You have five working days to clear your shipment through Customs after its arrival in the United States; otherwise, it will be sent, at your expense and risk, to a storage warehouse.

e) Money

There is no limit on the total amount of money you can bring into or take out of the United States. If you are carrying more than U.S. $10,000 into or out of the country at any one time, however, you must file a report with U.S. Customs. This rule applies to currency, traveller's cheques, money orders, and so on.

f) Prohibited and Restricted Items

Because U.S. Customs inspectors are stationed at ports of entry, they are frequently required to enforce laws and requirements of other U.S. government agencies in order to protect community health, to preserve domestic plant and animal life, and for other reasons.

There are several prohibited or restricted categories that you should be aware of. Here are a few of them:

- *Medicine and narcotics.* Narcotics are normally prohibited entry and are tightly regulated. However, if you require medicines containing habit-forming drugs or narcotics (e.g., cough medicine, diuretics, heart drugs, tranquillizers, sleeping pills, depressants, stimulants), you should
  - have all drugs, medicines, and similar products properly identified,
  - carry only the quantity that might normally be used for the length of your stay in the United States for health problems requiring such drugs or medicine, and
  - have either a prescription or a written statement from your personal physician that the medicine is being used under a doctor's direction and is necessary for your physical well-being while travelling or staying in the United States.

- *Pets.* Cats and dogs can be brought in, but they must be free of evidence of communicable diseases. If you plan to bring your pet, obtain a copy of the leaflet "Pets, Wildlife." Refer to item 14 in Appendix A.

- *Wildlife and fish.* These are subject to certain import and export restrictions, prohibitions, permits, and so on. Any part of certain types of wildlife or fish, or products and articles manufactured from them, could be affected, especially endangered species, which are prohibited from being imported or exported. If you are in doubt as to whether certain leather goods, skins, or furs are governed by the regulations, contact the U.S. Fish and Wildlife Service. Refer to item 17, Appendix A, for a contact address and brochure.

- *Food products.* Certain food products might be restricted. If you are in doubt, contact the U.S. Department of Agriculture Animal and Plant Inspection Service. Refer to item 16 in Appendix A.

- *Fruits, vegetables, plants.* Every fruit, vegetable, or plant being brought into the United States is supposed to be declared to the Customs officer in case it is a restricted item.

2. Returning to Canada

When you return to Canada after your U.S. Snowbird stay, there are various regulations that you must comply with. As far as the Canadian Government is concerned, if you have not been out of the country for more than six months, you are still a resident Canadian citizen. If you have been out of the country more than six months or you are a U.S. citizen resident in Canada, other customs regulations could apply. These customs regulations cover such matters as bringing back goods and vehicles. For vehicles, Transport Canada's regulations also must be considered. For further information, refer to the Canada Customs contact numbers and free explanatory publications outlined in item 2, Appendix A. Also refer to item 3 for information about Transport Canada. Obtain current information, since regulations can change.

Here is a summary of the key regulations:

a) Bringing Back Goods Purchased in the United States

Foreign goods for your personal use in Canada that you import from the United States must meet all import requirements and you must pay the appropriate duties after your exemption has been used. Each person is entitled to a duty exemption up to $500 in Canadian funds, as of June 13, 1995, after seven or more days' absence from Canada. There are no longer any calendar year restrictions; you can use this exemption as often as you want. You only pay duties on the value of goods over your exemption amount. Keep receipts for everything you might be declaring and convert the U.S. amount to the Canadian equivalent.

b) Bringing Back Cars, RVs, Trucks, and Other Vehicles Purchased in the United States

If you bought a new or used car, truck, trailer, or motor home in the United States, you will have to pay import assessments when you return to Canada. These include duty and excise tax if the vehicle is air-conditioned, or if it is a passenger vehicle weighing over 4,425 pounds (2007 kg). In addition, you would have to pay the federal goods and services tax (GST) of 7 percent and any applicable provincial sales or other taxes. Check with your provincial government.

The duty rate for eligible vehicles imported from the United States that fall under the Canada-U.S. Free Trade Agreement (FTA), that is, vehicles made in the United States or Canada, is 2.7 percent in 1995. If the vehicle was not made in the United States or Canada and therefore does not fall under the FTA, then the duty is 8.6 percent.

To determine the value of the vehicle for duty purposes, the original U.S. purchase price, including state sales tax and other applicable costs, will be converted into Canadian funds. That amount will vary, of course, depending on the exchange rate at the time. If you import a new vehicle within 30 days of the date it was delivered to you, the above formula applies, with no deduction for depreciation. If you purchased a new vehicle and imported it within one year of the date of delivery to you, however, you can deduct an amount for depreciation of the value of the car. Make enquiries. You can't obtain depreciation for a car that was purchased used. For a used car, the fair market value will be set according to vehicle values from a neutral source—for example, the U.S. or Canadian *Automobile Red Book*. If you have traded your old car in for a different car, the value of the new car will be a used value.

Make sure you have all receipts with you and any bill of sale. Ideally, have a current fair market value done on dealership letterhead, if you bought the vehicle from a dealership. You do not want to declare an artificially low value for the vehicle or have receipts that are clearly way below market value. **The reason: if you underestimate the vehicle value, Canada Customs can seize the vehicle and impound it until you pay a penalty of 40 percent of the correct value of the vehicle.** In that event, you have a 30-day period to make a written appeal, but it could take up to a year or more to adjudicate, and in the meantime you are out your car or penalty money. To avoid any stress or uncertainty, contact Canada Customs beforehand if you have any questions or doubts in your particular circumstances.

For further information about determining vehicle value for Customs purposes, contact the Canada Customs office closest to your expected point of entry or phone 1-800-461-9991 (toll-free in Canada only). Do this before you arrive at Customs. Refer to item 2 in Appendix A.

c) Transport Canada Vehicle Prohibitions
As of January 1, 1993, as a result of the FTA, there are no longer any Customs prohibitions on bringing a vehicle into Canada from the United States. There are restrictive importation rules for vehicles under Transport Canada regulations, however. Because of strict Canadian safety and emission standards, you may be prohibited from importing a vehicle that only meets U.S. standards, unless it is brought up to full Canadian compliance standards.

To satisfy yourself that the vehicle you want to import is eligible and to find out what documents you require, contact Transport Canada before you buy the vehicle. Phone 1-800-333-0558. This number is for the Registrar of Imported Vehicles and is toll-free from Canada and the United States. The registry was formed by Transport Canada in April 1995. There is an administrative charge of approximately $195–$245, plus GST, depending on your port of entry. This fee is to process the necessary approval documentation. Refer to item 3 in Appendix A for a list of free explanatory publications.

E. TIPS BEFORE LEAVING CANADA

- Take your passport and birth certificate with you if you are having an extended stay in the United States.

- If you are considering staying in the United States more than six months in the year, check with the U.S. Immigration and Naturalization Services (INS) and with an experienced cross-border tax accountant on the tax implications. Also check with a Canadian immigration lawyer experienced in U.S. immigration matters before you depart. Refer to Chapter 8, on selecting professional advisors.

- Check with U.S. Customs for the current policy on items you think might be prohibited or restricted in the United States. Ask about exemptions, shipping goods, and items that could be subject to duty.

- If you are considering buying a vehicle in the United States, check Customs and Transport Canada regulations for returning to Canada with the vehicle. Do this before you buy the vehicle.

- Check with Canada Customs on the current policy for bringing back goods purchased in the United States. What items are duty-free and what items require that you pay duty?

- Take receipts for items that have a high dollar value, in case you are challenged on your return to Canada. It is good to have proof that you bought a camera or expensive jewellery in Canada.

F. QUICK REFERENCE GUIDE TO RELEVANT PARTS OF THE APPENDICES

To help you obtain further information and contact numbers, here are the parts of the Appendices that are relevant to the contents of this chapter.

Appendix A: Items 2, 3, 6, 7, 12, 14, 15, 16, 17, and 22

CHAPTER

4

Housing and Real Estate

A. INTRODUCTION

There are many towns and RV or mobile home parks built specifically for retired people and Snowbirds in selected locations in the United States. Some of the advantages include the opportunity to live and socialize in a homogeneous community; planned social activities such as bingo, dancing, crafts, card games, trips, and educational programs; recreational facilities such as tennis courts, exercise rooms, a swimming pool, and golf and shuffleboard areas; services such as maintenance services and shopping and transportation facilities; and religious services. Security is another reason for the popularity of retirement communities. Many have 24-hour security services, which keep watch on the residences and check all visitors when they enter or leave.

Retirement communities have some drawbacks, however. For example, some communities are becoming crowded and increasingly costly. Some people don't enjoy planned activities and lessons. Others feel too isolated in communities that are far away from urban centres.

By identifying your own needs and wants, speaking to others, and doing your research, you will quickly determine what choice is the right one for you.

This chapter provides an overview of the considerations you should keep in mind when buying a house, apartment, condominium, townhouse, time-share, mobile home, or recreational vehicle in the United States. Refer to Chapter 6 for a discussion of the tax consequences of renting or selling your house or condo and of owning real estate in the United States if you die.

For more detailed information on issues related to real estate, refer to my other books published by McGraw-Hill Ryerson, including *Home Buying Made Easy, Condo Buying Made Easy, Home Selling Made Easy, Mortgages Made Easy, Mortgage Payment Tables Made Easy,* and *Making Money in Real Estate.*

B. BUYING A HOUSE

You may wish to buy a house in the U.S. Sunbelt that you intend to live in while you are there and leave vacant or possibly rent out the rest of the time. Maybe you hope to move to the United States at some point to live there full-time.

Whatever your motivation, there are some key steps to follow. You have probably already owned a house at some point, but the following tips and cautions bear repeating as a reminder. Once you have determined your needs, location, price, and other matters, here are the other factors to consider. Many of these are equally applicable when selecting a condo. Certain factors may be more or less important or relevant than others.

1. Where to Find a Home for Sale

There are some preliminary considerations you need to work through before starting your search:

- Be clearly focused on what type of real estate you want in order to save time and stress.
- Target specific geographic area or areas. This means restricting your choices to specific communities or areas within a community. This makes your selection much easier and gives you an opportunity to get to know specific areas thoroughly. Obtain street maps of the areas.
- Know the price range that you want based on your funds and real estate needs.
- Determine the type of ideal purchase package that you want (e.g., price and terms) as well as your "bottom line" fallback position. What is the maximum you are willing to pay?
- Make comparisons and short-list choices. That way you can ensure that you get the best deal.

There are various methods of finding out about what real estate is for sale. The most common methods are: word-of-mouth, using a real estate agent, reading local or real estate newspaper ads, or driving through the preferred neighbourhood and looking for For Sale signs.

2. General Tips When Looking for a Home

- **Location**
  One of the prime considerations is the location. How close is the property to cultural attractions, shopping centres, recreational facilities, community and religious facilities, and transportation? How attractive is the present development of the area surrounding the property? What is likely to happen in the future? Is there ample access to parking? Check on the amount

of traffic on the streets in your area. Heavy traffic can be a noise nuisance as well as a hazard.

- **Pricing**
  The pricing of the property you are considering should be competitive with that of other, similar offerings. This can be difficult to determine unless you are comparing identical homes in a subdivision or condos in the same complex. If you are purchasing a condominium unit, for example, it is sometimes difficult to compare prices accurately without taking into account the different amenities that may be available in one condominium complex that are not available in the other—for example, tennis courts, swimming pool, and recreation centre. You may decide that you do not want these extra facilities, in which case paying an extra price for the unit because it has these features would not be attractive. At the same time, you have to look at the resale potential.

- **Knowledge of the home and neighbourhood**
  Surveys have shown that the average home buyer spends 17 minutes looking at the home before making the purchase decision, often making a decision on an emotional basis. Seventeen minutes is not enough time for anything other than a superficial look. You don't want to suffer from buyer's remorse. You want to look at the property on several occasions to obtain a fresh perspective. Look at it in the day and evening. Look at the house when the owner is not present so that you can examine it thoroughly and at a leisurely pace. Bring a friend or relative with you. Take pictures outside and inside, if necessary, to enhance your recall if you are serious about buying the place. Make sure you drive around the neighbourhood to get a feeling for the appearance and conditions of other homes in the vicinity. If you wish to place an offer, remember to include a condition relating to inspection by a professional home inspector.

- **Reasons for sale**
  One of the important factors to determine is why the property is for sale. Maybe the vendor knows something you don't that will have a bearing on your future interest. Or maybe the vendor is selling the home because of a desire to move to a larger or smaller home or a condo, because of loss of employment, or because of a serious illness or disability.

- **Property taxes**
  Compare the costs of property taxes in the area that you are considering with those of other, equally attractive areas. Different municipalities have different tax rates, and there could be a considerable cost saving or expense. Also enquire as to whether there is any anticipated tax increase and why. For example, if the area is relatively new, there could be future property taxes or special levies to establish schools or other community support services.

- **Transportation**

  If you drive a car, how much traffic is there and how long would the commute take at various times of the day? Is public transportation available within walking distance? How reliable and frequent is it? Whether it is a bus, subway, rapid transit, freeway, ferry, or other mode of transportation, the quality of transportation will affect the quality of your life, as well as the resale price.

- **Crime rate**

  Naturally this is an important issue. Check with the local police department for crime statistics in your area, and talk with neighbours on the street. Ask if there is a "block watch" or "neighbourhood watch" program in the area.

- **Services in the community**

  Depending on your needs, you will want to check on the different services available in the community. A community will often be characterized by the local services. Is there adequate police, fire, and ambulance protection? Is there a hospital in the area? Are there doctors and dentists located in the vicinity? How often is garbage collected and streets maintained? Is mail delivered to your door or to a central mailbox location on your street or in your neighbourhood? If you wish to join an organization or club, is it close? Does the area cater to seniors or Snowbirds? Are there community centres or public parks nearby? Is there a place of worship of your faith in the neighbourhood? If the house or condo is proximate to a commercial development, are noise and traffic a problem? What types of businesses, stores, or services are nearby?

- **Climate**

  If you are buying for personal use, the issue of climate is important. Certain areas of your city or community may have more rain and higher wind than others, depending on climate patterns. Check with a local, state, or national weather bureau.

- **Parking**

  Is parking outdoors, in a garage, in an open carport, or underground? Is there sufficient lighting for security protection? Is it a long walk from the parking spot to your home? Is there parking space available for a recreational vehicle or second car? Is there ample parking for visitors in the lot or on the street? Is there a private driveway or back lane connected to the garage or carport? Is street parking restricted in any fashion (e.g., residents' parking only)? Is the restriction enforced? Do you need to buy a permit?

- **Topography**

  The layout of the land is an important consideration. If there is a hill along the property, water could collect around the base of the house, causing drainage problems. If water collects under the foundation of the house and there is only soil under the foundation, the house could settle.

- **Condition of building and property**
  Obtain an objective and accurate assessment of the condition of the property. Having an independent building inspector look at it is one recommendation; you can find a building inspector in the Yellow Pages of the phone book. In addition, the vendor should answer specific questions, posed by either the building inspector or you. You also want to make sure you include appropriate conditions in your agreement of purchase and sale for obtaining or confirming information.

- **Type of construction**
  Is the building constructed of wood, brick, concrete, stone, or other material? Is this important for fire safety concerns you might have?

- **Common elements and facilities**
  If you are buying a condominium unit, review all the common elements that make up the condominium development. Consider whether these elements are relevant to your needs as well as what maintenance or operational costs might be required to service these features.

- **Noise**
  Thoroughly check the levels of noise. Consider such factors as location of highways, driveways, parking lots, playgrounds, and businesses. If you are buying a condominium, also consider the location of the garage doors, elevators, and garbage chutes, as well as the heating and air-conditioning plant or equipment.

- **Privacy**
  Privacy is an important consideration and has to be thoroughly explored. For example, you want to make sure that the sound insulation between the walls, floors, and ceilings of your property is sufficient to enable you to live comfortably without annoying your neighbours or having your neighbours annoy you. If you have a condominium or townhouse unit, such factors as the distance between your unit and other common areas, including walkways, parking lot, and fences, are important.

- **Storage space**
  Is there enough closet and storage space? Is the location and size suitable? Are the kitchen, hall, and bedroom closets big enough for your needs? Is the basement or other storage area enough for sports and other equipment, tools, and outdoor furniture?

- **Heating / cooling**
  How is the house heated or cooled, directly and indirectly? Is the system efficient for your needs (e.g., does it use natural gas, oil, forced air, hot water, radiators, electric baseboard, wood-burning stove, or fireplace)? How old is the furnace? Has it been serviced regularly and is it still covered by warranty? Do you have any air-conditioning or ceiling fans? Is there a heat exchanger system in the fireplace? What are the annual heating/cooling bills?

3. Questions to Ask

Some of the common questions that should be asked are as follows. Address these to your lawyer, real estate agent, vendor, and building inspector.

a) Questions of a General Nature

- Does the property contain unauthorized accommodation?
- Are you aware of any registered or unregistered encroachments, easements, or rights of way?
- Have you received any notice or claim affecting the property from any person or public body?
- Are the premises connected to a public water system?
- Are the premises connected to a private or a community water system?

b) Questions about the Structure of the Dwelling

- Are you aware of any infestation by insects or rodents?
- Are you aware of any damage due to wind, fire, or water?
- Are you aware of any moisture and/or water problems in the basement or crawl space?
- Are you aware of any problems with the heating and/or central air-conditioning system?
- Are you aware of any problems with the electrical system?
- Are you aware of any problems with the plumbing system?
- Are you aware of any problems with the swimming pool and/or hot tub?
- Are you aware of any roof leakage or unrepaired damage?
- How many years old is the roof?
- Are you aware of any structural problems with the premises or other buildings on the property?
- Are you aware of any problems related to the building's settling?
- Are you aware of any additions or alterations made without a required permit?
- Has the wood stove or fireplace been approved by local authorities?
- To the best of your knowledge, have the premises ever contained urea formaldehyde insulation (UFFI)?
- To the best of your knowledge, have the premises ever contained asbestos insulation?
- To the best of your knowledge, is the ceiling insulated?
- To the best of your knowledge, are the exterior walls insulated?

c) Questions Regarding a Condominium Property

- Are there any restrictions on pets, children, or rentals?

- Are there any pending rules or condominium bylaw amendments that may alter the uses of the property?
- Are there any special assessments voted on or proposed?

C. BUYING A CONDOMINIUM OR TOWNHOUSE

Many people purchase a condominium to live in. Living in a condominium is not right for everyone, though, since it involves not only individual ownership of the unit and shared ownership of other property but also adherence to rules and regulations and shared rulership. But many people prefer condominium living over the alternatives, especially since many condominiums are adult oriented and don't permit children to live there unless they are just visiting. Other condominium projects are geared specifically to retired people, providing security and social activities, for example.

Condominiums may be detached, semidetached, row houses, stack townhouses, duplexes, or apartments. They can even be building lots, subdivisions, or mobile home parks. In general terms, the most familiar format for a condominium is an apartment condominium, that is, one level, or a townhouse condominium, which is two or more levels. Whatever the style, a residential unit is specified and is owned by an individual in a freehold (owning the land) or leasehold (leasing rights to the land only) format. The rest of the property, including land, which is called the common elements in most provinces and states, is owned in common with the other owners. Common elements generally include walkways, driveways, lawns and gardens, lobbies, elevators, parking areas, recreational facilities, storage areas, laundry rooms, stairways, plumbing, electrical systems and portions of walls, ceilings and floors, and other items. An owner would own a fractional share of the common elements in the development. If there are 50 condominium owners, then each individual owner would own one-fiftieth of the common elements as tenants in common. The legislation of each province or state can vary, but it is always designed to provide the legal and structural framework for the efficient management and administration of each condominium project.

The part of the condominium that you own outright is referred to as the unit in most provinces and states. You have full and clear title to this unit when you purchase it (assuming you are buying a freehold, not a leasehold, property), and the property is legally registered in your name in the land registry office in the province or state. The precise description of the common elements, and exactly what you own as part of your unit, may differ from development to development, but it is stipulated in the documents prepared and registered for each condominium. Part of the common elements may be designated for the exclusive use of one or more of the individual unit owners, in which case they are called limited common elements. In other words, they are limited for the use only of specific owners. Examples include parking spaces, storage lockers, roof gardens, balconies, patios, and front and back yards.

A condominium development is administered by various legal structures set out in provincial or state legislation. Snowbirds who purchase a recreational or resort condominium tend to own it outright and leave it empty when not in use or rent it by using the condominium corporation or   management company as an agent, using a real estate agent, or renting it independently.

In any situation of shared ownership and community living there are advantages and disadvantages. An overview of these follows.

a) Advantages

- Ready availability of financing, similar to a single-family home.

- Range of prices, locations, types of structures, sizes, and architectural features available.

- Availability of amenities such as swimming pool, tennis courts, health clubs, community centre, saunas, hot tubs, exercise rooms, and sun decks.

- Benefits of home ownership in ability to participate in the real estate market and potential growth in equity.

- Freedom to decorate interior of unit to suit personal tastes.

- Enhancement of security by permanence of neighbours and, in many cases, controlled entrances.

- Elimination of many of the problems of upkeep and maintenance often associated with home ownership, since maintenance is usually the responsibility of a professional management company or manager.

- Often considerably cheaper than buying a single-family home because of more efficient use of land and economy of scale.

- Reduction of costs due to sharing of responsibilities for repair and maintenance.

- Enhancement of social activities and sense of neighbourhood community by relative permanence of residents. In many cases, the residents are other Snowbirds.

- Elected council that is responsible for many business and management decisions.

- Participation of owners in the operation of the development, which involves playing a role in setting and approval of budget, decision making, determination of rules, regulations, and by-laws, and other matters affecting the democratic operation of the condominium community.

b) Disadvantages

- May be difficult to accurately assess the quality of construction of the project.

- A loss of freedom may be experienced through restrictions contained in the rules and bylaws (e.g., restriction on the right to rent, on pets, on duration of stay of visitors, or on use of a barbecue on the patio).

- People live closer together, creating problems from time to time; problem areas include the five P's: pets, parking, personality, parties, and people.

- One could be paying for maintenance and operation of amenities that one has no desire or intention to use.

- Management of the condominium council is by volunteers, who may or may not have the appropriate abilities and skills.

Condominiums are a popular form of housing, especially for older Canadians or those who have retired. The many benefits will ensure that the demand for this type of housing will grow. Make sure you obtain objective legal advice from a real estate lawyer before you make a final decision to purchase a condominium. Refer to the previous section for tips on what to look for when buying a home.

D. BUYING A TIME-SHARE

Resort time-sharing originated in Europe in the 1960s, when high costs and demand for limited resort space created the need for a way to ensure accommodation for a certain period of time each year. Time-shares are usually sold by the week and include fully furnished accommodation with maintenance and maid service. The concept was adopted in Florida in the 1970s to revive the sluggish condominium industry. Since then, time-shares have grown rapidly, with thousands of this type of resort throughout Canada, the United States, and the world. These resorts range from Ontario cottage country resorts to Florida condos to Mexican beach villas. Hundreds of thousands of people have purchased time-shares. At some time or another you have probably seen the ads: "Luxury Lifestyle at Affordable Prices!" "Vacation the World!" "Trade for Exotic Climes!" "Buy Your Own Vacation Dream Home!"

Other frequently used terms that are synonymous with time-sharing include *resort time-sharing, vacation ownership, multi-ownership, interval ownership,* and *shared vacation plan.* The time-share concept has been applied to numerous other areas, such as recreational vehicle and mobile home parks.

There are two main categories of time-shares: *fee simple ownership* and *right to use.*

1. Fee Simple Ownership

There are different formats. One option is to own a portion of the condominium, such as one-fiftieth of the property. Each one-fiftieth portion entitles you to one week's use of the premises per year. Other people also buy into the property. Frequently you are allocated a fixed week every year. In other instances, you could have a floating time, with the exact dates to be agreed upon according to availability. In some cases, you might purchase a quarter- or half-interest. If the complete property is sold, you would receive your proportional share of any increase in net after-sale proceeds. You would also normally be able to rent, sell, or give your ownership portion to anyone you wished.

2. Right to Use

This concept is much like having a long-term lease, but with use for just a one-week period every year. This arrangement is similar to prepaying for a hotel room for a fixed period every year for 20 years in advance. In other words, you don't have any portion of ownership in the property; you only have a right to use it for a fixed or floating time period every year. Condominiums, recreational vehicle parks, and other types of properties offer right-to-use time-shares.

The opportunity for return on your money in a right-to-use time-share is limited or nonexistent. This is because there is generally very little demand in the after-sale market, as well as other restrictions on resale or pricing of the resale.

In practical terms, time-sharing is primarily a lifestyle choice. Here are some of the disadvantages and cautions to be aware of:

- You may tire of going to the same location every year, since your needs may change over time.
- The time-share programs that include an exchange option (e.g., switching a week in a different location) are not always as anticipated in availability, flexibility, convenience, or upgrade fee.
- Make sure you know what you are getting. Some people who purchase the right-to-use type think they are buying a fee simple ownership portion.
- Be wary of hard-sell marketing. In most instances, the dream fantasy is heavily reinforced, and "free" inducements, such as a buffet dinner or an evening dinner cruise with a large group of other people, are used to entice you to hear a sales pitch first. High-pressure sales pitches, with teams of salespeople, can go on for hours. The sales representatives can be very persuasive, if not aggressive, and often use very manipulative techniques to get you to sign a credit card slip as a deposit. The "freebies" would generally cost you from $10 to $25. It is an illusion to think you are going to get

something for nothing. At best, you will be subjected to an intense one-on-one sales approach. At worst, you will be out your deposit money if you change your mind, unless there is a time period during which you may cancel. Otherwise, trying to get your money back afterwards, if you suffer from "buyer's remorse," is extremely difficult, if not impossible, especially if the time-share is outside Canada.

- Time-share sales in Canada and some U.S. states are sometimes covered by consumer protection, ensuring your right to get your money back by "rescinding" (cancelling) the contract within a certain time period.
- There is usually a regular management fee for maintaining the premises.

Time-shares are a dream for some but a nightmare for others. Speak to at least three other time-share owners in the project you are considering to get their candid opinion before you decide to buy. Never give out your credit card as a deposit, and don't sign any documents requested of you without first speaking with a local real estate lawyer. You can obtain a lawyer's name from the local lawyer referral service or provincial or state bar association; refer to Chapter 8. You might also want to check with the local Better Business Bureau before you make a decision. Don't let yourself be pressured. Sleep on the idea for a while, and if the deal seems too good to be true, it probably is. Remember, act in haste, repent at leisure.

If you want more details on time-shares in Canada, contact the Canadian Resort Development Association (CRDA) in Toronto at 1-800-646-9205 or (416) 960-4930. Ask for their free publication, *A Consumers Introduction to Internal Ownership and Vacation Club Membership*. Also ask if a particular development is a member of CRDA and if there have been any complaints.

If you are buying in the United States, contact the American Resort Development Association in Washington, DC, at (202) 371-6700. Ask for their free publication, *A Consumer's Guide to Resort and Urban Timesharing*. If you are interested in RV or mobile home time-share options in the United States, refer to item 40 in Appendix A. Most of these companies will permit you to stay at their locations for a nominal fee to see if you like them. Make enquiries.

E. BUYING A MOBILE HOME / MANUFACTURED HOME

Mobile homes, now frequently referred to as manufactured homes, are a very popular form of housing for Canadian Snowbirds. Some people live in a mobile home in Canada as well as one in the United States. The term "mobile home" can be confusing. It is not an RV and has no wheels, though it is manufactured to be moved by a large truck and set up on a permanent foundation, referred to as a pad. It is meant to be like any other house, except that it can be readily moved to a new location if desired. In some cases, a basement is built and the mobile home is set on top.

Mobile homes generally come in two widths. The single width is about 10 to 16 feet (3 to 5 m) wide and sometimes as long as 64 feet (19.5 m). The double homes are built in two sections and when combined are approximately twice as wide as a single. This type of unit can be very spacious and in many respects have the rooms, features, and appliances of a regular house. You can either buy a mobile home and have it put on the location of your choice or buy one already on a site. You have to be careful when selecting a mobile home. You must make sure it meets safety standards. Some older mobile homes contain flammable materials or are poorly designed and may not even be insurable, so check with your insurance company beforehand. Most mobile homes are in parks that are set up as permanent communities, even though many of the residents may be Snowbirds who only live there for six months a year. These private parks provide water, sewer, and electricity hook-ups and frequently have other features, such as a recreation and social centre, a swimming pool, tennis courts, a golf course, and security personnel. Some parks may have from 200 to 1,000 or more mobile homes.

Some parks are restricted to retired people, others to Snowbirds; some combine seasonal and permanent residents. RVs are permitted in some parks and not in others. There is a variety of different formats for these parks, which are regulated by local and/or state bylaws. In some rural locations there are few restrictions; in urban settings separate parks are established specifically for mobile homes. Some have communities that are independent and include their own facilities, whereas others use the facilities of the closest community.

Before deciding to buy a mobile home, you may want to rent one for a season to see if you like the concept and the area. Talk to other mobile home owners to get their advice on makes and models. Check with the Association of Mobile Home Owners. Refer to item 20 in Appendix A for Sunbelt state associations. These associations can provide you with invaluable information, insurance, and the names of mobile home parks in their state. They also lobby for the interests of mobile homeowners in their respective states. Also refer to item 19 for state travel park associations.

Finally, before you sign any documents to buy a mobile home or rent a park location, check with a real estate lawyer in the area for your protection. Your lot lease and mobile home warranty and contract can be reviewed for clauses or exclusions that you might not understand or want.

F. BUYING A RECREATIONAL VEHICLE (RV)

Owning an RV is a growing trend, especially among people aged 55 and up. Nearly half of the nine million RVs on the road in the United States are owned by people over 55. There are many reasons for the popularity of RVs with this age group. People in this age group have the time, discretionary income, and desire to see and experience the small towns, big cities, popular attractions, and natural beauty of North America. RVs provide an enjoyable, comfortable, and economical way to take it all in and provide an opportunity to meet new people on the road. Other advantages include spontaneity and convenience. RVs can be kept packed with essentials and ready to travel at a moment's notice. Comfort is another factor. RVs can have complete living, dining, sleeping, and bathroom facilities to provide travellers with all the amenities of home while on the road, as well as slide-out rooms for expansion.

An RV is defined as a motorized or towable vehicle that combines transportation and temporary living quarters for travel, recreation, and camping. RVs do not include mobile homes. There are many types of RVs, with a wide range of prices for new RVs, from $2,000 for the least expensive folding camping trailer to over $100,000 for a customized motor home. There are many price categories within this range. Used RVs of course cost less, and if you buy off season, you can get better deals. Here is a description of some of the specific types of RVs and the current average retail price in U.S. dollars.

1. Types of RVs

There are two main categories of RVs, towables and motorized:

a) Towable RVs

A towable RV is designed to be towed by a motorized vehicle (auto, van, or pickup truck) and is of such size and weight as not to require a special highway movement permit. It is designed to provide temporary living quarters for recreational, camping, or travel use and does not require permanent on-site hookup.

- *Folding camping trailer (average price, $4,352).* This is a recreational camping unit designed for temporary living quarters that is mounted on wheels and connected with collapsible sidewalls that fold for towing by a motorized vehicle. It provides kitchen, dining, and sleeping facilities for up to eight people. Some larger models come with full bathroom and heating/air conditioning options.

- *Truck camper (average price, $9,195).* This recreational camping unit is designed to be loaded onto or affixed to the bed or chassis of a truck and is constructed to provide temporary living quarters for recreational camping or travel use. Most provide kitchen, sleeping, and bathroom facilities for two to six people, heat, air-conditioning, and running water. The unit can be easily loaded onto a truck bed in a few minutes.

- *Conventional travel trailer (average price, $11,965).* This unit typically ranges from 12 to 35 feet (3.6 to 10.6 m) in length and is towed by means of a bumper or frame hitch attached to the towing vehicle. It provides temporary living quarters for four to eight people, with kitchen, toilet, sleeping and dining facilities, electrical and water systems, and modern appliances. The unit is available in conventional and two-level fifth-wheel models.

- *Fifth-wheel travel trailer (average price, $18,475).* This unit can be equipped the same as the conventional travel trailer but is constructed with a raised forward section that allows a bilevel floor plan. This style is designed to be towed by a vehicle equipped with a device known as a fifth-wheel hitch.

b) Motorized RVs

- *Custom van conversion (average price, $24,976).* This refers to a complete or incomplete automotive van chassis that has been modified by the RV manufacturer to be used for transportation and recreation. Modifications may include the addition of windows, carpeting, panelling, seats, sofas, reclining captain's chairs, closets, stereo systems, and accessories.

- *Van camper (average price, $39,585).* This is a panel-type truck to which the RV manufacturer has added any two of the following conveniences: sleeping, kitchen, or toilet facilities. The truck also includes 100-volt hookup, fresh water storage, city water hookup, and a top extension to provide more head room.

- *Motor home (compact) (average price, $29,873).* This unit is built on an automotive manufactured cab and chassis having a gross vehicle weight ratio (GVWR) of less than 6,500 pounds (3000 kg). It may provide any or all of the conveniences of the larger units.

- *Motor home (mini-low profile) (average price, $38,309).* This unit is built on an automotive manufactured van frame with an attached cab section having a GVWR of 6,500 pounds (3000 kg) or more, with an overall height of more than 8 feet (2.4 m) (low profile is less than 8 feet). The RV manufacturer completes the body section containing the living area and attaches it to the cab section.

- *Motor home (high profile) (average price, $62,583).* The living unit has been entirely constructed on a bare, specially designed motor vehicle chassis. Kitchen, sleeping, bathroom, and dining facilities are easily accessible to the driver's area from inside. Three types—conventional motor homes, mini-motor homes, and van-campers—range from 17 to 40 feet (5 to 12 m) long. Motor homes sleep up to eight people.

If you are buying an RV in the United States, check to make sure that it is endorsed by the Recreational Vehicle Industry Association (RVIA). This endorsement shows that the RV has complied with applicable national safety standards, such as those of the American National Standards Institute. The address for the RVIA is located in item 33 in Appendix A. If you are buying an RV in Canada, make sure that it is endorsed by the Canadian Recreational Vehicle Association, showing that it has received Canadian Standards Association (CSA) safety approval. Ask about warranty coverage in the United States and Canada.

You should also check on various Canadian government regulations or legal implications if you buy an RV or car in the United States and wish to take it home with you to Canada. Refer to items 1, 2, and 3 in Appendix A.

You may not be sure if you want to buy an RV right away, so consider renting one to see if you like it. If you have some friends with RVs, ask to go along on a short trip with them. Also ask them about their RV experiences and tips they could give you. Refer to item 34 in Appendix A for U.S. RV rental companies. Check with your local RV dealer in Canada about rentals in Canada.

2. Where to Get Further Information

There is an immense amount of information available to assist you. Request the excellent free material from the Recreational Vehicle Industry Association (RVIA) in the United States. The association's toll-free phone number (United States only) is 1-800-47SUNNY (78669). Ask for their information kit and "Go Camping America Vacation Planner." You can write to the association at the address given in item 33 of Appendix A.

Appendix A contains many contact sources for RV information. Refer to items 32–43, which include information about RV campground directories and chains, clubs, resorts, publications, associations, rental sources, retail shows and scenic trips. Also refer to item 9 for provincial tourism offices, item 18 for state travel offices in the United States, and item 19 for state travel park associations. All this free information will help you plan your trip. Contact your automobile association as well for information, and refer to Appendix B for books on travel in the United States that might interest you.

G. TIPS BEFORE LEAVING CANADA

- If you are thinking of purchasing U.S. real estate, speak to your financial institution before you leave regarding their policy on financing U.S. property.

- Be wary about buying time-shares before leaving Canada without knowing the advantages and disadvantages of time-shares. Always check out some of the resorts you are thinking of using, without further financial obligation. Speak to others who have bought time-shares from the company selling them.

- If you are thinking of buying a house or condo or a mobile home in a specific location, have a real estate professional, agent, or owner send material to you to review before you depart. The more research you do before you leave, the more objective and realistic your final decision will be.

- If you want to be certain you like a particular area or type of housing, consider renting a house, condo, or mobile/manufactured home or RV in your first Snowbird season. This is a low-risk and highly effective way of making your decision. You can make all your enquiries, thoroughly review information, and speak to references before you leave.

H. QUICK REFERENCE GUIDE TO RELEVANT PARTS OF THE APPENDICES

To help you obtain further information and contact numbers, here are the parts of the Appendices that are relevant to the contents of this chapter.

Appendix A: Items 1, 9, 13, 18, 19, 20, 22, 23, 24, 26, and 32-43

Appendix B: Items 2, 5, 6, and 7

CHAPTER
5

Insurance Needs and Options

A. INTRODUCTION

Adequate insurance is necessary for your peace of mind and financial health. As a Snowbird, you need to know about various types of insurance. It is often confusing to try to understand all the options, benefits, features, and rates, as well as the exclusions, exemptions, and deductibles, but it is very important to understand the terms and concepts. You need to take the time to do your research so that you can make the right decisions to meet your needs and protect yourself from potential risks.

It is also important to shop around for comparable rates and coverage. The insurance market is highly competitive, and you will find considerable differences in price and in the quality of coverage offered by different insurance companies. It is always a good idea to obtain a minimum of three competitive quotes. For out-of-country insurance coverage, you need more of a comparison than that. You want to check out as many Canadian insurance programs as you can that offer the type of coverage you are seeking. You need a full range of comparisons to evaluate the relative strengths and weaknesses of varying coverage. The type of selection criterion to apply will be discussed later in this chapter. These comparisons will provide you with an objective basis for selection and make your final decision much less stressful. To eliminate misunderstanding, get confirmation in writing of any requests made by you to your insurer or insurance company, or of representations made by an insurance company representative to you. Keep copies of all correspondence between you and your insurance company, as well as any receipts for items to be claimed for reimbursement.

This chapter covers the various types of insurance you should consider, depending on your circumstances: out-of-country medical insurance, homeowner insurance, home office insurance, mobile/manufactured home insurance, automobile insurance, RV insurance, automobile roadside assistance, and life insurance.

B. OUT-OF-COUNTRY EMERGENCY MEDICAL INSURANCE

If you have a serious injury or illness in the United States and require emergency medical attention, you will be financially devastated unless you have out-of-country medical insurance. The need for this extra insurance protection is simple. Provincial health insurance plans vary by province, but each provides you with the necessary protection when travelling within Canada. Coverage by provincial plans outside Canada is nominal, however—maybe $75 to $125 Canadian funds per day for hospital care. Payments for doctors' services outside Canada, in Canadian funds, will not exceed the amount payable had you been treated in your own province. This is a very low amount compared with U.S. rates.

The problem is that health coverage in the United States is very different from the medicare coverage we are accustomed to in Canada. We are not accustomed to being personally billed, so we don't appreciate the real cost of treatment, which is paid by the government. In the U.S. system, private hospitals and doctors operate in a profit-oriented environment, and costs are much greater. In the United States, the average hospital stay often exceeds U.S. $1,500 a day and can run as high as U.S. $10,000 a day for intensive care. Certain emergency surgical operations can cost $100,000 or more. So who pays the shortfall if you have a medical emergency in the United States? You do. Unless, of course, you have wisely purchased supplemental health insurance *before* you leave Canada, for the duration of your U.S. stay, be it a day or six months. Keep in mind that this supplemental insurance covers emergency treatment for injury or illness only. It does not cover nonemergency treatment or services. It is not a substitute for Canadian medicare.

Premium rates vary greatly between insurers. The rate depends on factors such as the nature of the coverage, your age and existing medical condition, policy exclusions and limitations, the deductible portion of your policy, whether you have a preferred (for healthy people) or standard rate plan, and the duration of your stay in the United States. The premium range for a six-month extended-stay plan could range per person from $500 to $3,000 or more, depending on the above variables. Rates are normally set by the insurer between June and September each year for extended-stay Snowbird coverage. For competitive reasons, the insurer might drop the market rates after you have taken the policy out, but such a reduction should be passed on to you. Do not choose a plan based on price alone but consider such factors as benefits, limitations, exclusions, and deductibles.

For information about your provincial health department coverage and policy for out-of-country claims, refer to item 10 in Appendix A. Refer to item 11 for a detailed listing of companies in Canada providing out-of-country medical insurance. To obtain a comparison of the various features of the numerous insurance plans available to Canadians, refer to item 23 for the two newspapers produced for Canadian Snowbirds. They generally provide this comparison between June and October, when the various plans announce their policies and premiums for the Snowbird season.

1. Claiming Tax Credits

On the positive side, some financial relief might be available from the tax credits you can earn when you purchase medical insurance. Many people overlook this substantial saving, which could effectively reduce your premium by up to one-quarter. You earn credits of approximately 27 cents for each dollar of medical expenses (i.e., 27 percent) in any consecutive 12-month period that exceed either 3 percent of income or $1,614, whichever is less. This is a good reason to make sure you keep receipts of all your medical expenses.

For example, let's say a retired couple, through careful professional financial and tax planning, have split their retirement income so that they are both earning $20,000 a year. By doing this, they have lowered their marginal tax rates (rather than one spouse having a higher taxed income) and minimized the risk of reaching the clawback threshold on their Old Age Security (OAS) pension, which occurs after approximately $53,000 of individual net income. They can each claim credits for medical expenses exceeding $600 (calculated by taking 3 percent of $20,000) in any consecutive 12-month period, at the rate of approximately 27 percent. To clarify, this 27 percent figure consists of a combined federal and provincial tax credit benefit. The federal tax credit is 17 percent, but this results in a reduction and, therefore, a savings in provincial tax payable, since provincial tax is a portion of federal tax. Provincial tax rates vary. For example, the Ontario tax rate is currently 58 percent, so the savings would be 9.86 percent (58 percent of 17 percent). The total tax credit benefit for an Ontario resident, therefore, would be 26.86 percent (17 percent plus 9.86 percent). British Columbia tax is currently 52.5 percent, and Alberta tax is 45.5 percent.

Returning to the retired couple, if they are each paying, for example, $1,400 in insurance premiums, they would be eligible to claim credits of $216 each for a total savings of $432 ($1,400 – $600 = $800 x 27 percent). If the couple were earning a lower income than $20,000 a year each, they would have a larger credit and save even more money. Other eligible medical expenses, such as prescription drugs, dental work, or eyeglasses, may also be claimed.

2. Understanding Insurance Options

Many insurance plans are available, and it can be very confusing and frustrating trying to understand which plan is right for you. Keep in mind that one plan can't be all things to all people. You want to determine your needs and then shortlist two or three plans that meet your needs. Only then do you consider the issue of premium cost.

It is helpful to understand how the insurance system works, since several parties are involved. *Insurers* are the people you deal with directly. They are the companies or organizations that package a plan and arrange for an insurance company to underwrite it, or pay the claims. The companies that pay the claims are called *underwriters*. Sometimes the underwriters sell directly themselves or through travel agents. Sometimes underwriters insure plans for various insurers, which could be competing with each other. In that case, each plan tends to be customized for each insurer, so they are slightly different from each other. In case you have a medical emergency, the underwriter or insurer contracts with an *emergency medical assistance company* to provide information, guidance, and coordination of your medical care. In other words, the company helps deal with your emergency medical needs, telling you which hospital or doctor to go to and so on. Such companies have a 24-hour, 7-day hotline, generally toll-free, or they accept collect calls from anywhere in the United States. They also monitor your treatment and make other arrangements as required. Always keep a record of who you spoke with when phoning this emergency medical number.

To keep costs down, many underwriters have negotiated reduced rates with specific hospitals and doctors, and therefore you might be referred specifically to them. If your condition is safely stabilized, they will likely send you back to Canada by air ambulance to save themselves money, since your treatment would then be covered by Canadian medicare.

Here are the main issues and options you need to know about:

- **Full disclosure of personal health information**
  The issue of full disclosure of health information in your initial policy application cannot be overemphasized. If the insurer denies your claim, your explanation that you made a mistake, misunderstood, or didn't know will bear no weight. As far as the insurer is concerned, you could have been deliberately misleading the company in order to save money on premiums or to get the coverage in the first place. So don't be tempted to play with the facts. Insurers are entitled to see all your past medical history records, and they know what to look for.

  Money is money, and the fine print of the policy governs. No insurer is going to pay out a lot of money if it technically and legally doesn't have to.

- **Extended-stay and multi-trip plans**
  An **extended-stay plan** is intended to cover you for the duration of your Snowbird stay in the United States for a continuous period. The premium is based on the duration of your stay—for example, up to six months. You pay for the exact number of days you need. Refer to item 11 in Appendix A for companies offering extended-stay coverage.

  A **multi-trip plan** is designed for shorter-term stays in the United States. You arrange coverage for a packaged number of days—for example, a maximum single-duration stay not exceeding 90 days. This means you can travel and stay in the United States as many times as you like within the length of your policy coverage (say, up to six months), as long as any one trip does not exceed your maximum number of days per trip (e.g., 15, 30, or 90 days). As soon as you return to Canada for at least a day, the cycle starts again. For example, some people purchase a plan for 90-day periods and stay in the United States for six months but break up the stay by flying back to Canada before the first 90-day period expires—for example, at Christmas. A few weeks later they return to the United States for another period not exceeding 90 days. There could be some savings on insurance premium if this type of arrangement suits your lifestyle, even after taking the airfare into account. However, there could be a risk of loss of coverage if your medical condition changes or if you need to take new medication after you return to Canada and before you return to the United States. Check this out thoroughly.

These multi-trip plans are usually based on an annual premium, for example, covering a calendar year or 12 months from the time you take it out. If the plan is based on a calendar year, some companies prorate the premium; others don't. One of the main benefits of a multi-trip plan is that it covers spontaneous trips any time you go back and forth across the Canada-U.S. border. You can obtain multi-trip plans through travel agents, banks, and some credit card companies or insurers directly. Refer to item 11 in Appendix A for a list of out-of-country insurance companies. Many of these companies do not provide multi-trip plans but only extended-stay plans.

- **Top-up insurance**
  This concept means that you acquire additional supplemental emergency medical coverage to "top up" an existing out-of-country medical plan. This existing plan could be coverage you get as a retiree from a government plan, other employer plan, union or association plan, or credit card plan. There are risks, however, with the top-up approach. Some plans don't permit top-ups. There can be great differences in plan policies. There could be a lapse in time periods or amounts between coverage, or disputes between different insurers as to the issue of coverage. For example, if your basic medical plan coverage has a ceiling cap of $50,000 and lasts for a maximum number of days, and your "top-up" plan kicks in at the end of that time period, what happens if you have a catastrophic injury before the first plan lapses? You are only covered for $50,000, and your expenses could be $200,000. You would be out the difference. Another example is if the top-up company decides that your illness was pre-existing if you make a claim with your first insurer first. An alternative is to coordinate a basic plan and top-up plan from the same insurer.

The other reality is that generally it is less expensive and less risky to have just one plan cover everything. It certainly eliminates the uncertainty. It also saves the inconvenience and frustration of having to deal with two different claims procedures.

- **Subrogation clause**

  If you take out Snowbird insurance with one insurer, and the company finds out that you have existing insurance coverage through an employer or pension health plan, the Snowbird insurer can, in some cases, make a claim against that plan. This process is called subrogation. Most insurance policies state the right to do this. You may not want that to happen, since such a claim could dilute your fixed health benefits under your employer/union/association pension plan coverage.

  If this is an issue to you, make sure you discuss the matter with your prospective Snowbird insurer. Get an agreement in writing to avoid any misunderstanding. Some insurers will waive any claim, some will do so for a premium surcharge (e.g., 10 to 15 percent), and others will limit their subrogation claim to a certain ceiling (e.g., $3,000).

- **Payment of deductibles**

  To reduce the risk, many insurance companies will offer you premium discounts if you agree to pay a deductible up to a certain amount—for example, from $100 to $10,000. The larger the deductible, the larger the saving in premiums, perhaps 25 to 40 percent. You have to determine your own financial comfort level and the risk you are willing to take. Check to see if the deductibles are paid in U.S. or Canadian dollars. When comparing premium rates, take into account your net deductible outlay. If you have an employee retirement health benefit plan, check to see if it covers any deductibles.

- **What is included in your insurance policy coverage?**

  You want to make sure you know what protection you are getting for your money, so compare the same types of benefits when you are comparing policies. The main types of emergency-related (injury or illness) coverage paid for by the insurer in many policies include ambulance, hospital care, special nursing care, doctor and dental services, and necessary medication. In addition, reimbursement of emergency-related expenses that you have incurred, payment for transportation of a relative to your hospital, return of your car or RV to Canada, and return of your body to Canada if you die are frequently included. If you require further treatment but can safely be returned to Canada, the insurer will normally cover the cost of an air ambulance (medically equipped jet) or regular airline to take you back home.

- **What is excluded from your insurance coverage?**

  Certain medical or surgical treatment or diagnostic expenses are not covered by your medical emergency insurance in the United States. Some of the common expenses are pre-existing conditions (refer to the next item); unnecessary diagnostic procedures; treatment that can safely wait until you return to Canada; rehabilitative or continuing care treatment for substance abuse (e.g., drugs or alcohol); chronic conditions (e.g., diabetes, emphysema); cancer that was diagnosed before you left Canada; and elective nonemergency treatment such as treatment by a chiropractor, podiatrist, optometrist, or physiotherapist.

- **Pre-existing conditions**

  This issue is an important one for insurers, since it relates to risk. For example, if you had previous signs of angina, you might already be on medication. The risk to an insurer is that you could have a heart attack in the United States, resulting in medical treatment that could cost the insurer $100,000 or more. It's a calculated risk for the insurer, and different insurers deal with the risk in different ways.

  For example, some insurers will simply refuse to cover you. Others would cover you except for any emergency medical condition relating to your pre-existing condition. Some offer a co-payment plan. This means if emergency medical treatment is required in the United States for a pre-existing condition, then the insurer will share the expense. For example, the insurer might pay 70 percent of the cost and you would pay the remaining 30 percent. Another variation is that the insurer agrees to pay up to a maximum amount in the event of such a claim—for example, $50,000. You would pay the rest. This could be a crippling expense financially. Some insurers will accept a pre-existing condition if it has been stabilized, with or without medication, for 3, 6, or 12 months. Ask your insurer if seeing your doctor for monitoring a condition is considered treatment and has to be disclosed on your application or before you leave Canada. Find out from your doctor if changes in medication are really necessary for your health, since they could impair your Sunbelt insurance coverage. For example, some insurance companies will not insure you if you are on medication before you depart, unless that was disclosed and approved in advance of your departure. Obviously, you don't want to risk your health. Also find out whether you have to notify your insurance company if you pay for nonemergency medical treatment in the United States.

- **Reasons for rejection of a medical emergency expense claim**

  There are situations in which your insurance company could refuse to pay your claim. You could therefore be stuck with the bill, which could be massive. The reasons for rejecting a claim include pre-existing conditions that you have not disclosed; medical exclusions set out in the policy; failure to make a formal claim before a deadline; failure to notify the insurer by calling the medical emergency number within the policy time period (e.g., before entering the hospital or within 24 to 48 hours afterwards);

refusal to go to a hospital or doctor of the insured's choice; refusal to be returned to Canada for continuing treatment after your condition was medically stabilized; lapse of your policy coverage period; or dispute with an insurance company if you are using two companies for coverage.

If you are treated for an illness during a short trip home to Canada, and you subsequently have emergency medical treatment for that ailment in the United States, you could be deemed to have a pre-existing illness that the insurer was never advised about. As a result, the insurer could deny the claim. Before you decide on an insurer and before you leave Canada, check out all these issues and get answers to your questions in writing to avoid any misunderstanding.

3. Key Questions to Ask

Here is a checklist of key questions to ask before deciding on the insurance coverage. Not all of them are necessarily applicable in your situation, but you should have them all answered to determine whether you can be covered adequately as well as to determine the benefits or drawbacks of the coverage.

- What are the age restrictions?
- What pre-existing conditions are permitted and how long must they be stable?
- Are there different policy plans and options available and what are they?
- What restrictions and limitations does the policy have?
- Are there any sports activities I cannot participate in, such as scuba diving or mountain climbing?
- What exactly does the policy cover in detail?
- What is the amount of the policy coverage limit (e.g., $1 million, $2 million, or unlimited)?
- Is the insurance paid out in U.S. or Canadian dollars?
- May I select the doctor and hospital of my choice or does the insurance company make that choice?
- If I wish to select my own hospital and doctor despite restrictions, will the insurance company still pay a portion of the bills, and if so, what percentage?
- Do I (or a spouse or family member) have to notify the insurance company within a certain time of my illness or injury to be eligible for coverage (e.g., before I enter a hospital, or within 24 or 48 hours), and if so, what is the time period? Is this position waived if I am unconscious or incapacitated?

- If I forget to comply with the above deadline but could have complied with it, what is the penalty? Does the insurance company only pay a portion of the cost, or a certain maximum dollar amount?

- Does the insurance company have a toll-free or collect telephone number to coordinate my emergency treatment and care, that can be reached from anywhere in the United States? Do the representatives speak English, French, and other languages (depending on your needs)?

- Does the insurance company submit the claim directly to my provincial health insurance plan, or do I have to do it myself?

- Is there a limited time period for submitting claims after the emergency treatment has been completed, after which the claim could be denied? What is that period? With respect to insurer? With respect to provincial health department? What documentation is required, and what invoices or receipts for expenses am I required to keep and submit?

- Do I have to pay up front for any hospital and medical treatment and then seek reimbursement from my provincial health plan and insurance company later, or do the U.S. hospitals and doctors bill my provincial health insurance plan and/or insurance company directly? If I have to cover minor expenses, up to how much and what types of expenses?

- Do I have to notify the insurer of any monitoring of my existing condition, treatment for illness, or change in medication after I have been approved for coverage but before I leave Canada? Will these circumstances affect my coverage? What if I pay for such nonemergency treatment or medication change after I leave Canada for the United States? If I see my doctor during a short visit home to Canada at Christmas, do I need to notify the insurer before I return to the United States about any existing condition, monitoring, medication change, or treatment for an illness? Will that affect my coverage?

- Does the insurer offer full payment for emergency expenses for a stabilized medical condition, or only a part of the expense (e.g., co-insurance), and would I have to pay the rest? What percentage or maximum dollar amount would the insurer pay in this instance (e.g., 50 to 90 percent, or $25,000 to $100,000)?

- If coverage is from an employer, government, or union pension health plan, who is the contact person to determine my benefits? Can coverage details be obtained in writing?

- Does my existing out-of-country medical emergency plan from a past employer, union, or other source permit me to top it up with other insurance? Does the top-up insurer immediately take over after the basic policy reaches the maximum number of days or amount of coverage? Is there a subrogation clause, and if so, what does it say?

- Will a basic out-of-country emergency medical plan allow secondary top-up insurance coverage, if required?

- Will the use of a basic plan mean that the top-up plan will consider the treated condition a pre-existing one and refuse to pay?

- Does my existing retiree/government/union health plan restrict the amount of coverage (e.g., $100,000 maximum) or days (e.g., 30 days)?

- Will the insurance company completely waive any claim for subrogation against my retiree/employee/union health benefit plan and put that in writing? If not, will the insurer waive a subrogation claim for a premium surcharge and what is that surcharge (e.g., 10 to 15 percent), or will the insurer limit a subrogation claim to a certain ceiling (e.g., $3,000)?

- If I have extended-stay coverage rather than a multi-trip plan, will it impair my coverage in any way if I return to Canada for short periods during my six-month stay in the United States?

- If credit card medical coverage is being obtained, does it start on the day of departure and how long is the maximum coverage? Can I obtain all the plan benefits in writing?

- If I die, does my coverage include the expense of returning my body to Canada? My RV or car? My spouse?

- Am I reimbursed for certain additional medical/travel-related expenses, such as accommodation, meals, or transportation of my automobile back to Canada, if I have an accident or illness that is deemed by the insurer to be an emergency?

- If I am ill or injured, will the insurance company pay the air fare for an immediate family member, relative, or friend to visit me?

- Does the insurance company restrict the nature of the relationship of the person to visit me—for example, immediate family only?

- If I have to return to Canada because of my illness or injury, will the insurance company pay to have a person of my choice accompany me?

- If I am being treated for an injury or illness and the insurance company deems it safe for me to travel, can the insurance company arbitrarily arrange for me to fly back to Canada in a commercial plane or air ambulance jet so that medicare can take over? ·

- Will I have to pay a deductible if I have a claim? How much? In U.S. or Canadian dollars? And under what circumstances?

- Will I have to join an organization to access the medical insurance coverage, and how much will the annual dues be?

- Does the insurance policy cover any trip cancellation costs, baggage loss, or other losses?

4. Tips before You Leave Canada

- Take your provincial health care card.

- Take your out-of-country medical insurance policy and number and related documents.

- Take your emergency assistance phone number for your out-of-country medical insurance and carry it in your wallet or purse at all times.

- Take several photocopies of all your important papers before you go, leaving a copy with a relative and keeping a copy yourself. These papers include such items as your current prescriptions, medical history, birth certificate, passport, driver's licence, credit cards, provincial health care card, out-of-province emergency assistance policy, and emergency assistance phone number.

- See your doctor for a thorough examination before you leave Canada. Apart from having a current assessment of your condition, you then also have a reference date for verifying that you did not have a pre-existing illness in case you have a later dispute with your insurance company.

- Ask your doctor to give you a report that provides a range of medical and personal data, which will be helpful if you have a medical emergency in the United States. These data should include your name, address, home phone number, spouse's name, and doctor's name and phone number; the person to be notified in case of an emergency and that person's phone number; and your birthdate, social insurance number, provincial health insurance number, out-of-province supplementary insurance plan number, blood type, drug allergies, immunization details, medical history, existing conditions, and current medications.

- If you are currently taking medication covered by your provincial health plan, supplemental health plan, or previous employer health plan, ask your doctor to prescribe enough medication before you leave Canada so that you won't run out while you are in the United States.

- If you have friends or relatives who are going to visit you in the United States, make sure you caution them to obtain out-of-country medical insurance to cover them while they are in the United States. Many people going there for only a day or even for several weeks don't think of getting additional insurance protection. A medical emergency could therefore turn into an economic nightmare. A single or multi-trip type of plan coverage might be appropriate.

- Check to see what potential health risks you should be aware of before you go to a specific area—for example, intense sunlight, air pollution, strong water currents, or infectious or poisonous insects, reptiles, or plants.

C. HOMEOWNER INSURANCE

If you own a house or condominium in Canada, or in the United States as well, you should have a comprehensive homeowner policy that covers you for replacement cost if your home burns down. Your policy should also cover a range of potential risks, such as theft; vandalism; water damage due to frozen pipes, sewer backup, or snow and ice buildup; or acts of God such as floods, earthquakes, tornadoes, or hurricanes. Check with your insurance company about the types of optional coverage available. The lower the deductible amount, the higher the insurance premium, so you can save some money by increasing your deductible. Deductibles can range from $200 to $2,500. Or you may prefer to have a lower deductible and pay a slightly higher premium for it. It all depends on how much you can afford to pay if you have to make a claim. Some insurance companies give premium discounts to people over 50, or if smoke detectors and/or fire or burglar alarms are installed in the home. Make enquiries.

1. Ensuring That You Are Fully Covered

If you are going to live in the United States for up to six months, check with your insurance company beforehand to ensure that you are fully covered during your absence. Different insurance companies have different policies. For example, your coverage might require you to notify the company in writing that you will be gone and who your local contact person is, turn off and empty all your water taps before you go, have the house maintained at a certain temperature so that freezing won't occur, and have your home checked once a week by a friend or neighbour or someone else you select. That person should have your house key, information on how to contact you in case of a home emergency, and the name and contact person of your homeowner insurance company. If you don't have anyone who you can ask to check your home regularly during your absence, you do have other options. You can contact the Canadian Corps of Commissionaires, which has offices throughout the country and can monitor your home while you are away. You can arrange for them to visit your home once a week if you like, to check on the inside of the house, water your plants if you wish, and remove any junk mail. There is a nominal cost of about $10 a visit. Refer to item 28 in Appendix A. Another option is to contact a bonded private franchise company that has offices throughout Canada called Housesitters, which will perform the same type of service for a fee.

2. Tips before You Leave Canada

Here are some home security tips to consider before you leave Canada. Many of these are equally applicable if you have a home in a Sunbelt state:

- Keep a current inventory list of your belongings and other personal possessions.

- Keep receipts for valuable articles, such as cameras, jewellery, art, stereo equipment, and furniture.

- Take photographs or a video of your rooms and belongings for additional support if you have to make a claim.

- Mark your valuable assets for identification in case they are stolen. You can generally borrow a marker from your local police department.

- Keep a copy of your inventory list, receipts, and photographs in your safety deposit box in case your home burns down.

- Get extra coverage for expensive items such as jewellery, since the limit may be $2,000 for any claim.

- Don't leave a message on your answering machine that you are out of the country for six months.

- Cancel newspaper delivery while you are away.

- Arrange with Canada Post to forward your mail or hold it until your return.

- Arrange for a neighbourhood friend or student to clear away advertising flyers.

- Have a reliable neighbourhood friend or student clear the snow from your sidewalk or at least tramp it down.

- Store small valuables in a safety deposit box. Store expensive items (e.g., TV or stereo) with a friend or relative while you are away, or move them out of sight if they can be seen from a window.

- Use clock timers to activate lights and radios.

- Keep garage doors locked and windows covered.

- Secure air-conditioners and other openings into your home.

- Change your locks if keys are lost or stolen.

- Make sure door hinge bolts are inside the house; hinges can easily be removed if they are on the outside.

- Install one-inch deadbolt locks on exterior doors. Door knob locks are unreliable and easily forced.

- Insert a metal piece or fitted wood into sliding glass door tracks.

- Reinforce basement windows with bars.

D. HOME OFFICE INSURANCE

If you have a part-time or full-time home-based business in Canada, you want to make sure you are protected in case you have to make a claim for a loss or injury that is related to your business use. This coverage is added on to your existing homeowner coverage, and is very reasonably priced. Otherwise, your current policy would likely not cover any such claims. Most basic homeowner policies specifically exclude business use of the home without additional coverage. For example, if a business-related computer or other business equipment were stolen, or if someone visiting you on business were injured on your property or in your home, your basic insurance policy would not cover you.

E. MOBILE/MANUFACTURED HOME INSURANCE

If you have this type of dwelling, either in the United States or Canada, you can get insurance to cover the risks that are unique to these types of homes— for example, damage caused by faulty blocks or jack, damage to tie-down equipment, damage to adjacent structures (e.g., storage area), or damage from falling objects, such as tree branches. You also want to consider replacement cost coverage in case the whole dwelling is destroyed. Deal with an insurance company that specializes in this type of insurance protection. In the United States, check with a state association of mobile/manufactured home owners to get names of recommended companies. Refer to item 20 in Appendix A.

F. AUTOMOBILE INSURANCE

This type of insurance covers you for losses you might suffer due to damage to your car, car theft, vandalism, or fire. It also covers claims made against you if you have a car accident and damage someone else's car or property or injure other people.

You can reduce your insurance premiums by increasing the deductible portion of your policy. That is the portion you pay first if you make a claim with your insurance company. This amount ranges from $100 to $2,500. The lower the deductible amount, of course, the higher the premium. Another way of reducing your insurance premium is to have an accident-free claims history.

Here are some further points:

• It is prudent to carry a minimum of $1 million third-party liability coverage, and ideally more (e.g., $2–3 million). Third-party coverage means that you are covered if you cause an accident to a third party who then makes a claim against you. The premium difference between $1 million and $3 million is relatively small. If one or two people are seriously injured or die as a consequence of an accident that you were responsible for, the award against you could be millions of dollars, especially in the United States. You should have adequate insurance coverage for your peace of mind.

- Obtain under-insured motorist coverage (UMP). This type of coverage protects you in case you or your car is hit by a driver of a car with inadequate or nonexistent insurance coverage. You or a passenger could be seriously injured or permanently disabled or killed. In that event, you are covered for any claim up to the limit of your own third-party liability insurance coverage (e.g., $1–$3 million), subject to any state or provincial ceilings. If someone with inadequate or nonexistent insurance hit you and you didn't have the UMP coverage, you would have no protection. You could sue the driver of the other car, but most likely that person would have no assets and you would be totally out of luck. The premium for under-insured motorist coverage is low, e.g., $15–$30 a year.

- If you bought your car in Canada, you would obtain your insurance in Canada. This insurance covers you against any claims you make as a consequence of car accidents, damage, or theft in the United States. If you buy a car in the United States, however, you need U.S. insurance, which you would cancel and replace with Canadian insurance when you arrive back in Canada. You can get this U.S. insurance through your local automobile travel club in the United States (e.g., AAA) or through other private carriers.

- If any personal possessions are stolen from your car, other than a car radio, for example, your car insurance would not cover it. You would have to make a claim under your homeowner insurance policy, which normally has a deductible that you have to pay first. This deductible could be from $100 to $500 or more, depending on your policy.

- If you are travelling to Mexico, your Canadian auto insurance will not cover you. You need to obtain a separate insurance policy for the duration of the trip. This policy can be obtained from a local auto club (AAA) branch close to the Mexican border.

- If you were the cause of a car accident and your car is damaged so badly that it is considered a write-off, the insurance company can pay you either the depreciated or "book value" of the car or the replacement cost. Clarify with your insurance company the type of coverage you have. Generally, it is optional coverage with an additional premium if you want to receive replacement market value of the vehicle. The older the vehicle, the higher the replacement cost premium.

- If you have a part-time or full-time home-based or small business in Canada, make sure you have additional insurance coverage for business use of your personal car. It doesn't cost much extra. Otherwise, if there is an accident and the car was being used for business-related purposes, the insurance company will reject the claim.

G. RECREATIONAL VEHICLE (RV) INSURANCE

If you have an RV of any type, make sure you have adequate coverage. Check with your current auto insurance company, RV dealers, and your local CAA auto club for names of insurance companies that specialize in this type of coverage. You want to consider coverage for such occurrences as hitch failure and collision with a low-hanging tree, as well as coverage for replacement of the RV.

H. AUTOMOBILE ROADSIDE ASSISTANCE AND OTHER COVERAGE

This is an essential type of coverage, especially if you are travelling in the United States. Most people have auto coverage with a local branch of the CAA (Canadian Automobile Association). Refer to item 27 in Appendix A for contact numbers. There are many benefits of membership, including roadside assistance if your car won't start or if you are locked out of your car, for example. The plan also covers towing your car to a service station for repair if necessary, paying for hotel accommodation for a reportable accident up to a maximum amount, and paying a court bond up to a maximum amount if you have committed a traffic offence that requires a bond. There is a toll-free 24-hour CAA and AAA emergency phone number you can phone from anywhere in the United States or Canada for roadside assistance. You can also obtain free travel books, maps, and customized route destination guides by being a member of a CAA club. Your membership is recognized by all AAA club members in the United States. Ask for a free U.S. AAA club directory with contact numbers. Most CAA auto clubs have optional coverage packages over and above the basic membership benefits.

I. LIFE INSURANCE

You may not require any life insurance if you have sufficient life savings, investments, and pensions to meet your needs and your spouse's needs. Depending on your age and medical condition, you may not be eligible for life insurance in any event, or if you are, it could be at a very high premium rate with a low amount of coverage. Insurance companies base premiums on risk—the higher the age, the greater the risk.

The most common type of insurance for those over 55 is term insurance, which insures a person for a specific period of time or term and then stops. If you are a nonsmoker, the premium is lower. There are several companies that specialize in insuring those over 60 years of age, regardless of medical condition. The coverage tends to be low—for example, a maximum of $10,000—with an annual premium that is generally increased every year. If you require additional money to meet financial obligations on death, such as funeral expenses, you may want to consider that option. Most auto clubs provide coverage for accidental death from motor vehicle accidents. These premiums are generally very low.

You may already be covered by an insurance policy you had with your previous employer, even in retirement. In addition, your estate does receive death benefits from your government CPP, OAS, and Veterans' pension plans.

J. TIPS BEFORE LEAVING CANADA

- Refer again to the tips in sections B-4 and C-2 in this chapter.
- Thoroughly compare the premiums of at least three insurance companies in each area that you want coverage. Check on exclusions, limitations, deductibles, and coverage.
- Make sure that you fully understand the nature of your coverage and that it is confirmed in writing before you depart.
- Make sure that you have left your United States forwarding address with family or friends and a telephone contact number in case you need to be reached in an emergency.
- If you do not have a fixed address because you have a transient RV lifestyle, set up a routine of phoning home the first or middle of the month, or more frequently. This way, your key contact people in Canada know when you will be communicating.

K. QUICK REFERENCE GUIDE TO RELEVANT PARTS OF THE APPENDICES

To help you obtain further information and contact numbers, here are the parts of the Appendices that are relevant to the contents of this chapter.

Appendix A: Items 10, 11, 20, 27, 28, and 33

Appendix B: Item 3

CHAPTER
6

Tax Issues and Options

A. INTRODUCTION

Tax issues can be very confusing to many Canadians. When you also live in the United States part-time and own property or other investments there, it can become quite complex. That is because you can be affected by the tax laws of both countries. In the United States, for example, you could be liable under certain circumstances for income tax, capital gains tax, estate tax, and gift tax.

This chapter attempts to answer the common questions about tax that arise out of being a Snowbird. The following overview provides general guidelines only; competent professional tax advice is essential. Topics covered include determining if U.S. tax laws affect you, renting U.S. property, selling U.S. property, paying U.S. and Canadian taxes on death, and understanding recent changes in the Canada-U.S. tax treaty. Also covered are strategies for reducing taxes on U.S. vacation property, tax credit for out-of-country medical insurance, where to get tax advice and information, and tips before leaving Canada.

B. DO U.S. TAX LAWS APPLY TO YOU?

Even though you are a Canadian citizen and only living in the United States part-time, you could still be subject to U.S. taxation. Even if you are not required to pay U.S. tax, you could be subject to various U.S. filing requirements. In addition, the recent Canada-U.S. tax treaty includes substantial changes that will affect you, many of them beneficial. Some of the main changes are discussed in section F in this chapter. Since changes can occur at any time, be sure to get current professional tax advice.

If you are a U.S. citizen, however, or have been granted lawful permanent resident status (a green card) by the U.S. Immigration and Naturalization Service, the discussion in this section will not apply to you. If you are a citizen of a country other than Canada or the United States, or are a Canadian citizen working full-time in the United States under the Canada-U.S. Free Trade Agreement, some of the following comments may apply. If you fall into any of the categories just noted, contact the Internal Revenue Service (IRS) in Ottawa (refer to item 13 in Appendix A), or if you are in the United States, the IRS office in your area. If you are in the United States on business or for employment, contact Revenue Canada-Taxation and obtain a copy of the pamphlet Canadian Residents Abroad (refer to item 1 in Appendix A).

1. Resident vs. Nonresident Alien Tax Status

If you are a Canadian resident who spends part of the year in the United States, the IRS considers you a resident alien or a nonresident alien for tax purposes. It is important to know which category you fall into, since there are considerable tax implications. For example, resident aliens are generally taxed in the United States on income from all sources throughout the world, including, of course, Canadian income. Nonresident aliens are generally taxed only on income from U.S. sources. Not all nonresident aliens have to file, as will be discussed shortly.

2. Resident Alien under the Substantial Presence Test

The IRS considers you a resident alien of the United States if you meet the substantial presence test. Here is a brief overview of the implications of the time you have spent in the United States:

- If you were in the United States for 183 days or more in the current year, you meet the substantial presence test and are considered a resident alien of the United States.
- If you were in the United States for 31 to 182 days in the current year, you may meet the substantial presence test.
- If you were in the United States for less than 31 days in the current year, you don't meet the substantial presence test and are considered a nonresident alien of the United States.

The substantial presence test uses the number of days you have spent in the United States over the last three years, including the current year, to determine your tax residency status. Here is the formula to do your own calculation. If you regularly spent over four months (122 days) a year in the United States, and you have done so for the past three years, you would be a U.S. tax resident under the substantial presence test and you don't need to do the following calculation:

- Each day in U.S. in the current year counts as a full day
  (no. of days **x** 1)   = _____

PLUS

• Number of days in U.S. in the preceding year counts as
  one-third of a day (no. of days x 1/3)   = _____

PLUS

• Number of days in U.S. in the second preceding year
  counts as one-sixth of a day (no. of days x 1/6)   = _____

  Total number of days   = _____

When totalling all the days for each of the above three years, remember that the days don't have to be consecutive, and a part of a day constitutes a full day.

If the total is more than 182 days, you have met the substantial presence test and are considered a resident alien for tax purposes for the current year. If the total is 182 days or less, you are considered a nonresident alien for tax purposes for the current year.

3. Exemptions from the Resident Alien Status

If you meet the substantial presence test and want to be exempted from being considered a resident alien—in other words, be considered a nonresident alien—there are two possible exemptions you can claim:

a) Exemption under the Closer Connection Category of the U.S. Internal Revenue Code

You can avoid being considered a U.S. resident for tax purposes by meeting certain criteria:

• You must have spent less than 183 days in the United States in the current year and you must not have applied for, or received, permanent resident status (a green card). When calculating the days, you can claim exemptions for days that you had to remain in the United States because of a medical condition or days spent in transit between two foreign countries, for example. Enquire about other acceptable reasons for deleting days.

• Your tax home is in Canada. If you are not employed or self-employed, your tax home is where you regularly live, as shown by owning or renting a house, condo, apartment, or furnished room there. Your Canadian home must be available to you continuously throughout the year at all times, and not just for the period that you are not in the United States.

  If you are employed or self-employed, your tax home is the location of your principal place of business or employment, regardless of where you maintain your family home.

• You had a closer connection to Canada than to the United States during the current year. Various factors demonstrate that you maintain more significant ties to Canada than the United States. These factors include the location of the following:

- Your permanent residence
- Your family
- Your personal belongings, such as cars, furniture, clothing, and jewellery
- Your bank
- Where you carry on business (if applicable)
- Social, cultural, religious, or political organizations to which you belong and participate
- The jurisdiction where you vote
- The jurisdiction where you hold a driver's licence

b) Filing Requirements for Closer Connection Exemption

You need to file Form 8840 with the IRS by June 15 of the following year. Each person claiming the Closer Connection exemption must file. You need to do this each year. The form, called the Closer Connection Exemption Statement, sets out the number of days you spent in the United States, states that your tax home is in Canada, and lists the factors that establish your closer connection with Canada. After you file this form, the IRS will stamp it "certified received" and return it to you. There is usually no tax cost to filing. Keep this form in a safe place with your other records, since it will be the only proof that you have filed.

If you fail to file Form 8840 by the due date, you could be required to file a U.S. tax return if the IRS subsequently determines that you have met the substantial presence test. You would therefore be subject to penalties by the IRS for nondisclosure. Penalties could be up to $1,000 or more for each category of income involved, even though you could claim treaty protection from U.S. tax, as discussed in (c) below. You could be considered a resident alien for tax purposes and would not be able to claim the Closer Connection exemption.

To obtain Form 8840, contact the closest IRS office in your area, if you are in the United States. In Canada, contact the IRS office in Ottawa. See item 13 in Appendix A.

c) Exemption under the Canada-U.S. Tax Treaty

If you are a resident alien because you met the substantial presence test and you cannot claim the Closer Connection exemption, you may still be able to be treated as a nonresident alien under the Canada-U.S. tax treaty. You could be considered a nonresident alien if you are considered a resident of both the United States and Canada under each country's tax laws, your permanent home is in Canada, and your personal and economic ties are closer to Canada than the United States.

To determine if the above exemption applies to you, contact any Revenue Canada income tax office or the International Taxation Office. Refer to item 1 in Appendix A for the toll-free number. Also contact the closest IRS office if you are in the United States or the IRS office in Ottawa. Refer to item 13, Appendix A.

d) Filing Requirements for Canada-U.S. Tax Treaty Exemption
You must file a U.S. income tax return on Form 1040 NR for the year in question. The deadline is June 15 of the following year. You must report all U.S. source income, which might include interest, dividends, and rent. These are normally subject to withholding tax. You must file a statement, Form 8833, showing any income and taxes withheld. And you must explain that you are a resident of Canada and are not subject to regular income tax rates under the Canada-U.S. tax treaty.

4. Summary of Guidelines for Filing a U.S. Tax Return

* *Resident alien.* Generally, resident aliens have to file a U.S. tax return reporting worldwide income for the year. If you cannot be considered a nonresident alien under the Canada-U.S. tax treaty or the Closer Connection exemption, you need to file; contact the IRS.

* *Nonresident alien.* If you are a nonresident alien, your income that is subject to U.S. income tax is divided into two categories:

    – Income that is **effectively connected** with a trade or business in the United States, including income from the sale or exchange of U.S. real estate property. This income, after allowable deductions, is taxed at the same rates that apply to U.S. citizens and residents.

    – Income that is **not effectively connected** with a trade or business in the United States but is from U.S. sources, such as interest, dividends, annuities, and rents. This income is taxed at a flat rate of 30 percent or lower.

As a nonresident alien, you must file a U.S. tax return if you have income that is effectively connected, or not effectively connected, which did not have sufficient tax or had too much tax withheld at source.

C. RENTAL INCOME FROM U.S. REAL ESTATE

You may be renting out your U.S. property part-time or full-time. As a nonresident alien, you are subject to U.S. income tax on the rental income.

1. Tax on Gross Rental Income

The rents you receive are subject to a 30 percent withholding tax, which your tenant or property management agent is required to deduct and remit to the

IRS. It doesn't matter if the tenants are Canadians or other nonresidents of the United States, or if the rent was paid to you while you were in Canada. The Canada-U.S. tax treaty allows the United States to tax income from real estate with no reduction in the general withholding rate. Since rental income is not considered to be effectively connected, it is subject to a flat 30 percent tax on gross income, with no expenses or deductions allowed. The 30 percent withholding tax therefore equals the flat tax rate.

You need to file Form 1040 NR, U.S. Non-Resident Alien Income Tax Return, showing the gross rental income and withholding tax. Your tenant or property management agent must withhold the 30 percent nonresident tax from the gross rent and remit it directly to the IRS. He or she must complete Form 1042, Annual Withholding Tax Return for U.S. Source Income of Foreign Persons, as well as Form 1042-S, Foreign Persons' U.S. Source Income Subject to Withholding. For more information, contact the IRS and request publication 515, Withholding of Tax on Non-Resident Aliens and Foreign Corporations, and publication 527, Residential Rental Property. Refer to item 13 in Appendix A.

2. Tax on Net Rental Income

Since a tax rate of 30 percent of gross income is a high rate, you may prefer to pay tax on net income, after all deductible expenses. This step results in reduced tax and possibly no tax. The Internal Revenue Code permits this option if you choose to permanently treat rental income as income that is effectively connected with the conduct of a U.S. trade or business. You are then able to claim expenses related to owning and operating a rental property during the rental period—for example, mortgage interest, property tax, utilities, insurance, and maintenance. You can also deduct an amount for depreciation of the building. However, the IRS only permits individuals (rather than corporations) to deduct the mortgage or loan interest relating to the rental property if the debt is secured by the rental property or other business property. If you borrow the funds in Canada, secured by your Canadian assets, you would not technically be able to deduct that interest on your U.S. tax return. Obtain strategic tax planning advice on this issue.

To make this election, you need to file Form 1040 NR, U.S. Non-Resident Alien Income Tax Return, each year. In addition, attach a letter stating that you are making the election. You also need to include the following information:

- All of your real estate located in the United States
- The extent (percentage) of your ownership in the property
- The location of the property
- Any major improvements in the property

- Any previous applications you have made of the real estate net income election

After you have made the election, it is valid for all subsequent years, unless approval to revoke it is requested and received from the IRS. You need to file an annual return, however.

If you want to be exempt from the nonresident withholding tax and are making that election, you have to give your tenant or property management agent Form 4224, Exemption from Withholding Tax on Income Effectively Connected with the Conduct of a Trade or Business in the U.S. Contact the IRS for further information and the publications 515 and 527.

When you file your annual return, show the income and expenses, as well as the tax withheld. If you end up with a loss, after deducting expenses from income, you are entitled to a refund of the taxes withheld. The due date of your return is June 15 of the following year. It is important to file on a timely basis. If you fail to file on the due date, you have 16 months thereafter to do so. If you don't do so, you will be subject to tax on the gross income basis for that year—that is, 30 percent of gross rents with no deduction for any expenses incurred, even if you made the net income election in a previous year. This is an important caution to keep in mind. Many people don't arrange to have tax withheld at source or to file any U.S. tax forms on the premise that their expenses exceed the rental income and the net income election is always available.

D. SELLING OF U.S. REAL ESTATE

If you are a nonresident alien, any gain or loss that results from a sale or disposition of your U.S. real estate is considered to be effectively connected with a U.S. trade or business. The purchaser or agent of the purchaser is generally required to withhold 10 percent of the gross sale price at the time the sale transaction is completed and the balance of payment is made. The 10 percent holdback is to be forwarded to the IRS.

1. Waiver of Withholding Tax

If you anticipate that the U.S. tax payable would be less than the 10 percent withheld, you can apply to the IRS in advance to have the withholding tax reduced or eliminated by completing a withholding certificate. If the 10 percent had already been paid, you would still be entitled to a refund after you filed your U.S. tax return if the 10 percent was greater than the amount due.

You may be able to be exempt from withholding tax at all if the purchase price of your property is less than U.S. $300,000 and the buyer intends to use the property as a residence at least half of the time it is used over the subsequent two-year period. The buyer does not have to be a U.S. citizen or resident or use the property as a principal residence. To obtain this type of exemption, the buyer must sign an affidavit setting out the facts related above. If the purchase price is over U.S. $300,000 or the buyer is unwilling or unable to sign the affidavit, you can request the waiver from withholding discussed in the previous paragraph.

2. Filing Requirements

You are required to report the gain or loss on sale by filing Form 1040 NR, the U.S. Non-Resident Alien Income Tax Return. You would have to pay U.S. federal tax on any gain (capital gain). If you own the real estate jointly with another person, such as your spouse, each of you must file the above form. For more information, contact the IRS and ask for publication 519, U.S. Tax Guide for Aliens. Refer to item 13 in Appendix A.

In addition, you must report any capital gain on the sale of your U.S. property in your next annual personal tax return filing with Revenue Canada. Remember, you must report your worldwide income and gains and pay tax on 75 percent of any capital gain, converted to the equivalent in Canadian dollars at the time of sale. As you may already know, the $100,000 lifetime capital gains exemption (LCGE) is no longer available as an offset against any gains payable in Canada. The last tax year that you could use the LCGE was 1994.

E. U.S. AND CANADIAN TAXES ON DEATH

If you are a Canadian nonresident living part-time in the United States, you will be taxed at your death for any assets in the United States. You will be taxed by both U.S. and Canadian authorities. Assets might include real estate, stocks in a U.S. corporation, debt instruments issued by a U.S. corporation such as bond or debenture or interest in a partnership if the partnership is doing business in the United States.

1. U.S. Estate Tax

U.S. federal estate tax is based on the fair market value of the U.S. asset on the date of death. There may be state estate taxes as well, depending on the state. These can be up to 10 percent or more of the federal estate tax. Under the new changes to the Canada-U.S. tax treaty discussed in more detail in Section F, you can claim foreign tax credits on U.S. estate tax paid, against deemed-disposition capital gains income taxes owed in Canada. Naturally, you would convert the amount paid in U.S. dollars to the Canadian equivalent. In the past, you could not do this, therefore effectively being subjected to double taxation on the same assets by each country.

2. Canadian Capital Gains Tax

Canada does not have an estate or death tax as such. But Revenue Canada considers that you have disposed of your assets at the time of your death and taxes you on any capital gains on your assets, whether they are in Canada or the United States. As already mentioned, under the proposed changes to the Canada-U.S. tax treaty, you would be able to offset any U.S. federal tax paid against any Canadian capital gains tax due relating to those same assets in the United States. The benefit of this change should be kept in perspective, however. Canada only taxes on 75 percent of the capital gains of the U.S. property; that is, on 75 percent of the difference between the purchase price and the deemed value of the property or asset at the time of death. If the amount of the appreciation of the U.S. property is small, the benefit of applying the U.S. tax paid will be equally small. This is because U.S. estate taxes can go up to 55 percent and are applied against the gross value of the property. If a complete exemption from U.S. tax was not possible and you had to pay U.S. estate tax, the amount paid could significantly exceed the offset against Canadian tax due, resulting in a large but unusable U.S. tax credit.

With proper tax planning, Canadian residents can defer Canadian capital gains tax on death by leaving the property to a spouse or spousal trust.

F. PROPOSED CHANGES IN THE CANADA-U.S. TAX TREATY

After many years, major changes in the Canada-U.S. tax treaty are ready to be concluded. The amendments to the agreement, referred to as a protocol, were tentatively agreed to as of August 31, 1994, subject to official ratification by both governments. This is expected to take place by the end of 1995.

There are significant tax savings to most Canadian Snowbirds in the new agreement, as well as estate planning opportunities. Before the proposed changes, Canadians were subject to the risk of double taxation on the death of a Canadian resident with U.S. property and other assets. For example, the combined U.S. and Canadian tax liability at the time of death could, in certain situations, exceed 80 percent or more of the value of the asset. This would greatly reduce the assets left available in the estate.

The proposed changes will benefit most Canadians in many ways. Here is an overview of the highlights of the proposed Canada-U.S. treaty changes. Make sure you obtain advice about the most current status and any changes from a professional tax expert familiar with cross-border tax issues.

1. Retroactive to November 9, 1988

The changes are retroactive to November 9, 1988, meaning that they cover the estates of individuals who died after that date. Executors have one year from the date the new changes are formally ratified to file appropriate refund claims from either or both governments for U.S. estate tax paid or Canadian capital gains tax paid under the old rules.

2. U.S. Estate Tax Eligible for Foreign Tax Credit

Under the old rules, Canada did not recognize U.S. estate tax assessed and paid as a foreign income tax eligible for a foreign tax credit in Canada. Under the proposed changes, Canada will provide a credit for any U.S. tax paid to be applied against Canadian tax payable in the year of death on U.S. source income or capital gains.

3. Tax Credit Increased to U.S. $600,000

Before the changes being ratified, Canadian citizens (non-U.S. residents) with U.S. property having a value of more than U.S. $60,000 are subject to estate taxes. In contrast, U.S. citizens or residents are entitled to a U.S. $600,000 base exemption. U.S. federal tax is calculated on the gross value of the estate value at death, less any allowable deductions or credits. Credits included any state death taxes and a "unified credit," which was to exempt a certain base amount from tax, as noted above. Under the proposed tax treaty changes, the unified tax credit has been raised from U.S. $13,000 to U.S. $192,800. This effectively raises the estate tax exemption from $60,000 to $600,000 on assets.

A portion of the exemption you will be allowed will depend on the percentage of your "gross estate" that is located in the United States at the time of your death, according to a formula:

$$\frac{\text{Gross U.S. estate}}{\text{Gross worldwide estate in U.S. \$}} \times \text{U.S. \$600,000 exemption} = \underline{\hspace{2cm}}$$

Your gross worldwide estate includes assets in the United States and Canada, including the value of RRIFs, RRSPs, and certain life insurance proceeds.

For example, let's say a person has a U.S. condominium worth U.S. $200,000 (gross U.S. estate) and a gross worldwide estate of U.S. $500,000. Applying the formula just described, the credit would cover two-fifths of the $600,000 exemption, that is $240,000:

$$\frac{\$200,000}{\$500,000} \times \ \$600,000 = \$240,000$$

If the above individual's worldwide estate is U.S. $1 million, the credit would cover one-fifth of the $600,000, or $120,000 of the U.S. gross estate:

$$\frac{\$200,000}{\$1,000,000} \times \ \$600,000 = \$120,000$$

The balance, $80,000 ($200,000 − $120,000), would be subject to U.S. estate tax.

You could be eligible for a higher exemption than the U.S. $600,000 under certain circumstances. For example, you could also receive a marital tax credit of the same amount, as well as a limited exemption for personal property.

4. Marital Tax Credit

If a property is left to a non-U.S. citizen spouse, a second tax credit may be available, based on the previous calculation. The basic exemption is effectively doubled if all of the U.S. property is left to the surviving spouse. In this scenario, it is assumed that both spouses are citizens and residents of Canada and are seasonal residents in the United States. If the U.S. property did not all go to the surviving spouse, the additional exemption would be prorated accordingly.

5. Exemption for Personal Property

If a Canadian resident's gross estate is less than U.S. $1.2 million, U.S. estate tax will apply only to a small range of assets, basically real estate. Therefore, other U.S. assets, such as stocks, bonds, boats, cars, and personal-use home furnishings, are excluded from U.S. estate tax. Certain U.S. personal business property or stocks in U.S. real estate holding companies are included in U.S. estate tax calculations.

6. Social Security Benefits

If you are considering retiring in the United States, the proposed new changes will affect you.

Under the old treaty, social security benefits received are not taxable in the country that issued them (e.g., Canada) and only half of the benefit is taxable in the other country (e.g., the U.S.). The proposed new treaty changes that. Now social security benefits paid from one country will be taxable exclusively by that country (e.g., Canada), and will no longer be taxed in the other country (e.g., the U.S.). This means that those who have retired to the United States full-time will not be subject to U.S. tax any longer on Old Age Security (OAS), Canada Pension Plan (CPP), or Quebec Pension Plan (QPP). Canada is proposing to amend the tax laws, however, to extend the nonresident withholding tax of 25 percent to such social security payments. If you are a Snowbird, not staying in the United States for more than six months, the changes do not affect you. You are still considered a permanent Canadian resident as far as Canada is concerned, so no withholding tax is deducted for social security payments sent to you in the United States during your Snowbird stay.

7. Withholding Tax on Interest

The general rule of withholding tax on interest income from U.S. sources is reduced from 15 to 10 percent for individuals as well as corporations. Withholding taxes on most cross-border direct dividends will be reduced from 10 to 7 percent in year 1 after ratification to 6 percent in year 2, and to 5 percent in year 3.

8. Gambling Winnings

Under the new changes, Canadians subject to U.S. income tax on gambling winnings will be allowed to offset against any allowable gambling losses to determine the net taxable amount payable. Naturally, you need to keep receipts and credible records of your losses.

9. Mutual Assistance in Collection Efforts

The proposed changes include a provision that Canada and the United States will assist each other in collecting revenue owing for taxes, interest, penalties, and costs. In practical terms, it will be much easier for the other country to collect taxes owing and harder for the taxpayer to avoid collection efforts from the other country.

G. STRATEGIES FOR REDUCING U.S. ESTATE TAX ON U.S. VACATION PROPERTY

The previous section discussed the changes in the Canada-U.S. tax treaty with respect to U.S. estate tax. These changes will probably eliminate the U.S. estate tax problem for most Snowbirds. In spite of the changes, however, there could be a situation where some people might still be paying an excess of U.S. estate tax over what they can offset in Canadian tax payable. For example, if you own an estate with a very high net worth, and a small percentage but high dollar value of the estate is in the United States, the recent Canada-U.S. tax treaty changes will be of limited benefit to you. The foreign tax credit changes will only have an effect if there are considerable capital gains on U.S. assets at the time of death. If you think this is your situation, you should consider some estate planning options to reduce any estate tax liability. Obtain expert professional tax advice customized to your situation, since the best solution may be complex.

There are advantages and disadvantages to the various strategies that follow. The purpose is just to make you aware of types of creative options that may be appropriate. Keep in mind that these are general guidelines only. You should not consider any of these strategies or other strategies without thoroughly discussing them with your professional advisors after they have done a detailed analysis of your U.S. and Canadian assets and financial affairs.

To lower your Canadian tax liability, you may also be able to claim the principal residence exemption on the sale of your U.S. property. This is assuming you were eligible to claim it—in other words, that it was a principal residence at least for part of the year. This claim, however, will reduce your ability to benefit from the full amount of your foreign tax credit for the U.S. estate tax paid, since you may have reduced your Canadian liability to be lower than your U.S. tax credit. You may therefore want to consider claiming only a portion of the principal residence exemption in order to maximize your foreign tax credits. Most of your exemption will therefore still be available for your Canadian home. This strategy and the calculations could be complicated, so make sure that you obtain tax advice from an expert familiar with both U.S. and Canadian taxes.

1. Joint Ownership of Property with Spouse or Family Members

The advantage of this option is that it splits the estate tax liability on death. Only your portion of the fair market value is taxed if you die. Because the value is reduced as a result of shared ownership, the tax liability is less. The owners of your property must show that they contributed to the purchase of the property in proportion to their ownership interest, unless you already own the property and wish to give a portion of it to your spouse or family members. There is an annual U.S. exemption of $100,000 for gifts to spouses, and you would only be giving a portion of the property value to your spouse. The gift would also reduce the amount of property value held by your spouse, thus reducing future taxable estate liability in the United States. You could also expand the annual gift exemption strategy by giving a part of the property each year beneath the annual exemption ceiling, if the property is of high value.

Canadian capital gains tax (CGT) would apply, however, to any gift of your U.S. second property (nonprincipal residence) to someone other than your spouse. The CGT is based on 75 percent of the proportional amount of the gain in current fair market value from the original acquisition price. The gift would be considered by Revenue Canada a "deemed disposition" of part of your U.S. property gain. For example, if the home went up in value by $100,000 in Canadian funds, and you were making a gift of half of the property, that would be a gain of $50,000 (half of the total gain). You would have to include 75 percent of that gain, or $37,500, in your tax filing for income in that taxation year. You would be paying Canadian tax on an artificial income from your second property.

In addition, if you decided to sell part of your U.S. property to friends or relatives, the U.S. capital gains tax would apply to that sale at fair market value. As mentioned in Section D, at the time of sale, you are required to remit 10 percent of the fair market value or purchase price to the IRS as a credit towards any U.S. capital gains tax that you may be required to pay when you file a U.S. tax return. Any excess amount paid would be refunded to you. If you receive payment from the buyer in instalments, however, you can spread the gain in both the United States and Canada over the number of years involved. You want to synchronize the payment structure to minimize the capital gains paid in both countries. There are foreign tax credits available for U.S. capital gains tax paid, to enable you to apply them against your Canadian tax payable.

2. Sale and Leaseback

If you want to avoid estate tax but continue living in your U.S. residence, you can sell the property at fair market value and then lease it back for a certain number of years with options for renewal. This would minimize or reduce taxes, such as Canadian and U.S. capital gains tax on any profit from the sale, U.S. estate tax on the value of any mortgage you receive from the purchaser as part of the purchase price package, and U.S. withholding tax for future U.S. income tax liability on any interest income you receive from a mortgage you accepted as part of the purchase price. Since everyone's situation is unique, make sure you get specific tax advice from a professional accountant.

3. Disposing of U.S. Property Prior to Your Death

This strategy may be desired if you want to defer selling the property right now, and thereby defer any U.S. and Canadian capital gains tax until a future time. At the same time, you could avoid any U.S. estate tax by having an option to purchase your U.S. property exercised before your death, if possible.

For example, you may wish to grant an option, for a fee, to a family member to purchase the U.S. property before or on a certain date. The price could be fixed at the time of the written option or a price formula could be included in the option document. You can include in the option that you have the power to nullify the deal if you wish. You need to have legal advice to ensure that the option is considered valid, including the payment of money for the granting of the option—for example, a nominal sum such as $100—from the person receiving the option. You should also grant a power of attorney (PA) to the person who has the option to purchase or to another party, depending on the circumstances. The PA would be specific to the sale and transfer of the property, pursuant to the terms of the option. You need to be in good mental health when you grant the PA. Make sure you see a local U.S. lawyer experienced in these matters. If you suddenly become ill or incapacitated, prompt action could be taken by the option holder to transfer the real estate out of your name to the option holder's name, thereby avoiding U.S. estate tax. The exercise of the option prior to your death subjects you to U.S. and Canadian capital gains tax (CGT). You pay Canadian CGT whether your property is transferred before your death or triggered by your death (deemed disposition). However, the U.S. CGT would most likely be creditable against Canadian CGT. Therefore, the combined amount of U.S. and Canadian capital gains taxes could be significantly less by the property being transferred before your death by the exercising of the option, than the combined amount of U.S. estate tax and Canadian capital gains tax that would arise on your death, if it wasn't transferred out beforehand.

If you suddenly die, however, no action could be taken under the option agreement and power of attorney. There could therefore be estate tax payable on the value of your U.S. real estate property in your name, subject to any of the proposed changes to the Canada-U.S. tax treaty discussed in Section F.

4. Buying Term Life Insurance

This is an option to help pay for any future estate tax liability shortfall. For many Snowbirds, however, it is not a realistic option, because it is either impossible to acquire or too expensive. Even if you could afford to acquire enough coverage, you would need to increase the face value, since the value of your estate goes up every year, along with the cost of your insurance premium. You should attempt to buy a policy that enables you to increase the face value up to a certain amount, without having to undergo a medical exam each time. If you can't obtain term life insurance, you may want to consider the cheaper accidental death insurance.

There are other strategies that may or may not be beneficial or necessary in your individual situation to reduce or eliminate U.S. estate taxes—for example, selling the U.S. property outright and renting, renting and not buying any U.S. property in the first place, holding the U.S. property in a sole purpose Canadian holding corporation, or taking out a non-recourse U.S. mortgage on the U.S. home. These options have advantages and disadvantages. Make sure you obtain tax advice from a tax expert skilled in U.S.-Canada tax strategies.

H. TAX CREDIT FOR OUT-OF-COUNTRY EMERGENCY MEDICAL INSURANCE PREMIUMS

Revenue Canada will permit you to claim, as a tax credit, up to 27 percent of the amount of your insurance premium, as long as it is deemed to be a qualifying medical expense. Refer to Chapter 5, Section B-1(a) for a more detailed discussion.

I. WHERE TO GET TAX ADVICE AND INFORMATION

Many sources of information and assistance are available to help you understand the tax issues and improve your decision-making.

- **Revenue Canada—Taxation** has many free guides, pamphlets, and interpretation bulletins covering a wide range of issues. They will also provide you with assistance on your tax return questions and on international tax issues, such as being a Snowbird in the United States. Refer to item 1 in Appendix A for a list of publications and contact numbers.

- **Revenue Canada—Customs** has informational brochures and will answer your enquiries relating to any taxes, such as duties and so on when you   are bringing goods back to Canada. Refer to item 2 in Appendix A and Chapter 3.

- **The U.S. Internal Revenue Service (IRS)** has many free publications and a toll-free enquiry number for assistance with the tax implications and filing requirements of being a Canadian nonresident alien of the United States or another category of temporary resident. Refer to item 13 in Appendix A.

- See **independent professional advisors** such as chartered accountants (Canada) or certified public accountants (United States) and lawyers who specialize in tax matters and are familiar with cross-border Canada/U.S. tax issues. As mentioned before, it is prudent to obtain two opinions, at least one from a Canadian expert and one from a U.S. expert. The more extensive and complex your investments or assets in the United States, the more important it is to satisfy yourself that the advice you are getting is consistent. If you are considering moving to the United States permanently, it is imperative that you receive opinions from tax experts on both sides of the border. For suggestions on what to look for in a professional tax accountant or lawyer, refer to Chapter 8.

J. TIPS BEFORE LEAVING CANADA

Here are some reminders of tax-related steps you should take before leaving on your extended vacation in the United States. Or make arrangements for these matters to be dealt with while you are away. There are significant deadlines that have negative tax or financial consequences if they are not met.

- If you pay the current year's income tax in quarterly instalments, make arrangements to have your December 15 and March 15 instalments paid on time.

- If Revenue Canada has not yet notified you of acceptance of your previous year's income tax return self-assessment, make sure you are notified of any ruling while you are gone. You only have 90 days to file a notice of objection if Revenue Canada rejects your return and does a reassessment. If you are staying in one place for the duration of your Snowbird vacation, you probably have mail forwarded to you regularly. If you have no fixed address because you are an RV nomad, have someone monitor your mail and notify you when you next communicate with that person.

- Remember some key deadlines that may occur while you are away. For example, December 31 is the deadline for an annual withdrawal from a Registered Retirement Income Fund (RRIF). March 1 is the deadline for any contributions to a Registered Retirement Savings Plan (RRSP).

- If you turn 71 in the current calendar year, make your RRSP contribution by December 31 of the current year, rather than by 60 days after the end of the year.

- Pay safety deposit fees, RRSP administration fees, accounting fees, investment counsel fees, charitable donations, and moving expenses by December 31 if you intend to claim them as deductions or credits in the tax return filing for the current year.

- If you have spent at least 31 days in the United States in the current calendar year and have spent substantial periods in the United States in the previous two years, you may be required to fill a treaty disclosure return or a Closer Connection statement before April 15 or June 15, respectively, of the following year, to avoid significant penalties.

- Before you leave Canada, select a professional accountant who can assist you, before you depart, on the cross-border tax issues you need to know. Leave your U.S. contact address and phone number with the accountant in case he or she needs to reach you, and contact the accountant before the end of December to see if there are any tax-related matters that have to be dealt with before the end of that month or in the next quarter of the following year.

K. QUICK REFERENCE GUIDE TO RELEVANT PARTS OF THE APPENDICES

To help you obtain further information and contact numbers, here are the parts of the Appendices that are relevant to the contents of this chapter.

Appendix A: Items 1, 2, 4, 8, 13, 14, and 15

Appendix B: Item 4

CHAPTER
7

Wills, Trusts, and Estate Planning

A. INTRODUCTION

Over the course of your life you will sign many documents. Your will is the most important document you will ever sign. With very few exceptions, everybody should have a will. A will is the only legal document that can ensure that your assets will be distributed to the beneficiaries of your choice, in the way that you wish, instead of by a government formula in the absence of a will. A will also ensures that your estate will be settled in a timely and efficient manner, rather than in a delayed fashion that will create a burden for your family. Combined with effective estate planning, a will can ensure that the least amount of tax is payable. There are no estate taxes or succession duties in Canada at this time. There are tax implications for dying in the United States, however, if you own property there; this is discussed in chapter 6. As a Snowbird living in the United States for an extended period, you should deal with your will, power of attorney, and estate planning matters before your departure.

It is estimated that only one out of three adults has a will, meaning that two-thirds of the time when people die their wishes are not met and the government has to become involved. There are various reasons for the failure of people to prepare a will. Some people just procrastinate by nature or have busy lives and simply never make writing a will a priority. Others do not appreciate the full implications of dying without a will or even put their mind to the issue. And some people simply resist the reality that they are mortal. The contemplation of the finality of death is discomfiting to many people, and therefore they resist dealing with issues connected to death. Preparing a will and dealing with estate planning means facing the issue of mortality in a direct way.

Of those who do have a will, many do not review it regularly or modify it according to changing circumstances. Typically, people first think of their will at predictable stages of their lives, such as when they get married, when their first child is born, the first time they fly without their children, or upon news of the sudden death of a friend or relative. After the will has been completed, they forget about it. Not updating it can be as bad as not having a will at all. It can cause the beneficiaries a lot of grief, stress, time, and expense when these problems are easily avoided by regular review and updating of the will. Other people do their own will, with potentially serious implications if it is not done properly.

Your will comes into effect only after your death and is strictly confidential until that time. You can rewrite or amend the will at any time. In fact, the need to keep your will up to date cannot be overemphasized, since circumstances can change at any time. Some people prepare a will and never review it later. This can be a very serious oversight. A lot can happen over time, and a will should be reviewed every year, ideally at the same time—for example, on the first day of the new year or on some other special event or another set date. In addition, you should review your will when special circumstances arise in case your personal wishes have changed or when you are planning your estate. For example, your family needs or marital status may have changed, your assets may have increased or decreased, you may have moved to a new province or bought a U.S. Sunbelt condo or house, or new government tax or other legislation may have been introduced that should prompt you to look at your estate plan again. For example, when the federal government changed the tax laws in the 1992 and 1994 budgets, it removed the $100,000 personal capital gains exemption offset against real estate investment and other capital gains. People who owned second properties, such as a cottage or a second home, were affected. Those who did not revise their strategies quickly could lose money in the future on the sale of the cottage or house after any capital gains tax, or the deceased's estate could pay a higher tax on the capital gain in the property at the time of death, assuming that the property was in the deceased's name.

As a caution, this chapter provides general guidelines only. The laws and terminology relating to will preparation or estate planning can vary from province to province and state to state and can change from time to time. Federal and provincial income tax legislation continually changes. Seek professional advice. Refer to Appendix C.

B. WHAT'S IN A WILL?

Depending on the complexity of your estate, your finances, and personal affairs, your will can be short and simple, or long and complex. Here is an outline of the main contents of a basic will:

- Identification of person making the will.
- Statement that the current will revokes all former wills and codicils. A codicil is a supplementary document to a will that may change, add to, or subtract from the original will.
- Appointment of an executor and trustee (this is discussed in more detail later).
- Authorization to pay outstanding debts. This includes funeral expenses, taxes, fees, and other administrative expenses before any gift of property can be made.
- Disposition of property.
- Special provisions (such as trusts or alternative beneficiaries).
- Funeral instructions.

C. WHAT HAPPENS IF THERE IS NO WILL?

If you don't have a will, or don't have a valid will, the outcome could be a legal and financial nightmare and an emotionally devastating ordeal for your loved ones. Not having a will at the time of death is called being intestate. It means you have not left instructions for how you want your assets to be dealt with on your death and you have not appointed anyone to be legally in charge of your estate. Accordingly, provincial and state (if you are a Snowbird with assets in the United States) legislation covers that situation. The court eventually appoints an administrator. If no family member applies to act as administrator, the public trustee or official administrator is appointed. Your estate will be distributed in accordance with the formulas of the laws of your province or state, which are inflexible and may not reflect either your personal wishes or the needs of your family or loved ones. Although the law attempts to be fair and equitable, it does not provide for special needs. For example, a home or other assets could be sold under unfavourable market conditions in order to effect the necessary distribution of assets that the law requires. In addition, the settling of your estate could be a long and expensive matter.

If you have assets in both Canada and the United States, you will have two separate probates governed by the laws of the province and state where you had assets. Your heirs could end up paying taxes that might easily have been deferred or reduced. There may not be enough worth in the estate to pay the taxes. Your family could be left without enough cash for an extended period of time. During this period, your assets may suffer a loss because of a lack of proper safeguards. There may be a delay in the administration of your estate and added costs such as an administrator bond. A bond is similar to an insurance policy in case the administrator makes a mistake.

The consequences of not having a will are not the type of memory or legacy most people would choose to inflict on their children, spouse, or relatives. At the time of a death and during the natural grieving process, the survivors do not want the stress and uncertainty of there not being a will. You should leave them cherished memories, including the foresight, consideration, and love shown by having a valid will that reflects current realities and your wishes. Simply put, there is no logical reason not to have a will.

D. WHAT IS A "LIVING WILL"?

A "living will" is designed for those who are concerned about their quality of life when they are near death. It is a written statement of your intentions to the people who are most likely to have control over your care, such as your family and your doctor. Make sure you convey your wishes to your family and your family doctor. Have a copy of the living will where it can be readily obtained—for example, in your wallet or purse. Give a copy to your spouse and family doctor. You should also review your living will from time to time.

The purpose of a living will is to convey your wishes in the event that there is no reasonable expectation of recovery from physical or mental disability. Such a will requests that you be allowed to die naturally, with dignity, and not be kept alive by artificial means or "heroic medical measures." At present, a living will is merely an expression of your wishes only and is not legally binding on your doctor or the hospital in charge of your care in Canada. However, some provinces, such as Quebec, Ontario, and Manitoba, have legislation on the issue of living wills. These provinces officially endorse the concept, if your written instructions are correctly done.

To obtain a sample living will with instructional booklet and/or videotape, contact:

Centre for Bioethics
University of Toronto
88 College Street
Toronto, ON M5G 1L4
Tel: (416) 978-2709

The cost of the booklet on living wills is $5, or $24.95 for two booklets plus a videotape.

In the United States, most states recognize a properly drawn living will. Except for Michigan, New York, and Massachusetts, all the U.S. states, including the Sunbelt states, have some form of legislation dealing with living wills. For further information and to obtain a free living will form customized for the Sunbelt state you reside in, contact:

Choice in Dying
200 Varick Street
10th Floor
New York, NY 10014
Tel: (212) 366-5540
Tel: 1-800-989-9455 (U.S. and Canada)

If you are a Snowbird, you should consider two living wills. One should be recognized in Canada and comply with any provincial legislation; it should also be generic enough for provinces in Canada without legislation. The other living will would be prepared for your extended stay in the United States and comply with appropriate U.S. state legislation or be generic enough to express your wishes for the three states that do not have specific living will legislation. You may also wish to consult a lawyer in Canada and, if you are living in the United States as a Snowbird, a U.S. lawyer as well, if you desire further information on this issue. Refer to Chapter 8.

E. PREPARING A WILL AND SELECTING A LAWYER

There are basically three ways to have your will prepared: write it yourself, have a lawyer do it for you, or have a trust company arrange a lawyer to do it for you. A brief overview follows. When you read the section on the reasons for seeing a lawyer, you will see the compelling need to protect your estate and personal wishes by doing so.

1. Writing Your Own Will

This is the poorest choice, because it could have many defects and inadequacies that could result in legal, financial, and administrative grief for your family, relatives, and beneficiaries. How you expressed your wishes may very well be legally interpreted differently from what you intended because of ambiguity. Worse still, any ambiguous clause in the will could be deemed void or the whole will could be considered void for various technical reasons. Some people do their own will by drafting it from scratch or by using a "standard form" for a will purchased in a bookstore or stationery store. The risk is very high when you try to save money and do it yourself rather than using a skilled professional. It is false economy, and depending on your situation, you could have a lot to lose. Many people assume that a "simple" will that they complete will suffice. What may appear to be simple to a layperson, however, could require more complex decisions and wording. Each person's situation is unique. There are better and inexpensive alternatives to provide you with peace of mind, as outlined in the next two subsections.

2. Hiring a Lawyer and Other Specialists

Wills, in almost all cases, should be prepared by a lawyer familiar with wills because he or she is qualified to provide legal advice and is knowledgeable about how to complete the legal work required in drafting a will. If your will is properly and professionally drafted, it will be valid in the United States and will cover your U.S. assets. If you have assets in both the United States and Canada, there will be a probate in both countries on your death. Your estate will require a lawyer in each country. Probate is governed by the laws and taxes of the province and state in which you have assets.

Depending on the complexity of the estate, however, a lawyer may not have the expertise to advise you on other, nonlegal issues, such as tax, investments, and retirement. If that is your situation, you should enlist the expertise of the other specialists, such as a professionally qualified accountant who specializes in tax, specifically a chartered accountant (CA) or certified general accountant (CGA). A lawyer specializing in wills could recommend a tax expert. You can also look in the Yellow Pages of the telephone book for accountants with these designations. Ask to speak to a tax specialist.

If you are selecting a financial planner as well to help manage your finanacial affairs, make sure that you check that person's credentials, expertise, and reputation. Ask for referrals from your lawyer or accountant and have any advice verified for the tax, legal, and administrative implications by your lawyer, accountant, and trust company.

For a discussion of how to select a lawyer, accountant, or financial planner, see Chapter 8.

The legal fee for preparing a basic will is very modest, generally between $100 and $150 per person. If your estate is complex, of course, this fee could be higher because of the additional time and expertise required. A "back-to-back" will is a duplicate reverse one for husband and wife and is generally a reduced price.

3. Main Reasons for Consulting a Lawyer When Preparing a Will

To reinforce the necessity of obtaining a legal consultation before completing or redoing a will, just look at some of the many situations in which legal advice is specifically required because of the complex legal issues and options involved. By not dealing with these issues, you could have serious legal and financial problems on your death.

- You want to live in the United States or elsewhere for extended periods of time—for example, to retire and travel south in the winter months. The issue of your technical domicile, or permanent residence, at the time of your death has legal and tax implications for your will. This is discussed in detail in Chapter 6.

- You own or plan to own foreign real estate, in the United States or elsewhere.

- You have a will that was signed outside Canada or plan to do so.

- You are separated from your spouse but not divorced.

- You are divorced and want to remarry.

- You are divorced and paying for the support of your former spouse and your children.

- You are living common-law, will be entering a common-law relationship, or are leaving an existing one.

- You are in a blended family relationship, with children of each spouse from previous relationships.

- You have children from a previous relationship and an existing one.

- You own your own business or part-own a business with other partners.

- Your estate is large and you need assistance with estate planning long before your death to reduce, delay, or eliminate taxes on your death.

- You have a history of medical problems and so someone could attack the validity of your will on the basis that you did not know what you were doing when you signed the will or were not capable of understanding the financial matters covered in the will.

- You want to have objective, unbiased, and professional advice rather than making choices in a vacuum or possibly being in an environment where you could be influenced by others who have a vested interest in the contents of the will, or you do not want to feel under duress or pressure from relatives or family members when preparing your will.

- You want to forgive certain people for debts they owe you, or make special arrangements for the repaying of debts or mortgages to your estate should you die before the debt or mortgage is paid back to you.

- You want certain events to occur that are complicated and have to be carefully worded, such as having a spouse or friend receive a certain income or use a home until he or she remarries or dies, at which time the balance of the money or the house would go to someone else.

- You want to set up a trust arrangement to cover various possibilities. Trusts are discussed later in this chapter.

- You want to make special arrangements to care for someone who is incapable of looking after himself or herself, or who is unable to apply sound financial or other relevant judgement—for example, a child, an immature adolescent, a gambler, an alcoholic, a spendthrift, or someone who has emotional, physical, or mental disabilities or limitations or who is ill.

- You wish to disinherit a spouse, relative, or child. There are several reasons for disinheriting someone. For example, you may have lent a lot of money to one child out of several, the money was not repaid, promises were broken, and a serious estrangement occurred. The unpaid money substantially reduced your estate, and to keep peace with the rest of the family you may want to remove the debtor child from sharing in the proceeds of your estate or reduce that child's portion by the amount of the debt. Another, more positive reason might be that all your children are now wealthy on their own and don't need your money at all. You may therefore want to give the majority of your estate to charitable causes that interest you.

- You wish to appoint a guardian to look after any children you are responsible for, in case you and your spouse die together.

- You have several children and you want to provide the opportunity for one specific child to buy, have an option to buy, or receive in the will the house, business, or farm or a specific possession or asset of your estate, and you want to set up the appropriate procedures and wording to enable your wishes to occur.

When viewing your own situation at this point or where you project your circumstances might be in the near future, there could be at least one if not many different reasons to consult with a legal expert on the topic of wills customized for your needs and wishes.

4. Using a Trust Company

A trust company can offer extensive services related to wills and estate planning, generally in conjunction with a lawyer of your choice or a lawyer recommended by the trust company. Always make sure that you obtain independent legal advice. A trust company can administer a trust set up as part of your estate planning or act as your executor. Everyone's needs vary, and after obtaining advice you may not require a trust company. Compare a minimum of three trust companies before deciding who to deal with. The decision is a critically important one, and you want to feel confident in your choice. Look in the Yellow Pages of your phone book under "Trust Companies."

5. Granting Power of Attorney

Many lawyers draft a power of attorney at the same time that they prepare a will. The purpose of a power of attorney is to designate a person or a trust company to take over your affairs if you can no longer handle them because of illness or incapacitation, for example. This is normally referred to as an "enduring power of attorney." Another reason is that you may be away for extended periods on personal or business matters or on a vacation. You may want to give someone the authority to sign documents on your behalf regarding the sale of your home while you are away. This is normally referred to as a "specific power of attorney," which is limited in scope and time. Considering the benefits of a power of attorney is important if you have substantial assets that require active management. You can revoke the power of attorney at any time in writing.

If you do not have a power of attorney and are unable to manage your financial affairs because of illness, accident, or mental infirmity, an application has to be made to the court by the party who wishes permission to manage your affairs. This party is referred to as a committee. If another family member does not wish to take on this responsibility, a trust company can be appointed, with court approval. Committee duties include filing with the court a summary of assets, liabilities, and income sources, along with a description of the person's needs and an outline of how the committee proposes to manage the accounts or structure the estate to serve those needs. In addition, continuing asset management is required to meet any changes in circumstances or needs, as well as record-keeping and accounting functions, all subject to the direction of the court.

F. SELECTING AN EXECUTOR OR TRUSTEE

One of the most important decisions you will make is your choice of executor to fulfill your instructions in your will. Your executor acts as your "personal representative" and deals with all the financial, tax, administrative, and other aspects of your estate, including assembling and protecting assets, projecting future cash needs, handling all tax requirements, distributing the assets of the estate, and acting as a trustee for the continuing management of the assets of your estate. As you can see, it would be difficult to find a layperson or family member who would have the range of skills and expertise needed to adequately fulfill all the functions that might be required. An executor should either be an expert or retain specialists in potentially diverse areas such as law, income tax, real estate, asset evaluation and management, accounting, financial administration, and insurance. Not only can the process be time-consuming and complicated, it can also expose the executor to personal legal liability if errors are made. The executor is accountable to all beneficiaries.

1. Selecting an Executor

A will takes estate planning only so far. It is up to the executor to settle the estate to the satisfaction of the beneficiaries. Generally, there are two kinds of executors. One type is the professional executor, such as a lawyer, accountant, or trust company. The other type is the inexperienced layperson, generally a relative or family friend familiar with your personal life.

Many people consider being asked to be an executor an honour, a reflection of the trust and respect in the relationship. Unfortunately, in the emotional context of a death, however, conflicts can and do occur between executors and beneficiaries. The conflicts can arise if the executor is perceived as being overzealous or indifferent, being authoritarian or showing favouritism, lacking necessary knowledge, making decisions too hastily, or lacking tact, sensitivity, or insight in dealing with people.

An executor can retain the services of a lawyer, of course, and use a trust company as an agent. Another possibility is to appoint a co-executor. If the will names more than one person to administer the estate, they are referred to as co-executors. They have equal rights and responsibilities in administering the estate. For example, you could consider having a spouse and a trust company as co-executors. In addition, if you are naming an individual as an executor or a co-executor, make sure you have an alternative executor in the event the first one is unwilling or unable to act.

2. Selecting a Trustee

You may want to set up trusts that are operable during your lifetime. These are generally called inter-vivos trusts. You need to have a trustee manage the trust. Another type of trust is one that is operable upon your death, as outlined in your will. This is generally referred to as a testamentary trust.

Through your will, you can appoint an individual or trust company to administer assets of your estate that you identify for later distribution. For example, you may wish to appoint a trustee to manage a portion of your assets for an extended period of time. If you are selecting a layperson to be the executor, you may not want the same person to be the trustee. There could be a potential conflict of interest for various reasons, and different skills could be required.

You can also set up trust funds in a variety of ways, depending on your objectives. You may wish the beneficiaries to have regular monthly payments of the income generated from the original capital of trust money. This could be the situation if you are leaving money to an educational or charitable organization. Conversely, you could have that monthly payment provision in favour of a surviving spouse, with the stipulation that payments cease if he or she remarries. The remaining capital goes elsewhere. If you are setting up a trust for young children, payments are usually made to parents or guardians for the maintenance and education of the child. For such a trust, there should be a provision allowing the trustee to deplete the capital of the trust fund, as required, to meet the needs set out in the trust provisions. Another option is to invest the trust funds until a specified event and then release the total funds. For example, if a child has been financially irresponsible, you may wish to have the funds held until he or she is more mature, say, 35 or 40 years old. If you wish to keep a gift in your will secret, there are various ways of doing that. Speak to a lawyer who is experienced in dealing with trusts.

Trustees are normally given the power in the will to undertake many duties, including taking in money, investing money, selling assets, and distributing the estate proceeds in accordance with the trust terms. It is important the trustee maintain a balance between the interests of income beneficiaries and beneficiaries subsequently entitled to the capital. In addition, a trustee should maintain accounts and regularly issue accounting statements and income tax receipts to beneficiaries, make income payments to beneficiaries, and exercise discretion on early withdrawal of capital where permitted, to meet special needs of beneficiaries. Finally, the trustee makes the final distribution of the trust fund to beneficiaries on the death of the income beneficiary and/or when beneficiaries reach a certain age designated in the terms of the will, or based on other conditions in the will.

You can see why trust companies perform a vital role. An individual may not have the long continuity required, because of death or lack of interest or ability, for the 10, 15, 20, 25, or more years required. It is an onerous role to place on an individual. The benefits of using a trust company are discussed in section G of this chapter.

3. Fees and Expenses

There are various fees associated with probating a will, settling an estate, or dealing with a trust. If you die in the United States and have assets there, such as a condo, you would have probate in both countries with a duplication in costs. The main costs are as follows:

- **Compensation for executors/administrators**
  In most cases an executor or administrator is entitled to a fee for his or her time and services provided. The maximum fee is normally 3 to 5 percent of the value of the estate. The beneficiaries or the court must approve the accounts prepared for compensation, and the amount comes out of the estate. An executor who is also a beneficiary could be denied a fee unless the will makes it clear that the gift to the executor is given in addition to, not instead of, executor's fees.

- **Legal fees**
  A lawyer can assist in locating and collecting assets, make any necessary application to court and prepare related documents, get the assets transferred into the name of the executor or administrator, prepare accounts, distribute funds, obtain releases, and file tax returns.

  Legal fees are considered a proper expense and may be paid out of estate funds, subject to approval of the court or the beneficiaries. A lawyer may charge a fee for itemized services rendered or a lump-sum fee of generally up to 2 percent of the value of the estate for certain basic services. This is a maximum percentage, not a standard rate. If any legal issue arises, such as the validity or meaning of a will, or if an application to the court is made, legal fees will be extra and are normally billed out at the lawyer's hourly rate. This could be between $150 and $200 or more an hour.

- **Probate fees**
  These are also known as court fees. They are established by provincial or state legislation. They do not form part of the executor's compensation, nor do they include legal fees associated with administering the estate. The probate fees can range from low to high, depending on the province or state. Check with a Canadian and a U.S. lawyer. The value of the estate is used as a base when determining the probate fee. It is paid to the provincial and/or state government.

- **Trustee fees**
  These would generally be negotiated separately, especially if a trust company is involved, and confirmed in writing. The services involved in managing a trust were discussed earlier.

- **Additional fees and costs**
  Naturally, income-tax-related costs and financial costs are extra.

  If a beneficiary of the estate thinks that the administration fee charged by an executor is excessive, he or she can ask the executor to "pass accounts" in a court of law. The executor must present an accounting of the work done to the court and ask a judge to set the fees. The final fee may be higher or lower than the fee that the executor initially requested. When beneficiaries are infants or children, the executor may be required to pass accounts because minors cannot give their approval for the actions of the executor. If the executor or beneficiary believes that the legal fees are excessive, they can be challenged. This is called "taxing" a lawyer's account. The account is generally taxed before the registrar at the courthouse. Procedures may differ in your community.

  Selecting the right executor for your needs will enhance the smooth disposition of your assets and the administration of your estate. It will also reduce the stress your family will be under. Selecting the wrong executor for your needs will result in the opposite outcome. To be on the safe side, use a professional to act as an executor or trustee, or appoint a family member to be a co-executor or co-trustee if the circumstances warrant it or you wish that to occur. Remember to shortlist three prospects and/or trust companies before you decide who will act as your executor and/or trustee.

G. BENEFITS OF USING A TRUST COMPANY AS EXECUTOR OR TRUSTEE

Many people prefer to name a trust company in the will as their executor for a variety of reasons. You may choose to select an individual executor as a co-executor with the trust company or stipulate that a designated trust company act for you if the named executor is unwilling or unable to act. There are various options and implications you can explore and discuss with your lawyer and/or trust company.

Following are the main benefits of a trust company. Compare these benefits to the capabilities of a personal friend, relative, or family member acting as an executor in your given situation.

- **Experience and expertise in will and estate planning**
  A large portion of any trust company's operation involves acting as an executor. A trust company's staff can regularly advise you about coordinating the contents of your will with the other financial affairs, needs, and personal changes in your life, since they are closely interrelated, and in conjunction with your legal and tax advisors. This broad expertise should enable the trust company to administer the estate economically and efficiently. Part of estate planning involves establishing objectives for estate distribution, taking into consideration any legislation concerning provision for dependents. In addition, planning involves determining what taxes would be payable by the estate or beneficiaries and considering procedures for minimizing or providing for these taxes.

- **Continuity of service**
  The appointment of a trust company ensures continuity of service during the full period of administration of the estate. This is particularly important if the estate involves a trust responsibility that might have to be administered for many years (e.g., if young children are the beneficiaries). A trust company will designate only their most experienced staff to deal with the administration of estates. The staff must combine both business ability and capacity for human understanding and empathy. These qualities enable them to deal tactfully and fairly with each beneficiary.

- **Accessibility**
  A trust officer is assigned a specific estate and is personally responsible for providing customized and responsive service.

- **Full attention to the needs of your estate**
  With a trust company as executor, the operation of estate administration is smooth, since infrastructure and continuity exists. If a layperson is an executor, that person's attention to the executor duties may be influenced by other personal interests, age, ill health, procrastination, or excessive stress due to the demands of fulfilling expectations in an area where he or she has no experience, expertise, or interest.

- **Portfolio management**
  A trust company can provide expertise for your estate's investment needs, such as cash management or operating a business.

- **Ensuring of control when that is important**
  There could be instances when a professional, neutral, and experienced executor or trustee must deal with issues in the will that require an element of control—for example, releasing funds over time to a child who is an adult but lacks financial responsibility. Another example is managing a business until the appropriate time to market and sell it. Trust companies have access to this type of expertise and can competently deal with any situation that might come up.

- **Confidentiality**
  Trust company staff are trained to treat the estate administration and related client business in the strictest confidence.

- **Sharing of responsibility**
  If you decide to name a friend or relative as joint executor, the trust company assumes the burden of the administration but works together with your other executor to make joint decisions.

- **Financial responsibility and security**
  Most trust companies in Canada are well established and are backed by substantial capital and reserve accounts. Reputable trust companies also strictly segregate estate assets from general funds. In addition, a trust company is covered by insurance if there is a mistake or oversight due to negligence or inadvertence.

- **Funding capacity**
  A trust company can work with your family to provide for their immediate financial requirements and needs immediately after your death.

- **Specialized knowledge**
  Because of the increasingly complex nature of tax and other legislation issues relating to an estate, as well as a wide variety of options available, a trust company employs a staff of experts to review and advise on matters or issues that arise. Specialists offer expertise in tax, legal, insurance, investment, and other areas.

- **Ability to act as a trustee**
  This means that the trust company protects your interests after you die. For example, the company might manage your investments or capital and make payments to designated beneficiaries as required over time. If there are minor children, children from a previous marriage, or situations in which the estate assets have to be controlled for an extended period of time, for example, a trustee could be giving out necessary funds from your estate over a period of 20 years or more.

- **Group decisions**
  If vital matters come up that involve a major decision, a trust company will use the collective expertise of a variety of senior staff and specialists to arrive at a decision.

- **Fees and savings**

  Most trust companies will enter into a fee agreement at the time your will is prepared. Trust company fees are determined by legislative guidelines and the courts, in most provinces. The same guidelines also apply to a private executor. There can also be savings due to efficiency by having an experienced trust company perform the executor duties. This would not, of course, include fees involved in regular estate management or the maintenance of trusts set up during the will planning process and included in the will. Obtain quotes from the trust company.

- **Avoidance of family conflict**

  In any family situation there could be personality or ego conflicts, or friction due to issues dealing with control, power, money, distribution of family possessions or assets, resentment due to past financial favours to certain children or forgiveness of loans to others, unequal distribution of the estate to family members, or a multitude of other potential conflict areas. A trust company acts as a neutral, objective, and professional catalyst in pre-empting, ameliorating, or resolving potential disagreements affecting the administration or distribution of the estate. Based on practical experience, a trust company understands and anticipates the many potential personal, family, financial, emotional, and psychological dynamics that may be operating following a death and the administration of the wishes set out in the will.

- **Peace of mind**

  There is a great reduction in stress to know that the estate will be administered competently, professionally, promptly, and in accord with your stated wishes. An experienced trust company can provide this peace of mind and feeling of security.

  There are clear advantages to using the services of a trust company in many situations, not only to act as an executor, but also to act as a trustee. As mentioned earlier, you may wish to appoint a spouse or family member as a co-executor or co-trustee in certain situations. Remember to interview a minimum of three trust companies before you decide which one you want to deal with. Always have your own lawyer, from whom you can obtain independent legal advice on will or trust matters. Make sure your lawyer has expertise in this area.

H. ESTATE PLANNING AND TRUSTS

1. Reasons for Estate Planning

Estate planning refers to the process required to transfer and preserve your wealth in an orderly and effective manner. Trusts are often at the centre of the strategic planning process. There are many types of trusts. A living trust, referred to as an inter-vivos trust, is established while the creator of the trust is still alive and is a very common type of trust. Trusts are set up with various instructions and conditions that the trustee must follow. There are tax and non-tax reasons for setting up a trust. A trust enables you to set aside money for a specific person or beneficiary under specific conditions. It is a powerful instrument, and great care must be taken in setting one up, since it enables you to exercise "control from the grave." Trusts vary widely. Some give the trustee wide discretion; others are rigid. Once again, a properly drafted will is the foundation of a strategic estate plan.

From a tax perspective, your estate planning objectives include:

- minimizing and deferring tax on your estate

- minimizing taxes on your death so that most of your estate can be preserved for your heirs

- moving any tax burden to your heirs to be paid only upon the future sale of the assets

There are various techniques for attaining the above objectives. Some of these are:

- arranging for assets to be transferred to family members in a lower tax bracket

- establishing trusts for your children to maximize future tax savings

- setting up estate freezes, generally for your children; this means that you reduce the tax they pay in the future on the increased value of selected assets

- making optimal use of the benefit of charitable donations, tax shelters, holding companies, or dividend tax credits

- taking advantage of special income tax options to minimize tax or payments on your present assets

Federal and provincial governments are always looking for ways of increasing revenue. One way is to tax what has been exempted before. Proper estate planning can anticipate these events and therefore reduce, delay, or save tax.

2. Stages of Estate Planning

Estate planning is a continuing process, as your circumstances, needs, and wishes change. Regardless of your age, the issue of estate planning, in conjunction with your will, is an essential element of life planning. There are different stages in a person's life, though, when certain issues may arise that require different estate-planning strategies.

In the later stages of life, you could be approaching retirement or already be retired. As you get older, there could be health concerns or medical needs that you or your spouse have. Your assets are probably at their peak. Your children may be married and may or may not need your financial support. Alternatively, you may have a child who is out of work or divorced or separated and requires financial support for him- or herself or his or her children. Here are the basic steps you want to consider:

- *Assess your financial status and your personal needs, goals, priorities, and wishes.* If you are reading this book, you are probably already a Snowbird or plan to become one. You may also want to do a lot of travelling by car, RV, or other means. You may wish to sell your existing home and move to a condominium in a quiet, retirement-oriented community in Canada or the United States with activities that challenge and stimulate as well as provide a socializing dimension. Many people "cash out" by doing this; in other words, they have so much equity in their home that after their new purchase they still have lots of money left. If you are considering any of the above real estate options, refer to Chapter 4. Complete Appendix C, a checklist for retirement, financial, and estate planning.

- *Review your will.* You need to balance the needs of your spouse against those of your children. You may wish to enjoy your lifestyle and retirement fully and leave whatever is left to your children. Alternatively, you may wish to leave a trust for your grandchildren or give additional money to a favourite charity or other worthwhile cause. If your children are already financially independent, these options may be attractive to consider. You may want to completely disinherit a child for other reasons. Make sure your lawyer words the will carefully to minimize the chance that it could be contested.

- *Reconsider your executor and trustee.* Make sure that your executor will completely fulfill your needs. For a variety of reasons, an immediate family member or relative may not be the best choice as executor or trustee. For example, there could be personality conflicts between someone chosen as executor or trustee and other members of the family. You may therefore wish to retain a trust company to act as your executor and trustee. You could name a responsible family member as a co-executor and co-trustee, if you so wished.

- *Obtain professional advice on minimizing taxes.* The issue of tax is always an important one, and the size of your estate can have considerable tax consequences. Federal and provincial income taxes are due when you die. There are tax consequences of having U.S. assets, but there are steps you can take in advance to minimize or eliminate them; refer to Chapter 6. Although Canada, unlike the United States, has no succession duties at present, several provinces are considering them. Unless you have taken steps to minimize taxes on your death, taxes could seriously deplete your estate. Obtain advice from your lawyer, professional tax accountant, and trust company.

3. Reducing Probate Fees and Taxes

Assets of your estate that are passed on through your will and go through the probate process are subject to probate fees. Some provinces have a ceiling, whereas other provinces do not. As a reminder, whenever an executor asks the court to confirm or validate the executor's right to deal with an estate, the executor applies for what is referred to as a Grant of Probate. This permits the executor to deal with the assets of the estate. At the time that this formal confirmation is made, the probate fees are due. If the executor did not go through this legal confirmation process, many people, regulatory or government agencies, or banks could become concerned that the will is invalid or that there could be a later will, and thus they refuse to recognize the executor's authority. Even if no will exists, the courts must formally and legally confirm the authority of an administrator to administer the estate, and a probate fee must still be paid.

You can minimize the amount of probate tax paid by removing assets from your estate. Clearly, if after professional consultation you choose to do this, you must be sure to leave enough assets or funds in your estate to pay the tax. These strategies have to be viewed, though, in the context of your overall estate plan. For example, if you have a business, part of your estate plan could be to place most of your assets beyond the reach of potential creditors. Otherwise, in theory, your estate could be at risk of attack by creditors. In addition, you may not want certain assets to remain in the estate, since these assets could be frozen pending the probate of the estate. Obtain professional advice from your lawyer, accountant, and trust company on the various issues that concern you, such as relinquishing control, your marital situation (particularly if you are separated or living common-law), whether you have children, tax consequences, legal or creditor considerations, and many other issues. There are some key techniques to move assets out of an estate before death or to automatically transfer them directly to a beneficiary at the time of death, thereby avoiding going through the will and probate. For example:

- Register property jointly so that it automatically passes to the survivor and not through the estate. In other words, the asset is not affected by the will. Examples are a joint tenancy in real estate or a joint bank account.

- Designate beneficiaries on your life insurance policies, RRSPs, RRIFs, annuity programs, and employee pension plans. If you are designating beneficiaries, check to see if you can easily change the beneficiary during your lifetime, without the consent of the beneficiary if you so wanted. This could be relevant in case of a marital estrangement. Some provinces don't allow you to name a beneficiary of an RRSP.

- Establish trusts during your lifetime to transfer title to property before your death.

The main financial purpose of an estate plan is to keep taxes and expenses as low as possible and pay as much as possible to your beneficiaries. You don't want to automatically make decisions as described just to reduce probate fees when other strategies could better suit your overall estate-planning objectives. You may wish to consider other strategies, such as:

- Using a testamentary trust to split income among your beneficiaries. This type of trust operates through the provisions of your will at the time of your death.

- Using the $500,000 capital gains deduction for the sale of shares in a privately held Canadian business by selling the asset to family members and thereby crystallizing the tax-free gain while you are still alive. Collateral documentation for you to retain control of the operation or management of the business could be negotiated and signed, including the remuneration package. This deduction is still available, but could be changed in any federal budget.

- Using strategies to protect certain family assets, in a marital breakdown, from being deemed to be marital property. This is relevant if you have married a second time and wish to protect the interests of the children of the first marriage, as well as the rights of your second spouse.

4. Death Benefits Available through the Canada Pension Plan

A surviving spouse will probably be entitled to two benefits under the CPP. One is called a death benefit and comes in a lump-sum payment, with a ceiling. The second benefit is called the survivor's benefit and depends on the age of the surviving spouse. There is a ceiling per month for a person over 65, and the survivor receives it for life. The survivor is also entitled to his or her own CPP benefits, but the two benefits have a ceiling. Check with your local CPP office for more information. Refer to Chapter 2.

I. TIPS BEFORE LEAVING CANADA

- Make sure that your will is current and reflects your wishes.

- Keep a copy of your will in your safety deposit box, as well as with your lawyer and/or trust company. Tell a close, trusted family member where your safety deposit box is located and who your lawyer is.

- Review your selection of executor and trustee, and consider the benefits of a trust company for those roles, as sole executor and trustee or co-executor and co-trustee.

- Have your Canadian lawyer confirm, or confirm with a lawyer in the

Sunbelt state you live in, that according to the laws of the state your Canadian will covers any U.S. real estate assets.

- Consider the benefits of a power of attorney, either to handle specific matters during your absence or to deal with any incapacity on your part.

- Consider the benefits of a living will. Make sure you have left copies of such a will with key relatives, your spouse, and your doctor. Carry a copy in your purse or wallet and in the glove compartment of your car. If you are seriously ill or in an accident, you want the document to be accessible.

- Ensure that you have adequately arranged your estate-planning needs to reduce probate fees and other taxes.

- If you do not already have a will or power of attorney, select a lawyer skilled in those areas and have the documents completed before you leave.

- If you do not already have a professional accountant who is skilled in cross-border tax issues, select one and obtain advice before you depart.

J. QUICK REFERENCE GUIDE TO RELEVANT SECTIONS OF THE APPENDICES

To help you obtain further information and contact numbers, here are the parts of the Appendices that are relevant to the contents of this chapter.

Appendix A: Items 1 and 13.

Appendix B: Sections 3 and 4.

Appendix C

CHAPTER
8

Selecting Professional and Other Advisors

A. INTRODUCTION

Professional advisors are essential to protect your interests. They can provide knowledge, expertise, and objective advice in areas in which you have little experience. It is important to recognize when it is necessary to call in an expert to assist you. Because of the costs associated with hiring a lawyer, accountant, or financial planner, some people are inclined to try the do-it-yourself approach, but this decision can be shortsighted and detrimental to their financial interests. For instance, the person who processes his or her own income tax return rather than hiring a professional tax accountant may miss out on tax exemptions that could save much more than the cost of the accountant's time. Or a person who does his or her own will or power of attorney could end up having the will or power of attorney deemed invalid because of a technicality. Alternatively, lack of professional tax and estate planning could mean that you pay a lot more tax during your lifetime and on your death than is necessary.

Professional advisors you may need include lawyers, accountants, financial planners, and others. They serve different functions, and you have to be very selective in your screening process. The right selection will enhance your peace of mind, reduce taxable income, and protect your legal and financial health. The wrong selection will be costly in time, money, and stress.

B. GENERAL FACTORS TO CONSIDER

There are many factors you should consider when selecting a professional advisor. The person's professional qualifications, experience in your specific area of need, and fee for services are factors you will want to consider. It is helpful to prepare a list of questions about these factors, plus others relating to your specific needs. By doing so, you won't forget them and can pose the questions to each of the prospective advisors. List the questions in order of priority in case you run out of time. You want to control the agenda. You also want to see if the advisor is proactive—that is, asks you questions—rather than being strictly reactive—that is, expecting you to ask all the questions. Some people may feel awkward discussing fees and areas of expertise with a lawyer, for instance, but it is important to establish these matters from the outset, before you make a decision to use that person's services. Some of the most common general selection criteria include the following:

1. Qualifications

Before you entrust an advisor with your affairs, you will want to know that he or she has the necessary qualifications to do the job. These may include a lawyer's or accountant's professional degree, or if you are looking for a financial planner, professional training accreditation and experience in the person's professed area of expertise. The fact that the person is an active member of a professional association or institute usually means a continuing interest in seminars and courses to keep his or her professional training current.

2. Experience

It is very important to take a look at the advisor's experience in the area in which you need assistance. Such factors as the degree of expertise, the number of years' experience as an advisor, and percentage of time spent practising in that area are critically important. The amount of reliance you are going to place on someone's advice and insights is obviously related to the degree of experience he or she has in the area. For example, the fact that a lawyer might have been practising law for ten years does not necessarily mean that the lawyer has a high degree of expertise in the area in which you are seeking advice—for example, real estate law dealing with houses, condominiums, time-share properties, or immigration. Perhaps only 10 percent of the practice has been spent in that specific area. An accountant who has had 15 years' experience in small business accounting is not likely to have expertise in providing advice on tax planning strategies for individuals living part-time in Canada and the United States. It cannot be overemphasized how important it is to enquire about degree of expertise and length of experience in the specific area you are interested in. If you don't ask the question, you won't be given the answer that may make a difference between satisfaction and dissatisfaction.

3. Compatible Personality

When choosing an advisor, make certain that you feel comfortable with the individual's personality. If you are going to have a long-term relationship with the advisor, it is important that you feel comfortable with the degree of communication between the two of you. You should also find out about the advisor's attitude, approach, degree of candour, and commitment to meet your needs. A healthy respect and rapport will increase your comfort level when discussing your needs and will thereby enhance further understanding of the issues. If you don't feel that there is the chemistry you want, don't continue the relationship. It is only human nature to resist contacting someone you don't like, and that could compromise your best interests.

4. Objectivity

This is an essential quality for a professional advisor. If advice is tainted in any way by bias or personal financial benefit, that advice is unreliable and self-serving. That is why you want to get a minimum of three opinions on your personal situation before carefully deciding which professional to select.

5. Trust

Trust is a vital trait in the person you select to advise you. Whether the person is a lawyer, accountant, financial planner, or other investment advisor, if you don't intuitively trust the advice as being solely in your best interests, do not use that person again. You have far too much to lose in financial security and peace of mind to have any doubts whatsoever. By having a better understanding of how to cautiously select an advisor, you will increase the odds of selecting wisely and developing a relationship with a professional you know will be guided by your needs at all times. You cannot risk the chance that advice is governed primarily by the financial self-interest of the advisor, with your interests as a secondary consideration.

6. Confidence

You must have confidence in your advisor if you are going to rely on his or her advice to improve your decision making and minimize your risk. After considering the person's qualifications, experience, personality, and style, you may feel a strong degree of confidence and trust that he or she will be totally objective. If you do not, don't use the person as an advisor; seek someone else as soon as possible.

7. Fees

It is important to feel comfortable with the fee being charged and the terms of payment. Is the fee fair, competitive, and affordable? Does it match the person's qualifications and experience? The saying "You get what you pay for" can be true of fees charged by lawyers, accountants, and financial planners. For instance, if you need a good tax accountant to advise you on minimizing taxes, you may have to pay a high hourly rate for the quality of advice that will save you thousands of dollars.

Most initial meetings with a lawyer, accountant, or financial planner are free or carry a nominal fee. Ask in advance. This meeting provides an opportunity for both parties to see if the advisory relationship would be a good fit.

8. Comparison

It is important that you not make a decision about which advisor to use without first checking around. It is a good rule of thumb to see a minimum of three advisors before deciding which one is right for you. You need that qualitative comparison to know which one, if any, of the three you want to rely on. Seeing how they each respond to your list of prepared questions is a good comparison. The more exacting you are in your selection criteria, the more likely it will be that a good match is made and the more beneficial that advisor will be for you.

C. SELECTING A LAWYER

There are many situations in which you might require a lawyer in Canada or the United States—for example, having to do with wills, living wills, powers of attorney, trusts, estates, buying or selling of real estate, time-shares, leases, contracts, insurance or accident claims, legal disputes, or immigration matters. If you have a business, you will need a lawyer to assist you.

For the most part, you will deal with a lawyer in Canada for the above needs. There are situations, however, where you would require a U.S. lawyer— for example, if you are buying a condo or time-share in the United States, or if you are signing legal documents in the United States. In certain situations, your lawyer in Canada would coordinate services with your U.S. lawyer.

Although your lawyer is trained to give legal advice about your rights, remedies, and options, it is you who must decide on the action to be taken.

1. Qualifications

a) Canada
Lawyers in Canada generally have a Bachelor of Laws degree (LL.B) from a recognized Canadian university and must be licensed to practise by the provincial law society in the province where they are practising.

b) United States
Lawyers in the United States (sometimes referred to as attorneys) generally have a Bachelor of Laws degree (LL.B) or a Juris Doctorate degree (JD) and must be licensed by the state bar association in the state they are practising.

2. How to Find a Lawyer

Methods of finding lawyers include referrals by friends, a banker, or an accountant, or through the Yellow Pages. There is also an excellent service called a lawyer referral service you should consider.

In *Canada*, most provinces have a lawyer referral program that is usually coordinated through the Canadian Bar Association. Simply look in the telephone directory under "Lawyer Referral Service" or contact the Law Society or Canadian Bar Association branch in your province. The initial meeting is usually free or carries a nominal fee (e.g., $10).

In the *United States,* similar lawyer referral systems are available, operated by the state or local bar association. Look in the telephone directory.

3. Understanding Fees and Costs

Whatever costs a lawyer incurs on your behalf and at your request will be passed on to you as an expense.

There are various types of fee arrangements, depending on the nature of the services provided. To avoid any misunderstanding, always ask about fees at the outset, as well as any applicable federal or provincial or state taxes that are added to those fees.

The main fee options include hourly fee, fixed fee (e.g., for routine services), percentage fee (e.g., for probating an estate up to a certain maximum), or contingency fee (e.g., for a personal injury claim in a car accident; if the lawyer attains a settlement, he or she receives a percentage of that, but if no settlement is made, there is no fee).

D. SELECTING AN ACCOUNTANT

You should speak with a tax accountant to advise you on matters dealing with tax and estate planning, including the possible use of trusts, in order to minimize taxes during your life and tax consequences on your death. Depending on the size and nature of your estate, there could be considerable tax issues and consequences involved.

A Canadian tax accountant will probably meet your needs, if he or she is familiar with the Canadian and U.S. tax consequences of holding U.S. real estate or other investments and dying in the United States. Many large chartered accountancy (CA) firms in Canada have tax experts who are familiar with cross-border tax and estate-planning issues. They also have associate offices in the United States. However, you may wish to get a second opinion from a certified public accountant (CPA) in the United States who is a tax expert familiar with U.S. and Canadian tax consequences. To locate such a professional, as well as a CPA who is also an expert on financial planning, refer to Section E in this chapter.

1. Qualifications

a) Canada

In Canada, anyone can call himself or herself an accountant. One can also adopt the title "public accountant" without any qualifications, experience, regulations, or accountability to a professional association. That is why you have to be very careful when selecting the appropriate accountant for your needs. There are two main designations of qualified professional accountants in Canada that could provide tax and estate planning advice: Chartered Accountant (CA), and Certified General Accountant (CGA). Accountants with the above designations are governed by provincial statutes.

b) United States

In the United States, contact a certified public accountant (CPA) for tax and estate-planning advice if you have assets in the United States. A CPA is similar to a CA in Canada. Some CPAs have a specialty designation in personal financial planning (PFS), which could include knowledge of U.S. and Canadian tax and estate-planning issues. This is important; otherwise, decisions could be made in a vacuum, with adverse tax consequences.

2. How to Find an Accountant

One of the main purposes of having an accountant is to tailor strategic tax and estate planning to your needs. It is therefore prudent to seek advice from a professional accountant who specializes in tax matters exclusively, since tax and estate planning are highly specialized areas. Again, "the rule of three" applies; be sure to speak to three different tax experts before choosing an accountant. When you are phoning an accounting firm, ask which accountant specializes in tax and estate-planning matters. Most initial meetings are free, without any further obligation. Keep in mind that all professional tax experts do not have the same mindset. Some are very conservative in their advice, whereas others are very bullish. Some enjoy the professional and intellectual challenge of knowing where the fine line is and adopt an aggressive approach to tax planning strategies. Others are more reluctant to do this. In all instances, we are talking about using accredited professional accountants. They have too much to lose to advise you improperly. But you will definitely find differences in style and attitude. The quality and nature of the advice could make a profound difference in the tax and estate savings you enjoy. That is why you need to compare accountants. You will have a much better idea who will meet your needs after you have interviewed three or more accountants.

You can obtain names of accountants and their specialties from their professional associations. Ask for referrals from friends, a lawyer, or a banker. Look in the Yellow Pages. Whatever sources you use, apply the preceding selection criteria.

3. Understanding Fees and Costs

Accountants' fees vary depending on experience, specialty, type of service provided, size of firm, and other considerations. The fee can range between $100 and $200 or more per hour for tax and estate-planning advice.

E. SELECTING A FINANCIAL PLANNER

Some people may wonder if they need to use a U.S. financial planner as well as a Canadian financial planner. It really depends on the circumstances. For the most part, a Canadian financial planner will meet your needs, since you are a resident of Canada and most, if not all, of your assets and investments are in Canada. If you are a U.S. citizen or plan to live in the United States full-time, however, or if you have assets or investments in the United States, then there are cross-border tax and estate-planning considerations and you should obtain tax and legal advice in those areas. There are chartered accountants and lawyers in Canada who have expertise on these issues; refer to Sections C and D. Also, many Canadian financial planners have a network of tax and legal professionals who are experts in the U.S. tax implications and can advise you. At the current Canadian/American exchange rate you are also saving about 30 percent in fees by using Canadian experts.

If you have U.S. assets or investments, however, it is prudent to obtain a second opinion from a U.S. tax accountant and financial planner familiar with cross-border tax and estate issues. Getting a second opinion can be reassuring if you get consistent advice. If not, you want to find out why not.

1. Qualifications

When you are choosing a financial planner, keep in mind that anyone can call himself or herself a planner; no federal, provincial (except for Quebec), state, or local laws require qualifications such as those imposed on other professionals, including accountants and lawyers. Several associations and organizations grant credentials that signify a planner's level of education; since criteria can change from time to time, however, check with the association involved. Some of the most commonly recognized designations follow.

a) Canada

- *Registered Financial Planner (RFP).* This designation is awarded to members of the Canadian Association of Financial Planners (CAFP— Toronto) who have engaged in the practice of financial planning for a minimum of three years and who have satisfied certain educational requirements. An individual with an RFP must regularly take professional development courses and must be covered by professional liability insurance. An RFP is also governed by a professional code of ethics and can be disciplined for breaching that code. Many financial planners with an RFP also have a CFP designation (see below), as well as such credentials as CA, MBA, LL.B, CLU, ChFC, or CFA.

- *Chartered Financial Planner (CFP).* The CFP designation is awarded by the Canadian Institute of Financial Planning (Toronto). It has no official connection with the CAFP, although many RFPs also have a CFP, as noted above. The CFP program takes approximately two years to complete and covers such topics as law, advanced financial planning, financial economics, financial management, and tax and estate planning. Planners with a CFP have demonstrated that they have successfully completed a study program, have passed examinations, and are interested in a broad and integrated approach to financial affairs. To obtain a CFP, the individual must have been involved in the financial planning field for a minimum of two years.

b) United States

- *Registered Financial Planner (RFP).* The International Association of Registered Financial Planners confers the RFP title on financial planners who have had at least four years' experience in planning, a college degree in business, economics, or law, and either a CFP (Certified Financial Planner), ChFC (Chartered Financial Consultant), or CPA (Certified Public Accountant) designation, as well as a securities or insurance licence.

- *Certified Financial Planner (CFP).* This designation is earned by people who have been licensed by the International Board of Standards and Practices for Certified Financial Planners, Inc. (IBCFP). The majority of these licensees have taken a self-study program administered by the Denver-based College for Financial Planning. These people must then pass a certification exam over several months to prove their expertise in financial planning, insurance, investing, taxes, retirement planning, employee benefits, and estate planning. In addition to passing the tests, a CFP must possess a certain amount of work experience in the financial services industry, have a defined amount of college education, participate in a continuing education program, and abide by a strict code of ethics.

- *Registry of Financial Planning Practitioners (Registry Financial Planner).* The Atlanta-based International Association for Financial Planning (IAFP) has established the Registry of Financial Planning Practitioners. To become a member of the registry, a planner must hold a CFA, CFP, ChFC, or CPA or a degree that has a strong emphasis on financial services, complete a minimum number of hours of continuing education credits every two years, possess three years of experience, and obtain letters of recommendations from clients, among other requirements.

- *Personal Financial Specialist (PFS).* The PFS is awarded only to people who are already Certified Public Accountants (CPAs). Within the American Institute of Certified Public Accountants (AICPA), those with a PFS concentrate on financial planning. They must be members in good standing of the AICPA, possess at least three years of personal financial planning experience and demonstrate special expertise by passing a comprehensive financial planning exam.

2. How to Find a Financial Planner

There are several ways of locating a financial planner. Referral by a friend, accountant or lawyer is one way. Looking in the Yellow Pages is another. One of the most effective ways is to contact a financial planning professional association.

There are several financial planning associations in Canada and the United States that will provide you with names and other educational information.

a) Canada

Canadian Association of Financial Planners
60 St. Claire Avenue East, Suite 510
Toronto, Ontario M4T 1N5
Tel: (416) 966-9928

The association will give you the contact phone number for the chapter in your province. By contacting this number, you will be sent a free publication called *A Consumer Guide to Financial Planning.* You will also be sent a roster of members who have been awarded the Registered Financial Planner (RFP) designation in your province. This list shows experience, and services provided, lists any financial products sold, and states the method of payment—for example, fee for service, commission, or both.

b) United States

International Association for Financial Planning (IAFP)
2 Concourse Parkway, Suite 800
Atlanta, Georgia 30328
Tel: (404) 395-1605 or 1-800-945-IAFP (4237)

Represents financial planners and will refer you to member planners in your area. Will also send you free copies of its various publications.

The Institute of Certified Financial Planners
7600 E. Eastman Avenue, Suite 301
Denver, Colorado 80231
Tel: (303) 751-7600 or 1-800-282-7526

Represents financial planners who have passed the CFP test. Will refer you to several planners in your area as well as send you free informational brochures.

National Association of Personal Financial Advisors (NAPFA)
1130 Lake Cook Road, Suite 105
Buffalo Grove, Illinois 60089
Tel: (708) 537-7722 or 1-800-366-2732

Represents financial planners who work for fees only and collect no commissions from the sale of products. Will refer you to fee-only planners in your area as well as send you free informational brochures.

American Institute of Certified Public Accountants
201 Plaza 3
Jersey City, New Jersey 07311-3881
Tel: (201) 938-3000 or 1-800-862-4272

Represents and maintains standards for CPAs. Can help you find a local tax-oriented accountant or an accountant who provides financial planning services and who has a personal financial specialist (PFS) designation. Will also send a free copy of various informational brochures.

3. How to Select a Financial Planner

After you've decided to seek the services of a financial planner, you may have other questions: Which professional is right for me? How do I identify a competent financial planner who can coordinate all aspects of my financial life? Just as you select a doctor or lawyer, you should base your decision on a number of factors: education, qualifications, experience, and reputation.

When selecting your financial planner, choose one you can work with confidently. You are asking this person to help shape your financial future, and you are paying him or her to do so. It is your responsibility and right to fully enquire about the planner's background, numbers of years in practice, credentials, client references, and other relevant information.

Call the planner and ask for a meeting. Use this opportunity to get a sense of your compatibility and to discover exactly how the planner will work with you. Ask questions about financial planning that will give you a basis for comparison with other planners you have contacted. In short, get the information you need to feel confident that this person is right for you and your needs.

Once again, it is recommended that you meet with at least three planners before you make your final selection. To work effectively with a planner, you will need to reveal your personal financial information, so it's important to find someone with whom you feel completely comfortable.

Research shows that consumers rate "trust" and "ethics" as the most important elements in their relationship with financial advisors. In fact, survey respondents gave this response twice as often as they mention good advice and expertise.

By asking the following questions, you should get the information you need to make your decision on which financial planner to hire. As you think of others, add them to your list. Keep in mind how the answers fit your personal needs.

4. Questions to Ask a Financial Planner

- *How long has the planner been working with clients in the comprehensive financial planning process?*

- *What did the planner do before becoming a financial planner?* Most planners come from fields related to financial services. If he or she started out as a lawyer, accountant, insurance agent, or other specialist, that background will most likely affect the advice the planner gives.

- *What are the planner's areas of expertise?* Ideally, these should include investments, insurance, estate planning, retirement planning, and/or tax strategies.

- *What services does the planner provide?* Most planners will help you assemble a comprehensive plan, but some specialize in particular areas of finance. The services you should expect include cash management and budgeting; estate planning; investment review and planning; life, health, and property/casualty insurance review; retirement planning; goal and objective setting; and tax planning. Ask about each service specifically.

- *Who will you deal with regularly?* You might see the planner only at the beginning and end of the planning process and work with associates in between. Ask if this will be the arrangement, and ask to meet the personnel involved. Also enquire about their qualifications.

- *What type of clientele does the planner serve?* Some planners specialize by age, income category, or professional group.

- *Will the planner show you a sample financial plan he or she has done?* The planner should be pleased to show you the kind of plan you can expect when the data-gathering and planning process is complete. Naturally, any plan you are shown would not reveal client names or confidential information.

- *Does the planner have access to other professionals if the planning process requires expertise beyond the scope of the planner?* Most financial planners are generalists and frequently consult with other professionals from related fields for added expertise in specialty areas. A good planner has a network of lawyers, accountants, investment professionals, and insurance specialists to consult if questions arise.

- *Does the planner just give financial advice, or does he or she also sell financial products?* As discussed earlier, there are several different types of advisors.

- *Will the planner's advice include only generic product categories or specific product recommendations?* Some planners will name a particular mutual fund or stock, for example. Others will advise that you keep a certain percentage of your assets in stocks, bonds, and cash, leaving you to assess which bonds, stocks, and money market funds are appropriate.

- *Will the planner spend the time explaining his or her reasons for recommending a specific product and how it suits your goals, circumstances, and tolerance for risk?* Ask how the planner will monitor a recommended mutual fund or investment product after you've bought it. You should feel comfortable that the planner will take the time to ensure that you understand the strategy and products that are recommended.

- *Will the planner do independent analysis on the products or become dependent on another company's research? Does the practitioner have any vested interest in the products recommended?*

- *How will you follow up after the plan is completed to ensure that it is implemented?* A good planner makes sure that you take steps to follow your plan. The plan should be reviewed and revised as conditions in your life, tax laws, or the investment environment changes.

- *How is the planner compensated?* Some planners charge for the advice they give. Others collect commissions from the sale of products they recommend. Some both charge a planning fee and receive a sales commission. Make sure that you receive a written estimate of any fees you must pay. An explanation of compensation is covered in section 5.

- *Will the planner have direct access to your money?* Some planners want *discretionary control* of their clients' funds, which permits the planners to invest at their discretion. You have to be extremely careful, since there is a high degree of potential risk. If you do agree to it, make sure that the planner has an impeccable track record, is bonded by insurance, and is covered by professional liability insurance. Also limit the amount to be within your financial comfort zone and have it confirmed in writing.

- *Are there any potential conflicts of interest in the investments the planner recommends?* A planner must advise you, for example, if he or she or the planner's firm earns fees as a general partner in a limited partnership that the planner recommends. If the planner receives some form of payment, frequently called a referral fee, when he or she refers you to another firm, you want to know.

- *What professional licences and designations has the planner earned?* Enquire whether the planner holds a RFP, CFP, ChFC, CA, CGA, CPA, PFS, LL.B, or CFA. Also find out the planner's educational background.

- *Has the planner ever been cited by a professional or governmental organization for disciplinary reasons?* Even if the planner says that he or she has an impeccable professional track record, you can check with the provincial or state securities office, and the provincial or state financial planning associations.

5. How a Financial Planner Is Compensated

Generally, financial advisors are compensated in one of four ways: solely by fees, by a combination of fees and commissions, solely by commissions, or through a salary paid by an organization that receives fees. It is important to understand, and be comfortable with, the way your financial planner gets paid—and you need to make sure the planner's compensation method is suited to your particular needs and situation. In some cases, financial advisors may offer more than one payment option. Keep in mind that compensation is just one among many important elements that should figure into your decision about hiring a financial advisor.

Here's how these different methods work:

a) Fee-Only

Many lawyers, accountants, and fee-only financial planners charge an hourly rate, and your fee will depend on how much time the advisor spends on your situation, including time in research, reviewing the plan with you, and discussing implementation options. Others just charge a flat amount. Such planners usually offer a no-cost, no-obligation initial consultation to explore your financial needs. Some ask you to complete a detailed questionnaire and then provide a computerized profile and assessment of your situation and options for a nominal fee that can range from $200 to $500 or more.

Fee-only financial advisors typically advise you on investments, insurance, and other financial vehicles but do not benefit from commissions if you take their suggestions. The advantage of this type of arrangement is that the planner has no vested interest in having you buy one product over another, since there is no financial gain to be made personally from any specific recommendation. Some fee-only financial planners will help you follow through on their recommendations using mutual funds and other investments, if you so wish.

b) Commission-Only

Some financial advisors charge no fee for a consultation but are compensated solely by commissions earned by selling investments and insurance plus services necessary to implement their recommendations—for example, a life insurance policy, annuity, or mutual fund. A commission-only advisor will develop recommendations for your situation and goals, review the recommendations with you and discuss ways to implement these recommendations.

In some cases, the commissions are clearly disclosed—for example, a percentage front-end-load commission on a mutual fund. In other cases, the fees are lumped into the general expenses of the product, as with life insurance, so you won't know how much your planner makes unless you ask him or her. When you interview such a planner, ask him or her approximately what percentage of his or her firm's commission revenue comes from annuities, insurance products, mutual funds, stocks and bonds, and other products. The planner's answers will give you a sense of the kind of advice his or her firm usually gives.

Not only do you pay fees in the form of an up-front charge, but you could also pay regular charges that apply as long as you hold an investment. For example, some insurance companies pay planners trailing fees for each year a client pays the premiums on an insurance policy. In addition, some mutual funds levy fees, which are annual charges of your assets designed to reward brokers and financial planners for keeping clients in a fund.

Some companies reward commission-motivated planners with prizes of free travel or merchandise if their sales of a particular product reach a target level. Other arrangements award planners who attain certain target sales goals with noncash goods and services, such as assistance in paying for investment research.

Your planner might not like your questioning his or her cash payment and other perks. It is your right to know, however, whether the products you buy generate direct fees and indirect benefits for the planner. By knowing the full extent of your planner's compensation, you will be better able to decide whether his or her advice is self-serving or objective.

c) Fee plus Commission
Some planners charge a fee for assessing your financial situation and making recommendations and may help you implement their recommendations by offering certain investments or insurance for sale. They typically earn a commission on the sale of some of those products.

In some cases, planners are actually captives of one company, so they recommend only its product line. They may have a comprehensive product line or a small one. Other planners are independent and therefore recommend the mutual funds or insurance policies of any company with which they affiliate.

Like fee-only planners, fee-plus-commission advisors may charge a flat fee or bill you based on the amount of time they spend on your situation. Others use a fee scale, varying their fees according to the complexity of your financial situation.

Another form of compensation is called fee offset, meaning that any commission revenue your planner earns from selling you products reduces his or her fee for planning. If you buy so many products that your entire fee is covered, you should request a refund of the fee you paid for your basic plan.

d) Salary
Many banks, trust companies, credit unions, and other companies offer financial planning services. In most instances, the financial advisors on their staffs

are paid by salary and earn neither fees nor commissions. There could be other incentives, however, based on the volume and value of the business done, including a raise in salary or a promotion given at an annual performance review. Alternatively, there could be quotas to be met. The companies are compensated through the sale of investments and/or services.

All four compensation methods discussed have their advantages. You must choose the method that, combined with the other qualities of the advisor you select, best meets your needs. If you don't understand how your financial advisor is compensated, it's your responsibility and your right to ask. Question your financial advisor in as much detail as necessary until you are clear. As a smart consumer, you want to know what you're buying and how much you're paying for it, and you're entitled to that information.

An advisor who is honest and straightforward about compensation gives you the information you need to make smart financial decisions. Do not consider hiring a financial planner who will not disclose how he or she is compensated.

F. OTHER PEOPLE PROVIDING FINANCIAL AND INVESTMENT ADVICE OR INFORMATION

As discussed earlier, your first step is to have an objective financial planner assess your current financial situation and needs and give advice on fulfilling your long-term objectives and needs with an integrated and comprehensive financial plan. You don't want to make financial or investment decisions in a vacuum. There is too much to lose.

There are many other people in the financial and investment area however, that you might have dealings with or hear about at some point. Here is a brief summary.

1. Retirement Counsellor

A retirement counsellor specializes in clients who are generally over 50 years of age, that is, nearing retirement or actually retired. Types of investments sold include RRSPs, RRIFs, LIF annuities, GICs, and mutual funds. The main thrust of these investments should be preservation of capital and low or moderate risk.

2. Company Human Resource Personnel

If you have a pension plan from your employer, you should ask the people administering the plan to provide you with details of the plan. Also ask them to assist you in projecting the income you will receive from the plan and, after you retire, what additional benefits, other than pension income, you will be entitled to. Also ask if these benefits are guaranteed or if the employer can withdraw them at any time. Refer to the discussion of company pension plans in Chapter 2.

3. Government Pension Plan Personnel

Check with the federal and provincial governments to see what pension or financial assistance plans you may be currently eligible for, such as OAS, CPP, QPP, or GIS. Refer to Chapter 2 for more detail.

4. Bank, Trust Company, Credit Union

These financial institutions have an extensive range of investment products available in the area of mutual funds, GICs, term deposits, Canada Savings Bonds, and so on. With mutual funds, there is generally a wide selection of money-market funds, growth funds, income funds, and balanced funds to accommodate people's investment needs and risk tolerance.

The range of training and expertise of bank, trust company, or credit union personnel can vary. Staff members licensed to sell mutual funds can give very helpful advice about the nature and benefits of their particular products. Expect to get general advice, however, not comprehensive advice dealing with all your present and future needs. Many of these institutions have instructive pamphlets to give you a better understanding of general money-management strategies.

Many of the major financial institutions in Canada are expanding into collateral financial services beyond their traditional scope. This is being done through subsidiary companies in areas such as discount stock brokerages, investment portfolio management, estate planning, trusts, and asset management and insurance.

One of the services provided by most major financial institutions is called private banking services, or a similar name. The concept is the same. It involves giving customized, personalized, and integrated advice about a mixture of services and products — for example, straight banking, investment, wealth management, and trust and estate planning. To be eligible for this special service, you have to meet certain criteria, such as having a minimum of net worth and/or liquid assets available for investing. The criteria vary considerably, depending on the policy of the institution involved.

5. Insurance Agent or Broker

The primary goal of these advisors is to sell life insurance and other insurance company products such as annuities or segregated mutual funds. As a consequence, you may be limited to building a financial plan around an insurance policy. An agent is a person who sells the products of only one company, whereas a broker can sell the products of any company. Thus, the recommended solutions offered by an agent could be restricted to a small range of products, sold only by the company the agent is working for. An independent insurance broker, however, could offer a wide range of insurance-related products available from different companies.

6. Mutual Fund Broker

Since a broker makes a commission on any product sold to you, you have to satisfy yourself that it is the right type of product and the best choice of that product for your needs. A high degree of trust is necessary, since you don't want to feel a broker's recommendation is based on the size of the commission or other special incentives to sell you a fund from a particular fund company. Be cautious, since a broker may only have a mutual fund licence but promote himself or herself as a professional financial planner.

7. Stockbroker/Investment Advisor

Sometimes stockbrokers refer to themselves as "investment advisors." Although the advice is free, the client pays for it through commissions that his or her accounts generate. Some full-service brokers offer investment advice on a broad range of financial products, such as stocks, bonds, mutual funds, and mortgage-backed securities. Some stockbrokers don't want to deal actively with small investor accounts because of the time involved, but would probably recommend a mutual fund to serve your needs instead.

Many brokerage firms offer "managed" accounts, referred to as "wrap" accounts in the industry. With these accounts, your money is invested in several pooled portfolios, depending on your risk profile, and managed generally by an outside money manager rather than a broker. You normally pay a fixed annual fee, based on a percentage of the value of the money invested.

8. Discount Broker

Although these brokers charge significantly lower commissions than do full-service stockbrokers, they only buy and sell, based on your instructions. They do not give advice. Using discount brokers is only a realistic investment option if you know the stock and bond market thoroughly and can take the time to make prudent decisions by understanding and researching the market.

9. Deposit Broker

These individuals generally sell term deposits, GICs, annuities, and RRIFs; in some cases, they are licensed to sell mutual funds.

10. Investment Counsellor

This type of financial advisor generally only deals with wealthy clients wishing to invest a minimum of $250,000 to $1 million. This restriction is due to the time involved to customize and monitor an investment portfolio. Some investment counsellors will take on a lower investment portfolio. A management fee is generally a percentage, normally 1 to 2 percent, of the value of the assets in the portfolio. If the management skill results in an increase in value of the client's portfolio, the fee obtained increases accordingly.

G. TIPS BEFORE LEAVING CANADA

- Make sure your financial affairs are in good order before you depart.
- Select objective professional tax, legal, and financial planning advice as your situation and needs dictate before you depart.
- Seek advice on the various cross-border implications of being a Canadian citizen living part-time in the United States for up to six months.
- Obtain advice on your various retirement, pension, and investment needs before you head south.

H. QUICK REFERENCE GUIDE TO RELEVANT SECTIONS OF THE APPENDICES

To help you obtain further information and contact numbers, here are the parts of the Appendices that would be relevant to the contents of this chapter.

Appendix B: Sections 3 and 4.

APPENDIX

A

Sources of Further Information

One of the challenges and frustrations of researching information is knowing where to start. This Appendix can save you a great deal of time, energy, money, and hassle by providing you with contact numbers you may wish to phone.

Many of the numbers provided are toll-free. Those that are not toll-free may accept collect calls; there is no risk in asking. Most Canadian or U.S. government offices will accept collect calls. If you can't locate the phone number for a federal or provincial government office in Canada, phone Reference Canada at 1-800-667-3355. Its representatives are very helpful and resourceful in providing information.

Index of Topic Headings

1. Revenue Canada—Taxation
2. Revenue Canada—Customs
3. Transport Canada
4. Health Canada
5. Reference Canada
6. Canadian Consulates in the United States
7. Canadian Provincial Offices in the United States
8. Provincial Offices for Seniors
9. Provincial Tourism Offices
10. Provincial Health Departments—Out-of-Country Medical Claims and Information
11. Companies Providing Out-of-Country Medical Insurance
12. U.S. Consulates in Canada
13. U.S. Internal Revenue Service (IRS)
14. U.S. Customs Service
15. U.S. Immigration and Naturalization Service (INS)
16. U.S. Department of Agriculture—Animal and Plant Inspection Service

17. U.S. Fish and Wildlife Service
18. State Travel Offices in the United States
19. State Travel Parks Associations
20. Associations of Mobile Home Owners
21. National Seniors' Organizations
22. Canadian Snowbird Advisor Newsletter
23. Newspapers for Canadian Snowbirds
24. News for Canadian Snowbirds on Sunbelt Radio Stations
25. Health Newsletters
26. Local Chambers of Commerce
27. CAA Clubs and Branches
28. Canadian Corps of Commissionaires
29. Canadian Banks Offering Services to Snowbirds
30. U.S. Banks Offering Services to Snowbirds
31. Elderhostel
32. RV Buyers' and Users' Guides
33. RV Dealers' Associations
34. RV Rental Sources
35. U.S. Campground Directories
36. Campground Chains
37. Camping on Public Lands
38. Camping Clubs
39. Publications for RV Owners and Campers
40. Membership and Ownership Type of RV Resorts
41. Selecting a Tow Vehicle
42. RV Retail Shows
43. Scenic Byways in the United States

1. Revenue Canada—Taxation

There could be tax implications of living, working, investing, or owning assets in the United States. Contact your closest Revenue Canada office below for more information.

International Taxation Office
2540 Lancaster Road
Ottawa, ON K1A 1A8
Tel: 1-800-267-5177 (toll-free in Canada)
Tel: (613) 952-3741 (from Ottawa area or outside Canada)
Collect phone calls accepted from anywhere in the United States.

District Taxation Offices
Collect phone calls are accepted.

British Columbia

277 Winnipeg St.
Penticton, BC V2A 1N6
Tel: (604) 492-9200
1-800-565-5125

1166 W. Pender St.
Vancouver, BC V6E 3H8
Tel: (604) 689-5411
1-800-663-9033 (calls from Yukon
and northwestern British Columbia)

1415 Vancouver St.
Victoria, BC V8V 3W4
Tel: (604) 363-0121
1-800-742-6108

Alberta

220 - 4th Ave. S.E.
Calgary, AB T2G 0L1
Tel: (403) 221-8919
1-800-332-1410
(calls from southern Alberta)

9700 Jasper Ave., Suite 10
Edmonton, AB T5J 4C8
Tel: (403) 423-3510
1-800-232-1966
(calls from northern Alberta)
1-800-661-6451
(calls from Northwest Territories and
northeastern British Columbia)

Saskatchewan

1955 Smith St.
Regina, SK S4P 2N9
Tel: (306) 780-6015
1-800-667-7555

340 - 3rd Ave. N.
Saskatoon, SK S7K 0A8
Tel: (306) 975-4595
1-800-667-2083

Manitoba

325 Broadway Ave.
Winnipeg, MB R3C 4T4
Tel: (204) 983-6350
1-800-282-8079

Ontario

11 Station St.
Belleville, ON K8N 2S3
Tel: (613) 969-3706
1-800-267-8030

150 Main St. W.
P.O. Box 2220
Hamilton, ON L8N 3E1
Tel: (905) 522-8671
1-800-263-9200
(calls from area codes 416 and 905)
1-800-263-9210
(calls from area code 519)

385 Princess St.
Kingston, ON K7L 1C1
Tel: (613) 545-8371
1-800-267-9447

166 Frederick St.
Kitchener, ON N2G 4N1
Tel: (519) 579-2230
1-800-265-2530

451 Talbot St.
London, ON N6A 5E5
Tel: (519) 645-4211
1-800-265-4900

77 City Centre Dr.
P.O. Box 6000
Mississauga, ON L5A 4E9
Tel: (905) 566-6700
1-800-387-1700
(calls from area codes 519, 705,
and 905)

5001 Yonge St., Suite 1000
North York, ON M2N 6R9
Tel: (416) 221-9309
1-800-387-1700
(calls from area codes 519, 705,
and 905)

360 Lisgar St.
Ottawa, ON K1A 0L9
Tel: (613) 598-2275
1-800-267-8440
(calls from area code 613)
1-800-267-4735
(calls from area code 819)

185 King St. W.
Peterborough, ON K9J 8M3
Tel: (705) 876-6412
1-800-267-8030

32 Church St.
P.O. Box 3038
St. Catharines, ON L2R 3B9
Tel: (905) 688-4000
1-800-263-5672

200 Town Centre Court
Scarborough, ON M1P 4Y3
Tel: (416) 296-1950
1-800-387-5229
(calls from area code 905)
1-800-387-5183
(calls from area codes 519 and 705)

19 Lisgar St. S.
Sudbury, ON P3E 3L5
Tel: (705) 671-0581
1-800-461-4060
(calls from area code 705)
1-800-461-6320
(calls from area codes 613 and 807)

130 South Syndicate Ave.
Thunder Bay, ON P7E 1C7
Tel: (807) 623-3443
1-800-465-6981

36 Adelaide St. E.
Toronto, ON M5C 1J7
Tel: (416) 869-1500

185 Ouellette Ave.
Windsor, ON N9A 5S8
Tel: (519) 258-8302
1-800-265-4841

Quebec

100 Lafontaine St., #211
Chicoutimi, PQ G7H 6X2
Tel: (418) 698-5580
1-800-463-4421

44 du Lac Ave.
Rouyn-Noranda, PQ J9X 6Z9
Tel: (819) 764-5171
1-800-567-6403

3131 Saint-Martin Blvd. W.
Laval, PQ H7T 2A7
Tel: (514) 956-9101
1-800-363-2218

50 Place de la Cité
Sherbrooke, PQ J1H 5L8
Tel: (819) 564-5888
1-800-567-7360

305 René-Levesque Blvd. W.
Montreal, PQ H2Z 1A6
Tel: (514) 283-5300
1-800-361-2808

5245 Cousineau Blvd., Suite 200
Saint-Hubert, PQ J3Y 7Z7
Tel: (514) 283-5300
1-800-361-2808

165 vue de la Pointe-aux-lièvres S.
Quebec, PQ G1K 7L3
Tel: (418) 648-3180
1-800-463-4421

25 des Forges St., Suite 111
Trois-Rivières, PQ G9A 2G4
Tel: (819) 373-2723
1-800-567-9325

320 St-Germain E., 4th Floor
Rimouski, PQ G5L 1C2
Tel: (418) 722-3111
1-800-463-4421

New Brunswick

120 Harbourview Blvd., 4th Floor
P.O. Box 8888
Bathurst, NB E2A 4L8
Tel: (506) 548-7100
1-800-561-6104

126 Prince William St.
Saint John, NB E2L 4H9
Tel: (506) 636-4600
1-800-222-9622

Prince Edward Island

94 Euston St.
P.O. Box 8500
Charlottetown, PE C1A 8L3
Tel: (902) 628-4200

Nova Scotia

1256 Barrington St.
P.O. Box 638
Halifax, NS B3J 2T5
Tel: (902) 426-2210
1-800-565-2210

47 Dorchester St.
P.O. Box 1300
Sydney, NS B1P 6K3
Tel: (902) 564-7080
1-800-563-7080

Newfoundland

Sir Humphrey Gilbert Building
P.O. Box 5968
St. John's, NF A1C 5X6
Tel: (709) 772-2610
1-800-563-2600

Free Publications

General and Supplemental Income Tax Guides
* General Income Tax Guide
* Emigrants
* Capital Gains
* Rental Income
* Business and Professional Income
* RRSPs and Other Registered Plans for Retirement
* Preparing Returns for Deceased Persons
* Employment Expenses

Interpretation Bulletins

IT-29	United States Social Security Tax and Benefits
IT-31	Foreign Exchange Profits and Losses
IT-76R2	Exempt Portion of Pension When Employee Has Been a Non-Resident
IT-95R	Foreign Exchange Gains and Losses
IT-120RY	Principal Residence
IT-122R2	U.S. Social Security Taxes and Benefits
IT-161R3	Non-Residents—Exemption from Tax Deductions at Source on Employment Income (also ask for "Special Release")

IT-163R2	Election by Non-Resident Individuals on Certain Canadian Source Income
IT-171R	Non-Resident Individuals—Taxable Income Earned in Canada
IT-194	Foreign Tax Credit—Part-Time Residents
IT-221R2	Determination of an Individual's Residence Status (also ask for "Special Release")
IT-262R	Losses of Non-Residents and Part-Year Residents
IT-270R2	Foreign Tax Credit
IT-298	Canada-United States Tax Convention—Number of Days "Present" in Canada
IT-370	Trusts—Capital Property Owned on December 31, 1971
IT-372R	Trusts—Flow-Through of Taxable Dividends and Interest to a Beneficiary (1987 and Prior Taxation Years)
IT-395R	Foreign Tax Credit—Foreign-Source Capital Gains and Losses
IT-399	Principal Residence—Non-Resident Owner
IT-420R3	Non-Residents—Income Earned in Canada
IT-465R	Non-Resident Beneficiaries of Trusts
IT-506	Foreign Income Taxes as a Deduction from Income
IT-520	Unused Foreign Tax Credits—Carry Forward and Carry Back

Pamphlets
- Canadian Residents Going Down South
- Canadian Residents Abroad
- Are You Moving?
- How to Calculate Your RRSP Contribution Limit
- Gifts in Kind
- Tax Information for People with Disabilities
- Paying Your Income Tax by Installments

Information Circulars
- Registered Retirement Income Funds
- Away-from-Home Expenses
- Deferred Profit Sharing Plans
- Canada-U.S. Social Security Agreement
- Gifts in Right in Canada
- Consent to Transfer Property of Deceased Persons

2. Revenue Canada—Customs

It is important to know your rights and obligations when coming back from a trip to the United States. To save frustration and expense, check with the customs office before you leave. Phone 1-800-461-9999 (toll-free in Canada).

Regional Canada Customs Offices:

Pacific
1001 W. Pender St.
Vancouver, BC V6E 2M8
Tel: (604) 666-0459

Alberta
220 - 4th Ave. S.E., Suite 720
Calgary, AB T2P 2M7
Tel: (403) 292-4622

Central
Federal Building
269 Main St.
Winnipeg, MB R3C 1B3
Tel: (204) 983-3771

Southwestern Ontario
Walkerville P.O. Box 2280
Windsor, ON N8Y 4R8
Tel: (519) 645-4133

Hamilton
10 John St. S.
Hamilton, ON L8N 3V8
Tel: (416) 572-2818

Toronto
2nd Floor, 1 Front St. W.
P.O. Box 10, Station A
Toronto, ON M5W 1A3
Tel: (416) 973-6433

Ottawa
360 Coventry Rd.
Ottawa, ON K1K 2C6
Tel: (613) 991-0552

Montreal
400 Youville Square
Montreal, PQ H2Y 3N4
Tel: (514) 283-6632

Quebec
130 Dalhousie St.
Quebec, PQ G1K 7P6
Tel: (418) 648-3401

Atlantic
6169 Quinpool Rd.
Halifax, NS B3J 3G6
Tel: (902) 426-2667

Free Publications
* Bringing Back Goods from the United States. Under the North American Free Trade Agreement (NAFTA)
* Importing a Motor Vehicle into Canada
* Importing Goods into Canada? Documentation Simplified
* Importations by Mail
* I Declare

3. Transport Canada

There are technical requirements to consider if bringing a U.S.-purchased car or RV back to Canada (for example, emission control). Enquire before you go to the U.S., or before you buy a vehicle in the U.S. Transport Canada established a special registry in April 1995. Contact them at:

Registrar of Imported Vehicles
Tel: 1-800-333-0558 (toll-free in Canada and the U.S.)
13th Floor, 344 Slater St.
Ottawa, ON K1A 0N5
Tel: (613) 998-2174
Fax: (613) 998-4831

Free Publications
• List of Vehicles Admissable and Non-admissable from the U.S.
• Your Guide to Importing a Vehicle from the U.S. into Canada

4. Health Canada

There are many forms of federal government assistance to seniors, including pensions and other forms of financial assistance. Contact your local office (see the Blue Pages in your telephone directory) or the number below for further information.

Jeanne Mance Building
19th Floor, Tunney's Pasture
Ottawa, Ontario K1A 0K9
Tel: (613) 957-2991

Free Publications
• Seniors' Guide to Federal Programs and Services
• Your Guaranteed Income Supplement
• Your Old Age Security Pension
• Your Spouse's Allowance
• Canada's Seniors—A Dynamic Force
• New Horizons

5. Reference Canada

Reference Canada is your telephone referral and basic information service for federal government programs and services.

With Reference Canada, you no longer need to worry about how to track down information about the federal government. All it takes is a telephone call. Information officers are available to help you in either English or French.

All regions except Manitoba and Quebec: 1-800-667-3355
Manitoba residents: 1-800-282-8060
Quebec residents: 1-800-363-1363
Persons with a hearing impairment: 1-800-465-7735

In Quebec, also contact the Communication-Quebec office closest to your area. You can locate this number in the Blue Pages of your telephone directory.

6. Canadian Consulates in the United States

If you have any problems (for example, you lose your passport) that require Canadian government assistance, contact the closest Canadian consulate in the United States.

Washington
501 Pennsylvania Ave. N.W.
Washington, DC 20001
Tel: (202) 682-1740
Fax: (202) 682-7726

Atlanta
Suite 400, South Tower,
One CNN Center
Atlanta, GA 30303-2705
Tel: (404) 577-6810/577-1512
Fax: (404) 524-5046

Boston
Three Copley Place, Suite 400
Boston, MA 02116
Tel: (617) 262-3760
Fax: (617) 262-3415

Buffalo
One Marine Midland Center,
Suite 3000
Buffalo, NY 14203-2884
Tel: (716) 852-1247
Fax: (716) 852-4340

Chicago
Two Prudential Plaza
180 N. Stetson Ave., Suite 2400
Chicago, IL 60601
Tel: (312) 616-1860
Fax: (312) 616-1877

Dallas
St. Paul Place, Suite 1700
750 N. St. Paul St.
Dallas, TX 75201
Tel: (214) 922-9806
Fax: (214) 922-9815

Detroit
600 Renaissance Center, Suite 1100
Detroit, MI 48243-1798
Tel: (313) 567-2085
Fax: (313) 567-2164

Los Angeles
300 S. Grand Ave.
10th Floor, California Plaza
Los Angeles, CA 90071
Tel: (213) 687-7432
Fax: (213) 620-8827

Minneapolis
701 Fourth Ave. S., Suite 900
Minneapolis, MN 55415-1899
Tel: (612) 333-4641
Fax: (612) 332-4061

New York
1251 Avenue of the Americas
New York City, NY 10020-1175
Tel: (212) 596-1600
Fax: (212) 596-1793

Seattle
412 Plaza 600
Sixth and Stewart Streets
Seattle, WA 98101-1286
Tel: (206) 443-1777
Fax: (206) 443-1782

7. Canadian Provincial Offices in the United States

There could be situations in which you require the assistance of a representative of your province in the United States. If so, contact the office nearest you.

British Columbia
Government of British Columbia
2600 Michelson Dr., Suite 1050
Irvine, CA 92715
Tel: (714) 852-0201
Fax: (714) 852-0168

Alberta
Government of Alberta
23rd Floor, General Motors Building
767 Fifth Ave.
New York, NY 10153
Tel: (212) 759-2222
Fax: (212) 759-3682

Saskatchewan
Government of Saskatchewan
Saskatchewan Economic Development
630 Fifth Ave., Suite 2107
New York, NY 10111
Tel: (212) 969-9100
Fax: (212) 969-9549

Quebec
Bureau du Québec
245 Peachtree Center Ave.
Marquis One Tower, Suite 1650
Atlanta, GA 30303
Tel: (404) 880-0250
Fax: (404) 880-0253

Délégation du Québec
Exchange Place, 19th Floor
53 Stats St.
Boston, MA 02109
Tel: (617) 723-3366
Fax: (617) 723-3659

Délégation du Québec
Two Prudential Plaza
180 N. Stetson Ave., Suite 4300
Chicago, IL 60601
Tel: (312) 856-0655
Fax: (312) 856-0725

Délégation du Québec
11755 Wilshire Blvd., Suite 2200
Los Angeles, CA 90025
Tel: (310) 477-2217
Fax: (310) 477-3540

Délégation générale du Québec
Rockefeller Center
630 Fifth Ave., Suite 360
New York, NY 10111-0009
Tel: (212) 397-0200
Fax: (212) 757-4753

Québec Service du tourisme
17 W. 50th St.
New York, NY 10020-2287
Tel: (212) 397-0200

Bureau du tourisme du Québec
1300 - 19th St. N.W., Suite 2200
Washington, DC 20036
Tel: (202) 659-8991
Fax: (202) 659-5654

8. Provincial Offices for Seniors

To learn more about provincial services available to seniors, you may wish to contact the following offices:

British Columbia
Office for Seniors
B.C. Ministry of Health
1515 Blanshard St., 6th Floor
Victoria, BC V8W 3C8
Tel: (604) 952-1238
Fax: (604) 952-1282

Alberta
Seniors' Policy and Programs
Women's and Seniors' Secretariat
Alberta Community Development
16th Floor, Standard Life Centre
10405 Jasper Ave.
Edmonton, AB T5J 4R7
Tel: (403) 427-6358
Fax: (403) 427-1689

Saskatchewan
Policy and Planning Unit
Saskatchewan Social Services
1920 Broad St.
Regina, SK S4P 3V6
Tel: (306) 787-3621
Fax: (306) 787-1032

Manitoba
Manitoba Seniors' Directorate
803 - 155 Carleton St.
Winnipeg, MB R3C 3H8
Tel: (204) 945-6565
Fax: (204) 945-0013

Ontario
Office for Seniors' Issues
Ministry of Citizenship
Province of Ontario
76 College St., 6th Floor
Toronto, ON M7A 1N3
Tel: (416) 327-2422
Fax: (416) 327-2425

Quebec
Direction de l'intégration sociale
Ministère de la santé et
des services sociaux
Édifice Joffre
1075, chemin Sainte-Foy, 11e étage
Quebec, PQ G1S 2M1
Tel: (418) 643-6386
Fax: (418) 643-9024

New Brunswick
Office for Seniors
Health and Community Services
Province of New Brunswick
520 King St., 4th Floor
P.O. Box 5100
Fredericton, NB E3B 5G8
Tel: (506) 453-2480
Fax: (506) 453-2082

Nova Scotia
Nova Scotia Senior Citizens'
Secretariat
P.O. Box 2065
1740 Granville St., 4th Floor
Halifax, NS B3J 2Z1
Tel: (902) 424-4649
Fax: (902) 424-0561

Prince Edward Island
Health and Community Services
Agency
Government of Prince Edward Island
P.O. Box 2000
Charlottetown, PE C1A 7N8
Tel: (902) 368-6130
Fax: (902) 368-6136

9. Provincial Tourism Offices

If you are travelling by car or RV to and from the United States, you may want to plan to explore your own beautiful and diverse country on your way. Here is a list of toll-free phone numbers for provincial tourism offices. These offices will send you a detailed information package on your areas of interest, as well as an accommodations directory.

Tourism British Columbia
1-800-663-6000

Ontario Travel
1-800-ONTARIO (668-2746)

Alberta Tourism
1-800-661-8888

Tourism Québec
1-800-363-7777

Tourism Saskatchewan
1-800-667-7191

New Brunswick Tourism
1-800-561-0123

Travel Manitoba
1-800-665-0040

Nova Scotia Tourism
1-800-565-0000

10. Provincial Health Departments—Out-of-Country Medical Claims and Information

Contact your provincial health department about coverage for out-of-country medical expenses. You will need to obtain supplemental insurance from a private carrier. See Item 11.

British Columbia
Medical Services Plan
P.O. Box 2000
Victoria, BC V8W 2Y4
Tel: (604) 356-0180
1-800-663-7100
Fax: (604) 952-2964

Alberta
Alberta Health
P.O. Box 1360
Edmonton, AB T5J 2N3
Tel: (403) 427-0248
1-800-661-4806
Fax: (403) 427-1093

Saskatchewan
Department of Health
3475 Albert St.
Regina, SK S4S 6X6
Tel: (306) 787-3261
1-800-667-7523
Fax: (306) 787-3761

Manitoba
Manitoba Health
P.O. Box 925
Winnipeg, MB R3C 2T6
Tel: (204) 786-7221
1-800-282-8069
Fax: (204) 783-2171

Ontario
Ministry of Health
P.O. Box 9000
Kingston, ON K7L 5A9
Tel: (613) 546-3811
(Call your local office collect)
Fax: (613) 545-4399

Quebec
RAMQ
P.O. Box 6600
Quebec, PQ G1K 7T3
Tel: (418) 646-4636 (Quebec)
Tel: (514) 861-3411 (Montreal)
1-800-561-9749

New Brunswick
Health and Community Services
P.O. Box 5100
Fredericton, NB E3B 5G8
Tel: (506) 453-2161
Fax: (506) 453-2726

Prince Edward Island
Health and Community Services
Agency
35 Douses Rd.
Montague, PE C0A 1R0
Tel: (902) 368-5858
Fax: (902) 838-2050

Nova Scotia
Department of Health
P.O. Box 488
Halifax, NS B3J 2R8
Tel: (902) 424-5999
1-800-563-8880
Fax: (902) 424-0615

Newfoundland
Department of Health
P.O. Box 8700
Confederation Building, West Block
St. John's, NF A1B 4J6
Tel: (709) 729-4928
Fax: (709) 729-5824

Yukon
Health Services
P.O. Box 2703
Whitehorse, YT Y1A 2C6
Tel: (403) 667-5725
1-800-661-0408
Fax: (403) 668-3786

Northwest Territories
Department of Health
2nd Floor, ICC Building
Inuvik, NT X0E 020
Tel: (403) 873-7740
1-800-661-0830
Fax: (403) 979-3197

11. Companies Providing Out-of-Country Medical Insurance

Many companies provide out-of-country medical insurance to supplement provincial coverage. As the insurance underwriters may change from year to year, they are not mentioned here. Also, the same insurance company may be underwriting different organizations or companies with special packages. The market is very competitive, so thoroughly comparison-shop and look at features, benefits, premiums, limitations, exclusions, and deductibles. These factors can change each year, usually between June and September.

Associations

Canadian Association of Retired Persons (CARP)
1-800-561-7831

Canadian Grey Panthers
1-800-668-4545

Canadian Snowbird Association (CSA)
1-800-563-5104

International Association of Winter Visitors
1-800-661-8785

Auto Clubs

CAA Travel & Medical Insurance
Contact your local auto club. For phone numbers, refer to item 27, Appendix A.

National Auto League Health Pac
1-800-387-2298

Banks

Bank of Montreal Travel Protection Plan
1-800-661-9060

CIBC Travel Medical Insurance
1-800-263-6766

Hong Kong Bank of Canada Travel Insurance
1-800-387-5290

Royal Bank Travel Health Protector
1-800-565-3129

Scotiabank Medical Insurance Plan
1-800-263-0997

TD Bank Green Plan Travel
1-800-263-7769

Credit Unions

CUIS (Credit Union Insurance Services) Travel Insurance
1-800-263-5110

Trust Companies

Canada Trust Travel Medical Insurance
1-800-263-4008

Montreal Trust Insurance
1-800-263-0261

Municipal Trust Travel Insurance
1-800-465-5077

National Trust Travel Insurance
1-800-461-0557

Royal Trust Travel Insurance
1-800-387-5290

Other

John Ingle Insurance
1-800-387-4770

Blue Cross Plans

B.C. (through Medical Services Association)	Tel: (604) 737-5528
Alberta & Northwest Territories	1-800-661-6995
Saskatchewan	1-800-667-6853
Manitoba	1-800-262-8832
Ontario (as of February 23, 1995, called Liberty Health)	1-800-268-3763
Quebec	1-800-361-5706
Atlantic	1-800-561-7123

Good Holiday Travel Insurance
1-800-561-3323

Maritime Medical Travel Health Plan
Tel: (902) 461-2100

Medical Insurance for Long-Term Travel (MILT) Travel Insurance Specialists
1-800-563-0314

Medicare International
1-800-461-2100

Mutual of Omaha Insurance Company of Canada
1-800-268-8825

North American Life Assurance Co.
1-800-563-0314

Protection Plus Golden Age Insurance
1-800-387-0339

Travel Gold
1-800-663-5389

Travel Insurance Co-ordinators
1-800-663-4494

Travellers Choice Out-of-Canada Medical Insurance
1-800-665-8553

Travelrite Travel Insurance
1-800-563-8615

Voyageur Travel Insurance
1-800-668-4342

12. U.S. Consulates in Canada

You may have questions about travelling to the United States, in terms of any restrictions, limitations, or documentation required. Or you may want to invest in a business enterprise in the United States. If so, contact the closest U.S. consulate at the number below.

1095 W. Pender St.
Vancouver, BC V6E 2M6
Tel: (604) 685-4311
Fax: (604) 685-5285

#1050 - 615 Macleod Trail S.E.
Calgary, AB T2G 4T8
Tel: (403) 266-8962
Fax: (403) 264-6630

360 University Ave.
Toronto, ON M5G 1S4
Tel: (416) 595-1700
Fax: (416) 595-0051, (416) 595-5419

2 Place Terrasse Dufferin, C.P. 939
Quebec, PQ G1R 4T9
Tel: (418) 692-2095
Fax: (418) 692-4640

100 Wellington St.
Ottawa, ON K1P 5T1
Tel: (613) 238-5335, (613) 238-4470
Fax: (613) 238-5720

Suite 910, Cogswell Tower,
Scotia Square
Halifax, NS B3J 3K1
Tel: (902) 429-2480
Fax: (902) 423-6861

P.O. Box 65
Postal Station Desjardins
Montreal, PQ H5B 1G1
Tel: (514) 398-9695
Fax: (514) 398-0973, (514) 398-0711

13. U.S. Internal Revenue Service (IRS)

The IRS is equivalent to Revenue Canada. As there could be various tax implications to your stay in the United States, income derived in the United States, or assets owned in the United States, check with the IRS Canadian office.

IRS Canadian Office
60 Queen St., Suite 201
Ottawa, ON K1P 5Y7
Tel: (613) 563-1834
Fax: (613) 230-1376

Free Publications

These publications with related forms are available from any IRS office in the United States or the IRS office in Canada. If you are phoning from the United States, you can request these forms by phoning the following toll-free number: 1-800-TAX-FORM (1-800-829-3676).

#54	Tax Guide for U.S. Citizens and Resident Aliens Abroad
#448	U.S. Estate and Gift Tax Guide
#513	Tax Information for Visitors to the United States
#514	Foreign Tax Credit for Individuals
#515	Withholding of Tax on Non-Resident Aliens and Foreign Corporations
#519	U.S. Tax Guide for Aliens

#521   Moving Expenses
#523   Tax Information on Selling your Home
#527   Residential Rental Property
#593   Tax Highlights for U.S. Citizens and Residents Going Abroad
#910   Guide to Free Tax Services

14. U.S. Customs Service

You will have to comply with U.S. customs regulations when entering the United States. Make enquiries before you leave Canada.

For specific information on requirements and regulations that might affect you, contact the U.S. Customs office closest to your point of entry into the United States (for example, at an airport or border station).

As there are many entry points and therefore many phone numbers, contact directory information in the location that you are going to enter the United States.

Address for Free Publications
U.S. Customs Service
P.O. Box 7407
Washington, DC 20044

Free Publications
• U.S. Customs Directory
• International Mail Imports
• Customs Hints for Visitors (Non-residents)
• Tips for Visitors
• Pets, Wildlife
• Importing a Car

15. U.S. Immigration and Naturalization Service (INS)

For further information on remaining in the United States over six months a year, working in the United States as a business visitor or professional, or emigrating to the United States, contact the appropriate INS office below before entering the United States. If you are a U.S. citizen or the national of a country other than Canada, contact the INS. If you intend to enter the United States under a trader or investor category, contact the U.S. Embassy or a U.S. Consulate office in Canada.

Ports of Entry INS Offices

Peace Arch Inspection Station
P.O. Box 340
Blaine, WA 98230
Tel: (206) 332-8511, (206) 332-8512

U.S. Immigration Building
P.O. Box 165
Sweetgrass, MT 59484
Tel: (406) 335-2911

Detroit Tunnel
150 E. Jefferson Ave.
Detroit, MI 48226
Tel: (313) 226-2390

Peace Bridge
Rhode Island St.
Buffalo, NY 14213
Tel: (716) 885-3367

Thousand Island Bridge
P.O. Box 433, Road No. 1
Alexandra Bay, NY 13607-9796
Tel: (315) 482-2681

Ogdensburg Prescott Bridge
Ogdensburg, NY 13669
Tel: (315) 393-0770

65 W. Service Rd.
Champlain, NY 12919
Tel: (518) 298-3221, (518) 298-8433

P.O. Box 189
Military Rd.
Houlton, ME 04730
Tel: (207) 532-2906

One Maine St.
P.O. Drawer 421
Calais, ME 04619
Tel: (207) 454-2546, (207) 454-2547

Vancouver International Airport
P.O. Box 23046
Vancouver, BC V7E 1T9
Tel: (604) 278-2520

Air Terminal Building
2000 Airport Rd. N.W.
Calgary, AB T2E 6W5
Tel: (403) 221-1730

Edmonton International Airport
P.O. Box 9832
Edmonton, AB T5J 2T2
Tel: (403) 890-4486

Winnipeg International Airport
Winnipeg, MB R2R 0S6
Tel: (204) 783-2340

L.B. Pearson International Airport
P.O. Box 6011
Toronto, ON L5P 1E2
Tel: (416) 676-2563

Montreal International Airport
P.O. Box 518
Dorval, PQ H4Y 1B3
Tel: (514) 631-2097

16. U.S. Department of Agriculture—Animal and Plant Inspection Service

Certain types of fruits, vegetables, meats, animals, plants, and seeds are prohibited entry into the United States. Make enquiries at your closest U.S. customs office, or contact:

U.S. Department of Agriculture
6505 Bellcrest Rd.
Hyatts Ville, MD 20782
Tel: (301) 436-5524

Free Pamphlet
• Travelers' Tips

17. U.S. Fish and Wildlife Service

You are prohibited from buying, owning, or transporting certain types of live fish or animals, or products made from these animals. Ask for further information at your closest U.S. customs office, or contact:

Department of the Interior
Washington, DC 20240

Free Pamphlets
• Fish and Wildlife
• Facts About Federal Wildlife Laws

18. State Travel Offices in the United States

Use this listing of state travel offices to order free vacation information. One call, often to a toll-free number accessible from Canada as well as the United States, or a letter will let you explore a variety of American vacation destinations in the comfort of your home.

Although the quantity and variety of information available will vary from state to state, you will receive such items as maps, calendars of events, travel guides, and brochures containing information about accommodations, campgrounds, restaurants, attractions, recreational activities, and more.

For assistance in making specific travel arrangements, contact your local travel agent. Common Sunbelt states are noted with an asterisk (*).

Alabama Bureau of Tourism and Travel
P.O. Box 4309
Montgomery, AL 36103-4309
Tel: (205) 242-4169
1-800-ALABAMA

Alaska Division of Tourism
P.O. Box 110801, TIA
Juneau, AK 99811-0801
Tel: (907) 465-2010

* Arizona Office of Tourism
1100 W. Washington St.
Phoenix, AZ 85007
Tel: (602) 542-8687
1-800-842-8257

Arkansas Department of Parks and Tourism
One Capitol Mall, Dept. 7701
Little Rock, AR 72201
Tel: (501) 682-7777
1-800-NATURAL

* California Division of Tourism
P.O. Box 1499, Dept. TIA
Sacramento, CA 95812-1499
Tel: (916) 322-2881
1-800-TO-CALIF

Colorado Tourism Board
P.O. Box 38700
Denver, CO 80238
Tel: (303) 592-5410
1-800-COLORADO (265-6723)

Connecticut Department of Economic Development, Tourism Division
865 Brook St.
Rocky Hill, CT 06067
Tel: (203) 258-4355
1-800-CT-BOUND

Delaware Tourism Office
99 Kings Hwy., Box 1401, Dept. TIA
Dover, DE 19903
Tel: (302) 739-4271
1-800-441-8846

* Florida Division of Tourism
126 W. Van Buren St., FLDA
Tallahassee, FL 32399-2000
Tel: (904) 487-1462

Georgia Department of Industry, Trade and Tourism
P.O. Box 1776, Dept. TIA
Atlanta, GA 30301
Tel: (404) 656-3590
1-800-VISIT-GA

* Hawaii Visitors' Bureau
2270 Kalakaua Ave.
Honolulu, HI 96815
Tel: (808) 923-1811

Idaho Division of Tourism Development
700 W. State St., Dept. C
Boise, ID 83720
Tel: (208) 334-2470
1-800-635-7820

Illinois Bureau of Tourism
100 W. Randolph, Suite 3-400
Chicago, IL 60601
Tel: (312) 814-4732
1-800-223-0121

Indiana Department of Commerce/ Tourism and Film Development Division
One N. Capital St., Suite 700
Indianapolis, IN 46204-2288
Tel: (317) 232-8860
1-800-289-6646

Iowa Division of Tourism
200 E. Grand
Des Moines, IA 50309
Tel: (515) 242-4705
1-800-345-IOWA (for ordering
vacation kit only, U.S. only)
1-800-528-5265
(special events calendar)

**Kansas Travel and Tourism
Division**
700 S.W. Harrison St., Suite 1300
Topeka, KS 66603-3712
Tel: (913) 296-2009
1-800-2KANSAS

**Kentucky Department of
Travel Development**
500 Mero St., 22nd Floor, Dept. DA
Frankfort, KY 40601
Tel: (502) 564-4930
1-800-225-TRIP

Louisiana Office of Tourism
Attn.: Inquiry Dept.
P.O. Box 94291, LOT
Baton Rouge, LA 70804-9291
Tel: (504) 342-8119
1-800-33-GUMBO

Maine Office of Tourism
189 State St.
Augusta, ME 04333
Tel: (207) 289-5711
1-800-533-9595

**Maryland Office of Tourism
Development**
217 E. Redwood St., 9th Floor
Baltimore, MD 21202
Tel: (410) 333-6611
1-800-543-1036
(for vacation kit only)

**Massachusetts Office of Travel
and Tourism**
100 Cambridge St., 13th Floor
Boston, MA 02202
Tel: (617) 727-3201
1-800-447-MASS
(for vacation kit only, U.S. only)

Michigan Travel Bureau
P.O. Box 3393
Livonia, MI 48151-3393
Tel: (517) 373-0670
1-800-5432-YES

Minnesota Office of Tourism
121 - 7th Place E.
St. Paul, MN 55101
Tel: (612) 296-5029
1-800-657-3700

Mississippi Division of Tourism
P.O. Box 1705
Ocean Springs, MS 39566-1705
Tel: (601) 359-3297
1-800-WARMEST

Missouri Division of Tourism
P.O. Box 1055, Dept. TIA
Jefferson City, MO 65102
Tel: (314) 751-4133
1-800-877-1234

Travel Montana
Room TIA
Deer Lodge, MT 59722
Tel: (406) 444-2654
1-800-VISIT-MT

**Nebraska Division of Travel
and Tourism**
P.O. Box 94666
Lincoln, NE 68509
Tel: (402) 471-3796
1-800-228-4307

* Nevada Commission on Tourism
Capitol Complex, Dept. TIA
Carson City, NV 89710
Tel: (702) 687-4322
1-800-NEVADA-8

**New Hampshire Office of Travel
and Tourism Development**
P.O. Box 856, Dept. TIA
Concord, NH 03302
Tel: (603) 271-2343
1-800-386-4664

**New Jersey Division of Travel
and Tourism**
20 W. State St., CN 826, Dept. TIA
Trenton, NJ 08625
Tel: (609) 292-2470
1-800-JERSEY-7

*** New Mexico Department of
Tourism**
491 Old Santa Fe Trail
Sante Fe, NM 87503
Tel: (505) 827-7400
1-800-545-2040

**New York State Division of
Tourism, Department of
Economic Development**
One Commerce Plaza
Albany, NY 12245
Tel: (518) 474-4116
1-800-CALL-NYS

**North Carolina Division of
Travel and Tourism**
430 N. Salisbury St.
Raleigh, NC 27603
Tel: (919) 733-4171
1-800-VISIT-NC

**North Dakota Department of
Tourism**
Liberty Memorial Building,
604 E. Blvd.
Bismarck, ND 58505
Tel: (701) 224-2525
1-800-435-5663

**Ohio Division of Travel and
Tourism**
P.O. Box 1001
Columbus, OH 43266-0101
Tel: (614) 466-8844
1-800-BUCKEYE
(continental U.S. and all of Canada)

**Oklahoma Tourism and Recreation
Department, Travel and
Tourism Division**
500 Will Rogers Building, DA92
Oklahoma City, OK 73105-4492
Tel: (405) 521-3981
1-800-652-6552
(information requests only)

**Oregon Economic Development
Department, Tourism Division**
775 Summer St. N.E.
Salem, OR 97310
Tel: (503) 373-1270
1-800-547-7842

**Pennsylvania Office of Travel
Marketing**
Room 453, Forum Building
Harrisburg, PA 17120
Tel: (717) 787-5453
1-800-VISIT-PA

Rhode Island Tourism Division
7 Jackson Walkway, Dept. TIA
Providence, RI 02903
Tel: (401) 277-2601
1-800-556-2484

South Carolina Division of Tourism
Box 71
Columbia, SC 29202
Tel: (803) 734-0122
1-800-346-3634

South Dakota Department of Tourism
711 E. Wells Ave.
Pierre, SD 57501-3369
Tel: (605) 773-3301
1-800-DAKOTA

Tennessee Department of Tourist Development
P.O. Box 23170, TNDA
Nashville, TN 37202
Tel: (615) 741-2158
1-800-836-6200

Texas Department of Commerce, Tourism Division
P.O. Box 12728
Austin, TX 78711-2728
Tel: (512) 462-9191
1-800-88-88-TEX

Utah Travel Council
Council Hall/Capitol Hill, Dept. TIA
Salt Lake City, UT 84114
Tel: (801) 538-1030
1-800-200-1160

Vermont Department of Travel and Tourism
134 State St.
Montpelier, VT 05602
Tel: (802) 828-3236
1-800-338-0189, 1-800-837-6668

Virginia Division of Tourism
1021 E. Cary St., Dept. VT
Richmond, VA 23219
Tel: (804) 786-4484
1-800-VISIT-VA

Washington State Tourism Development Division
P.O. Box 42500
Olympia, WA 98504-2500
Tel: (206) 586-2088, (206) 586-2012
1-800-544-1800

West Virginia Division of Tourism and Parks
2101 Washington St. E.
Charleston, WV 25305
Tel: (304) 348-2286
1-800-225-5982

Wisconsin Division of Tourism
P.O. Box 7606
Madison, WI 53707
Tel: (608) 266-2161
1-800-372-2737 (in-state)
1-800-432-TRIP (out-of-state)

Wyoming Division of Tourism
I-25 at College Dr., Dept. WY
Cheyenne, WY 82002
Tel: (307) 777-7777
1-800-225-5996

19. State Travel Parks Associations

These associations are for the owners of travel parks, including the larger parks catering to Snowbirds who have extended stays (for example, up to six months). As a result, they tend to offer extensive services and amenities. Write to them for a directory of members. Just the most popular Sunbelt states are listed:

Arizona Travel Parks Association
1130 E. Missouri St., #530
Phoenix, AZ 85014
Tel: (602) 230-1125
Fax: (602) 433-9534

California Travel Parks Association
P.O. Box 5648
Auburn, CA 95604
Tel: (916) 885-1824
Fax: (916) 823-6331

Florida Association of RV Parks and Campgrounds
1340 Vickers Dr.
Tallahassee, FL 32303-3041
Tel: (904) 562-7151
Fax: (904) 562-7179

Texas Association of Campground Owners
P.O. Box 14055
Austin, TX 78761
Tel/Fax: (512) 459-8226

20. Associations of Mobile Home Owners

Many U.S. states have associations of people who own manufactured homes. Sometimes the homes are referred to as "mobile" homes. These home owners tend to live in their homes all year long, or if they are Snowbirds, up to six months a year. Benefits of membership in these associations include group rates for mobile home insurance, a regular newsletter or magazine, and government lobbying efforts on behalf of members. Contact numbers for the key Sunbelt state associations follow:

Arizona

Arizona Association of Manufactured Homeowners
20 E. Main St.
Mesa, AZ 85201
Tel: (602) 844-2208

California

Golden State Mobilehome Owners' League
3381 Stevens Creek Rd., Suite 210
San Jose, CA 95117
Tel: (408) 244-8134

Florida

Federation of Mobile Homeowners of Florida
4020 Portsmouth Rd.
Largo, FL 34641-3399
Tel: (813) 530-7539

Nevada

Mobilehome Owners' League of the Silver State
1928 Western, Suite 4
Las Vegas, NV 89102
Tel: (702) 384-8428

New Mexico

Mobilehome Owners' Association of New Mexico
3000 Aztec Rd. N.E., #147
Albuquerque, NM 87107
Tel: (505) 884-0776

Texas

Texas Manufactured Homeowners' Association
311 Laurel
San Antonio, TX 78212-3334
Tel: (210) 223-2378

21. National Seniors' Organizations

The following national organizations provide helpful contacts and networking for seniors. Many of these organizations offer Snowbird out-of-country health insurance, discounts on purchases such as medication and on lodgings, meetings, newsletters, advocacy efforts in lobbying various levels of government, and other member benefits. Fees tend to be nominal. Contact the organizations directly for further information. The four organizations noted with an asterisk (*) offer out-of-country insurance to Canadian Snowbirds.

Canada

Assemblée des aînés et aînées francophones du Canada
Pièce 1404, 1 rue Nicholas
Ottawa, ON K1N 7B7
Tel: (613) 563-0311
Fax: (613) 563-0288

* Canadian Association of
Retired Persons
27 Queen St. E., Suite 1304
Toronto, ON M5C 2M6
Tel: (416) 363-8748
Fax: (416) 363-8747

* Canadian Grey Panthers
50 Burnhamthorpe Rd. W., Suite 401
Mississauga, ON L5B 3C2
1-800-561-4739

Canadian Pensioners Concerned Inc.
National Office
7001 Mumford Rd., Suite 310
P.O. Box 35
Halifax Shopping Centre
Halifax, NS B3L 4N9
Tel: (902) 455-4709
Fax: (902) 455-1825

* Canadian Snowbird Association
180 Lesmill Road
North York, ON M3B 2T5
Tel: (416) 391-9000
1-800-265-3200
Fax: (416) 441-7020

Federal Superannuates'
National Association
233 Gilmour St., Suite 401
Ottawa, ON K2P 0P2
Tel: (613) 234-9663
Fax: (613) 234-2314

National Pensioners' and Senior
Citizens' Federation
3033 Lakeshore Blvd. W.
Toronto, ON M8V 1K5
Tel: (416) 251-7042
Fax: (416) 252-5770

One Voice—The Canadian Seniors
Network
350 Sparks St., Suite 1005
Ottawa, ON K1R 7S8
Tel: (613) 238-7624
Fax: (613) 235-4497

U.S.

American Association of Retired
Persons
601 E Street N.W.
Washington, DC 20049-0002
Tel: (202) 434-2277
1-800-424-3410 (U.S. only)
Fax: (202) 434-6483

* International Association of
Winter Visitors
P.O. Box 30458
Mesa, AZ 85275-0458
Tel: (602) 396-4040
1-800-346-6585
Fax: (602) 396-4953

22. Canadian Snowbird Advisor Newsletter

This newsletter discusses current issues of concern or interest to Canadian Snowbirds in an objective, candid, and practical style. The advice, tips, and strategies are designed to save you money, time, and stress by providing the main information a Canadian Snowbird needs to know. It is written by Canadian and U.S. experts and professionals, and covers topics such as cross-border (Canada/U.S.) tax issues, legal issues, immigration, customs, real estate, money management, and investment, as well as estate, financial, and retirement planning issues.

To obtain the newsletter and for further information, contact the Canadian Retirement Planning Institute Inc., #300 - 3665 Kingsway, Vancouver, BC V5R 5W2. Tel: (604) 436-3337; Fax: (604) 436-9155.

23. Newspapers for Canadian Snowbirds

To keep current on Canadian events, news, and information, as well as on issues that affect Snowbirds, subscribe to one or both of the publications below. They are published weekly during the Snowbird season (November 1 - April 30). Ask for a complimentary copy for review.

Canada News
P.O. Box 1729
Auburndale, FL 33823-1729
Tel: (813) 967-6450
1-800-535-6788

The Sun Times of Canada
515 W. Bay St.
Tampa, FL 33606
Tel: (813) 254-6620
1-800-253-4323

24. News for Canadian Snowbirds on Sunbelt Radio Stations

There are various radio programs containing news specifically for Canadian Snowbirds. The largest news program coverage is called *Canadian News with Prior Smith* and is heard in Florida, South Carolina, and Arizona each weekday. Most Florida stations also air the news magazine *Canada This Week* each Sunday. Consult stations for scheduling.

There are also radio news programs for Canadian Snowbirds heard in various communities in Southern California. Refer to the radio station list below. Stations, coverage, and scheduling may change. Most programs are on AM stations, some on FM, and others on both.

Florida

Station	Region	Dial Position	Broadcast Time(s) (Mon-Fri)
WGUL	Tampa Bay	860	10:35 A.M.
			3:35 P.M.
WGUL FM	New Port Richey, Dunedin, Clearwater, Largo	105.5	10:35 A.M.
			3:35 P.M.
WBRD	Bradenton	1420	9:30 A.M.
WTMY	Sarasota	1280	8:24 A.M.
WENG	Englewood, Venice	1530	12:20 P.M.
WKII	Port Charlotte, Punta Gorda, Southwest Gulf Coast	1070	9:53 A.M.
WDCQ	Fort Myers, Cape Coral, Naples	1200	12:15 P.M.
WODX	Marco Island, Naples	1480	12:06 P.M.
WFTL	Fort Lauderdale, North Miami to Pompano Beach	1400	2:00 P.M.
WPBR	Palm Beaches, Boca Raton	1340	9:00 A.M.
WPSL	Port St. Lucie, Fort Pierce, Stuart	1590	8:50 A.M.
WOKC	Lake Okeechobee	1570	8:30 A.M.
WAXE	Vero Beach	1370	10:00 A.M.
WMEL	Melbourne, Cocoa Beach	920	12:00 noon
WAMT	Titusville	1060	8:15 A.M.
WSBB	New Smyrna Beach	1230	9:00 A.M.
			5:00 P.M.
WROD	Daytona Beach	1340	11:55 A.M.
WAOC	St. Augustine	1420	11:50 A.M.
WDCF	Dade City	1350	8:15 A.M.
			12:15 P.M.
			3:15 P.M.
WZHR	Zephyrhills	1400	8:30 A.M.
WJCM	Sebring, Avon Park, South Central Florida	960	12:35 P.M.
			5:25 P.M.
WWBF	Bartow, Lake Wales, Lakeland	1130	8:30 A.M.
WHNR	Winter Haven, Kissimmee	1360	9:30 A.M.
WLBE	Leesburg, Orlando, Central Florida	790	12:15 P.M.
WOCA	Ocala, Silver Springs	1370	11:50 A.M.
WWJB	Brooksville	1450	9:30 A.M.
WEBZ FM	Panama City, Florida Panhandle	99.3	9:00 A.M.
			3:00 P.M.
WTKX	Pensacola	1230	9:30 A.M.

South Carolina

Station	Region	Dial Position	Broadcast Time(s) (Mon-Fri)
WRNN FM	Myrtle Beach	94.5	(Jan/Feb/Mar)

Arizona

Station	Region	Dial Position	Broadcast Time(s) (Mon-Fri)
KXAM	Phoenix, Mesa, Scottsdale, Sun City	1310	10:00 A.M.

California

Station	Region	Dial Position	Broadcast Time(s) (Mon-Fri)
KWXY	Palm Springs, Rancho Mirage, Palm Desert, Indian Wells,	1340 or 98.5	9:15 A.M. 3.15 P.M.

25. Health Newsletters

These monthly eight-page newsletters keep you current on health issues relevant to seniors, to enhance your well-being and quality of life. Ask for a complimentary copy.

The Johns Hopkins Medical Letter: Health After 50
550 N. Broadway, Suite 1100
Johns Hopkins
Baltimore, MD 21205

University of California at Berkeley Wellness Letter
P.O. Box 420148
Palm Coast, FL 32142

26. Local Chambers of Commerce

To obtain information from a local Chamber of Commerce about a community you are considering, phone the directory assistance operator in that community or contact the appropriate state Chamber of Commerce listed below:

Arizona Chamber of Commerce
1221 E. Osborn Road, #100
Phoenix, AZ 85014
Tel: (602) 248-9172
Fax: (602) 265-1262

California State Chamber of Commerce
1201 K St., 12th Floor
P.O. Box 1736
Sacramento, CA 95812
Tel: (916) 444-6670
Fax: (916) 444-6685

Florida Chamber of Commerce
136 S. Bronough St.
P.O. Box 11309
Tallahasee, FL 23202-3309
Tel: (904) 425-1200
Fax: (904) 425-1260

Nevada State Chamber of Commerce
P.O. Box 3499
Reno, NV 89505
Tel: (702) 686-3030
Fax: (702) 329-3499

The Association of Commerce and Industry of New Mexico
2309 Renard Place S.E., Suite 402
Albuquerque, NM 87106-4259
Tel: (505) 842-0644
Fax: (505) 842-0734

Texas State Chamber of Commerce
900 Congress Ave., Suite 501
Austin, TX 98701
Tel: (512) 472-1594
Fax: (512) 320-0280

27. CAA Clubs and Branches

There are many benefits to becoming a member of a local CAA Club that will also help you as a Snowbird. These include out-of-country insurance protection, travel books, and assistance with car problems in the United States and Canada. Contact the office closest to you for detailed information.

CAA National Office
Canadian Automobile Association
1775 Courtwood Cres.
Ottawa, ON K2C 3J2
Tel: (613) 226-7631
This is an administrative office only. For member services, contact any of the following CAA member clubs. Contact numbers may change over time.

British Columbia

Head Office
British Columbia Automobile Association
4567 Canada Way
Burnaby, BC V5G 4T1
Tel: (604) 268-5000
1-800-663-1956

Abbotsford
Tel: (604) 855-0530

Chilliwack
Tel: (604) 792-4664

Delta
Tel: (604) 599-1616

Kamloops
Tel: (604) 372-9577

Kelowna
Tel: (604) 861-4554

Langley
Tel: (604) 268-5950

Nanaimo
Tel: (604) 390-3533

Nelson
Tel: (604) 352-3535

New Westminster
Tel: (604) 268-5700

Penticton
Tel: (604) 492-7016

Port Coquitlam
Tel: (604) 944-7745

Prince George
Tel: (604) 563-0417

Alberta

Head Office
Alberta Motor Association
10310 G.A. MacDonald Ave.
Edmonton, AB T6J 6R7
Tel: (403) 430-5555
1-800-642-3810

Banff
Tel: (403) 762-2266

Calgary
Tel: (403) 590-0001, (403) 278-3530,
(403) 262-2345, (403) 240-5300,
(403) 239-6644

Camrose
Tel: (403) 672-3391

Saskatchewan

Head Office
CAA Saskatchewan
200 Albert St. N.
Regina, SK S4R 5E2
Tel: (306) 791-4321

Moose Jaw
Tel: (306) 693-5195

North Battleford
Tel: (306) 445-9451

Richmond
Tel: (604) 272-5930

Vancouver
Tel: (604) 268-5600, (604) 268-5800

Vernon
Tel: (604) 542-1022

Victoria
Tel: (604) 389-6700, (604) 744-2202

West Vancouver
Tel: (604) 268-5650

Edmonton
Tel: (403) 473-3112, (403) 474-8601,
(403) 484-1221

Fort McMurray
Tel: (403) 743-2433

Grande Prairie
Tel: (403) 532-4421

Lethbridge
Tel: (403) 328-1181

Medicine Hat
Tel: (403) 527-1166

Red Deer
Tel: (403) 342-6633

Prince Albert
Tel: (306) 764-6818

Regina
Tel: (306) 791-4322, (306) 791-4323

Saskatoon
Tel: (306) 955-4484, (306) 653-1833

Swift Current
Tel: (306) 773-3193

Weyburn
Tel: (306) 842-6651

Manitoba

Head Office
CAA Manitoba Motor League
870 Empress St.
Winnipeg, MB R3C 2Z3
Tel: (204) 987-6161
1-800-222-4357

Altona
Tel: (204) 324-8474

Ontario

Barrie
Tel: (705) 726-1803

Belleville
Tel: (613) 968-9832

Brampton
Tel: (905) 793-4911

Brantford
Tel: (519) 756-6321

Brockville
Tel: (613) 498-1105

Burlington
Tel: (905) 632-6772

Cambridge
Tel: (519) 622-2620

Chatham
Tel: (519) 351-2222

Cobourg
Tel: (905) 372-8777

Don Mills
Tel: (416) 449-9993

Dundas
Tel: (905) 627-7777

Yorkton
Tel: (306) 783-6536

Brandon
Tel: (204) 727-0561

Portage La Prairie
Tel: (204) 857-3453

Winnipeg
Tel: (204) 987-6202, (204) 987-6226

Espanola
Tel: (705) 869-3611

Gloucester
Tel: (613) 741-2235

Grimsby
Tel: (905) 945-5555

Guelph
Tel: (519) 821-9940

Hamilton
Tel: (905) 525-1210, (905) 385-8500

Islington
Tel: (416) 231-9967

Kingston
Tel: (613) 546-2596

Kitchener
Tel: (519) 894-2582, (519) 741-1160,
1-800-265-8975

Leamington
Tel: (519) 322-2356

London
Tel: (519) 685-3140,
(519) 473-3055

Mississauga
Tel: (905) 275-2501,
(905) 823-6800

Newmarket
Tel: (905) 836-5171

North Bay
Tel: (705) 474-8230

Oakville
Tel: (905) 845-9680

Orangeville
Tel: (519) 941-8360

Orillia
Tel: (705) 325-7211

Oshawa
Tel: (905) 723-5203

Ottawa
Tel: (613) 820-1890,
(613) 736-9696

Owen Sound
Tel: (519) 376-1940

Parry Sound
Tel: (705) 746-9305

Peterborough
Tel: (705) 743-4343,
1-800-461-7622

Pickering
Tel: (905) 831-5252

St. Catharines
Tel: (905) 688-0321

St. Thomas
Tel: (519) 631-6490,
1-800-265-4343

Sarnia
Tel: (519) 542-3493

Sault Ste. Marie
Tel: (705) 942-4600

Scarborough
Tel: (416) 439-6370,
(416) 752-9080

Simcoe
Tel: (519) 426-7230

Stoney Creek
Tel: (905) 664-8000

Sudbury
Tel: (705) 522-0000,
1-800-461-7111

Thornhill
Tel: (905) 771-3255,
1-800-268-3750

Thorold
Tel: (905) 984-8585,
1-800-263-7272

Thunder Bay
Tel: (807) 345-1261

Timmins
Tel: (705) 264-1021

Toronto
Tel: (416) 593-7360,
(416) 789-7466

Welland
Tel: (905) 735-1100

Willowdale
Tel: (416) 495-1802,
(416) 223-1751

Windsor
Tel: (519) 255-1212,
1-800-265-5681

Woodstock
Tel: (519) 539-5676

Quebec

Head Office
CAA Quebec
444 Bouvier St.
Quebec, PQ G2J 1E2
Tel: (418) 624-0708

Brossard
Tel: (514) 861-7575

Charlesbourg
Tel: (418) 624-0708

Chicoutimi
Tel: (418) 545-8686

Hull
Tel: (819) 778-2225

Laval
Tel: (514) 861-7575

Montreal
Tel: (514) 861-7575

Pointe-Claire
Tel: (514) 861-7575

St-Leonard
Tel: (514) 861-7575

Ste-Foy
Tel: (418) 624-0708

Sherbrooke
Tel: (819) 566-5132

Trois-Rivieres
Tel: (819) 376-9393

New Brunswick

Head Office
CAA Maritimes
737 Rothesay Ave.
Saint John, NB E2H 2H6
Tel: (506) 634-1400
1-800-561-8807

Fredericton
Tel: (506) 452-1987

Moncton
Tel: (506) 857-8225

Prince Edward Island

Charlottetown
Tel: (902) 892-1612

Nova Scotia

Dartmouth
Tel: (902) 468-6306

Halifax
Tel: (902) 443-5530

28. Canadian Corps of Commissionaires

If you need a reliable person to check on your home regularly during your absence, you may wish to contact the Corps of Commissionaires at the offices below.

National Headquarters
100 rue Gloucester St., Suite 503
Ottawa, ON K2P 0A4
Tel: (613) 236-4936
Fax: (613) 563-8508

Victoria and Vancouver Island
4248 Glanford Ave., 2nd Floor
Victoria, BC V8Z 4B8
Tel: (604) 727-7755
Fax: (604) 727-7355

British Columbia
404 - 198 W. Hastings St.
Vancouver, BC V6B 1H2
Tel: (604) 681-9207
Fax: (604) 681-9864

Northern Alberta
1730 - 10405 Jasper Ave.
Edmonton, AB T5J 3N4
Tel: (403) 428-0321
Fax: (403) 426-6573

Southern Alberta
#710, Alberta Pl., 1520 - 4th St. S.W.
Calgary, AB T2R 1H5
Tel: (403) 244-4664
Fax: (403) 228-0623

Northern Saskatchewan
493 - 2nd Ave. N.
Saskatoon, SK S7K 2C1
Tel: (306) 244-6588
Fax: (306) 244-6191

Southern Saskatchewan
Alpine Village Mall
122 Albert St.
Regina, SK S4R 2N2
Tel: (306) 757-0998
Fax: (306) 352-5494

Manitoba
301 One Wesley Ave.
Winnipeg, MB R3C 4C6
Tel: (204) 942-5993
Fax: (204) 942-6702

Ottawa
108 Lisgar St.
Ottawa, ON K2P 0C2
Tel: (613) 231-6462
Fax: (613) 567-1517

Kingston
614 Norris Court, Unit #9
Kingston, ON K7P 2R9
Tel: (613) 634-4432
Fax: (613) 634-4436

Toronto and Region
80 Church St.
Toronto, ON M5C 2G1
Tel: (416) 364-4496
Fax: (416) 364-3361

Hamilton
#609 Imperial Building
25 Hughson St. S.
Hamilton, ON L8N 2A5
Tel: (905) 522-7584
Fax: (905) 522-8011

London
815 Commissioners Rd. E.
(Western Counties Rd.)
P.O. Box 22066
London, ON N6C 4N0
Tel: (519) 681-8440
Fax: (519) 681-3465

Windsor
3381 Walker Rd.
Windsor, ON N8W 3R9
Tel: (519) 966-9651
Fax: (519) 966-9651

Quebec
2323 boul du Versant Nord,
Suite 208
Ste-Foy, PQ G1N 4P4
Tel: (418) 681-0609
Fax: (418) 682-6532

Montreal
Plaza Laurier, Suite 400
5115 ave. de Gaspé
Montreal, PQ H2T 3B7
Tel: (514) 273-8578
Fax: (514) 277-1922

New Brunswick and P.E.I.
111 Prince William St.
Saint John, NB E2L 2B2
Tel: (506) 634-8000
Fax: (506) 634-8657

Nova Scotia
1472 Hollis St.
Halifax, NS B3J 1V2
Tel: (902) 429-8101
Fax: (902) 423-6317

Newfoundland
3rd Floor
Terrace on the Square
(Churchill Square)
8-10 Rowan St.
St. John's, NF A1B 2X3
Tel: (709) 754-0757
Fax: (709) 754-0116

29. Canadian Banks Offering Services to Snowbirds

Many Canadian banks provide services and products to Snowbirds. A list of the correspondent banks in the United States, as well as trust and estate management and investor services, are noted. Contact the institutions directly to ask about the following: Snowbird services, programs for seniors, U.S. dollar chequing/savings accounts, U.S. dollar credit cards, mortgage loans for purchase of a U.S. residence, ATM access from U.S. to Canadian accounts, and so forth.

• **AMEX Bank of Canada**
1-800-654-2042 (Canada and the U.S.)

• Bank of Montreal

British Columbia
1-800-663-0241
Alberta
1-800-372-9579
Saskatchewan and Manitoba
1-800-665-0002

Ontario
1-800-387-1342
Québec
1-800-361-1854
Maritimes
1-800-565-7132

Correspondent Banks

Arizona:
 Bank of America, Bank One, First Interstate
California:
 Bank of America, First Interstate, Union Bank, U.S. Bank, Wells Fargo
Florida:
 Barnett, First Union, NationsBank, Sun Bank
Texas:
 Bank of America, Bank One, First Interstate, NationsBank, Texas
 Commerce

Trust and Estate Management

Through the Trust Company of the Bank of Montreal.

Investor Services

Through subsidiaries Nesbitt Burns and InvestorLine Service.

• Bank of Nova Scotia

For information, contact your local branch.

Correspondent Banks

Arizona:
 Bank of America, Bank One, First Interstate
California:
 Bank of America, Bank of California, Bank of Nova Scotia, Standard
 Chartered Bank, Union Bank, Wells Fargo
Florida:
 Barnett, NationsBank, Sun Bank
Texas:
 Bank One, NationsBank, Texas Commerce

Trust and Estate Management

Through subsidiaries Scotiatrust and Montreal Trust.

Investor Services
Full brokerage service through subsidiary ScotiaMcLeod; discount brokerage with Scotia Securities.

● **Canada Trust**
1-800-668-8888 (Canada and the U.S.)

Correspondent Bank
Owns First Federal Savings & Loans of Rochester, New York.

Trust and Estate Management
Full range of services.

Investor Services
Mutual funds through subsidiary CT Fund Services.

● **Canadian Imperial Bank of Commerce**
1-800-465-2422 (Canada and the U.S.)

Correspondent Banks
Arizona:
    Bank of America, First Interstate
California:
    Bank of America, First Interstate
Florida:
    Barnett, First Union, NationsBank, Sun Bank
Texas:
    NationsBank, Texas Commerce

Trust and Estate Management
Through subsidiary CIBC Trust Corp.

Investor Services
Through subsidiary Wood Gundy.

● **Royal Bank of Canada**
1-800-263-9191 (English)
1-800-363-3967 (French)

Correspondent Banks
Arizona:
    Bank One, Citibank

California:
    Bank of America, Bank of California, City National Bank, First Interstate
    Bank of California, Union Bank
Florida:
    Nationsbank, Royal Bank of Canada, Sun Bank
Texas:
    Texas Commerce

Trust and Estate Management
Through subsidiary Royal Trust.

Investor Services
Through subsidiary RBC Dominion Securities; discount brokerage through
Royal Bank Investor Trading.

• Toronto-Dominion Bank
1-800-465-2265 (Canada and the U.S.)

Correspondent Banks
Arizona:
    Bank One, First Interstate
California:
    Bank of America, First Interstate, Wells Fargo
Florida:
    Barnett, Sun Bank
Texas:
    Bank One, Texas Commerce

Trust and Estate Management
Through subsidiary TD Trust.

Investor Services
Through subsidiaries TD Asset Management and Evergreen Investment Ser-
vices; discount brokerage through Green Line Investor Services; Green Line
Mutual Funds.

30. U.S. Banks Offering Services to Snowbirds

Many U.S. banks in Sunbelt states offer Canadians such services as: seniors'
programs, investment services, U.S. dollar credit cards (to winter residents),
mortgage loans for a U.S. residence, personal loans and lines of credit, and
estate and tax planning. Contact the institutions below for more detail.

Bank Atlantic
Tel: (305) 764-3111
1-800-741-1700

Bank One
Tel: (602) 248-0608
1-800-366-BANK (2265)

Barnett Bank
1-800-441-2299 (from U.S.)
1-800-553-9024 (from Canada)

Citibank
1-800-374-9800

Dean Witter
Arizona:
Tel: (602) 945-4331
(collect from Canada)
1-800-347-5107 (from U.S.)
Florida:
Tel: (407) 394-8632
1-800-473-2020

Desjardins Federal SB
Tel: (305) 454-1001

Republic Bank
Tel: (813) 796-2900

Sun Bank
1-800-382-3232 (from Florida)
1-800-458-4984 (from Canada)

31. Elderhostel

Elderhostel is a nonprofit organization serving the educational needs of older adults. An extensive range of programs is offered in Canada and the United States, and internationally. Participants are usually retired or planning retirement and in their mid-to-late fifties and beyond. There are approximately 600,000 members in the United States and 70,000 in Canada. Membership and program catalogues are free.

Elderhostel U.S.
75 Federal St.
Boston, MA 02110-1941
Tel: (617) 426-7788
Fax: (617) 426-8351

For programs offered in the United States, Canada, and internationally. There are also programs for people with RVs. Note, the Canadian programs offered through this office in Boston are *different* ones than those offered by Elderhostel Canada. Produces 12 catalogues a year: 4 for the United States and Canada (combined), 4 for international programs, and 4 supplemental catalogues. To be placed on the mailing list for all 12 catalogues, send a cheque for $14 in Canadian funds to cover postage costs. Programs through Elderhostel U.S. are paid in U.S. dollars. Canadians who wish to participate in programs through Elderhostel U.S. must meet U.S. age eligibility requirements. At present the age minimum is 60 for one person and the spouse must be at least 50 years old. There is a different age requirement for Canada (see below).

Elderhostel Canada
308 Wellington St.
Kingston, ON K7K 7A7
Tel: (613) 530-2222
Fax: (613) 530-2096

For programs offered in Canada and internationally. Produces four catalogues a year. There is no fee to cover postage costs within Canada. Programs through Elderhostel Canada are paid in Canadian dollars. The age requirement in Canada is a minimum of 55 years for one person and at least 50 years for the spouse.

32. RV Buyers' and Users' Guides

When you begin shopping for your RV, buyers' guides and users' guides are invaluable sources of information. Buyers' guides categorize RVs by type, and provide model and manufacturer names, features, photos, and prices. Users' guides provide information to help you get the most from your RV. Many of these publications can be found at local bookstores and libraries. They can also be purchased directly from the publishers listed here.

Chevy Outdoors:
Practical Guide to RVs
The Aegis Group
30400 Van Dyke
Warren, MI 48093
(313) 575-9400
$3.00

RV Repair and Maintenance
Manual
T.L. Enterprises
3601 Calle Tecate
Camarillo, CA 93012
(805) 389-0300
$19.95 plus postage

RV How-To Guide
Woodall Publishing Co.
28167 N. Keith Dr.
Lake Forest, IL 60045
(708) 362-6700
$6.95 plus $2.50 postage

Woodall's RV Buyer's Guide
Woodall Publishing Co.
28167 N. Keith Dr.
Lake Forest, IL 60045
(708) 362-6700
$5.50 plus $2.75 postage

Woodall's RV Owner's Handbook
Woodall Publishing Co.
28167 N. Keith Dr.
Lake Forest, IL 60045
(708) 362-6700
Vol. 1: Illustrated introduction to RV basics, $7.95 plus $2 postage
Vol. 2: Illustrations on the operation of major RV systems, $7.95 plus $2 postage
Vol. 3: Emergency and money-saving repairs and preventive maintenance, $7.95 plus $2 postage

33. RV Dealers'Associations

United States

To find out more about U.S. RV dealers or rental agencies in your area or at your destination, contact the RV dealers' associations below for information about their members.

Arizona RV Dealers' Association
2038 N. Country Club Drive
Mesa, AZ 85201
(602) 834-9581

Florida RV Trade Association
401 N. Parsons Ave., Suite 107
Brandon, FL 33510-4538
(813) 684-7882

**Recreation Vehicle Dealers'
Association (National)**
3930 University Dr.
Fairfax, VA 22030
(703) 591-7130

**Recreation Vehicle Industry
Association**
P.O. Box 2999, Dept. SL
Reston, VA 22090-0999
1-800-47SUNNY (78669)

**Southern California RV Dealers'
Association**
1201 Baldwin Park Blvd.
Baldwin Park, CA 91706-5877
(818) 960-1884

Texas RV Association
3355 Bee Caves Rd., Suite 104
Austin, TX 78746-6751
(512) 327-4514

Canada

Contact the recreation vehicle dealers' association (RVDA) in your province to obtain information on RV dealers, clubs, magazines, and shows.

RVDA of British Columbia, Langley. Tel.: (604) 533-4200
RVDA of Alberta, Edmonton. Tel.: (403) 455-8562
RVDA of Saskatchewan, Regina. Currently being formed. Check with directory assistance

RVDA of Manitoba, Winnipeg. Tel.: (204) 256-6119
Ontario RVDA, Brechin. Tel.: (705) 484-0295
RVDA of Quebec, Montreal. Tel.: (514) 338-1471
RVDA of Nova Scotia, Dartmouth. Tel.: (902) 462-4747

34. RV Rental Sources

The growing popularity of RVs means outlets nationwide now rent motorhomes, folding camping trailers, and other vehicles. Many offer packages that include airline and railway connections for fly-drive and rail-drive plans. One-way and off-season rates are also available from some dealers.

Check your Yellow Pages under "Recreation Vehicles—Renting and Leasing" for local sources or try the following contacts for locations nationwide.

Cruise America
11 Westhampton Ave.
Mesa, AZ 85210
Tel: (602) 464-7300
1-800-327-7799
Nationwide motorhome rentals.

Go Vacations, Inc.
777 W. 190th St.
Gardenia, CA 90248
Tel: (310) 326-0555
1-800-487-4652
Local, national, fly-drives,
and one-way options.

Recreation Vehicle Rental Association
3930 University Dr.
Fairfax, VA 22030
Tel: (703) 591-7130
1-800-336-0355
"Rental Ventures," a 32-page brochure including a free copy of "Who's Who in RV Rentals," is available for $7.50 first class, $6.50 third class prepaid.

Rental Management Systems
1201 Baldwin Park Blvd.
Baldwin Park, CA 91706
(818) 960-1884

35. U.S. Campground Directories

Campground directories provide comparative information on camping locations across the United States, and their fees and facilities. Directories are available at local bookstores, public libraries, or directly from the publishers listed here. In addition, the National Association of RV Parks and Campgrounds, also listed below, has free individual state directories of its members for a nominal handling charge of $1 per state.

AAA Campbooks
(11 regional U.S./Canada editions)
Contact a local CAA or AAA
chapter for information.

**KOA Directory/Road Atlas/
Camping Guide**
Kampgrounds of America, Inc.
P.O. Box 30558
Billings, MT 59114
Tel: (406) 248-7444
$3 by mail or free at any KOA
campground in North America.

**National Association of RV Parks
and Campgrounds**
8605 Westwood Centre Drive, #201
Vienna, VA 22182
Tel: (703) 734-3000

**Trailer Life Campground &
RV Services Directory**
TL Enterprises
P.O. Box 6888
Englewood, CO 80155-6888
$19.95

**Wheelers Recreational Vehicle
Resort & Campground Guide**
Print Media Services
1310 Jarvis Ave.
Elk Grove Village, IL 60007
Tel: (708) 981-0100
$12.95 plus $2.50 postage

**Woodall's Campground
Directories**
Woodall Publishing Co.
28167 N. Keith Dr.
Lake Forest, IL 60045
Tel: (708) 362-6700
North American Edition, $16.95
plus $3.75 postage
Eastern edition, $10.95
plus $2.75 postage
Western edition, $10.95
plus $2.75 postage

Woodall's Camping Guides
Woodall Publishing Co.
28167 N. Keith Dr.
Lake Forest, IL 60045
Tel: (708) 362-6700
Eight regional editions:
each $6.95 plus $2.50 postage

**Yogi Bear's Jellystone Park
Campground Directory**
Leisure Systems, Inc.
6201 Kellogg Ave.
Cincinnati, OH 45230
1-800-558-2954

36. Campground Chains

Several well-known companies operate U.S.-wide chains of campgrounds
with dependable standards of quality and service. Properties range from safe,
convenient places to spend a travel night to full-service family resorts. Contact their national headquarters for information about locations in areas you
would like to visit.

**Best Holiday Trav-L-Park
Association**
1310 Jarvis Ave.
Elk Grove Village, IL 60007
Tel: (708) 981-0100

Kampgrounds of America (KOA)
P.O. Box 30558
Billings, MT 59114
Tel: (406) 248-7444

Leisure Systems, Inc.
Yogi Bear's Jellystone Park
Camp-Resorts
6201 Kellogg Ave.
Cincinnati, OH 45230
1-800-558-2954

37. Camping on Public Lands

Camping facilities on public lands are generally simple and rustic but set amid some of the most spectacular scenery in the United States.

Thousands of campsites can be found on lands supervised by U.S. federal agencies including the National Park Service, USDA Forest Service, Bureau of Land Management, and U.S. Army Corps of Engineers. These sites are convenient to scenic byways, waterways, trails, and numerous outdoor recreation activities. Parks managed by state and local governments also offer a wealth of camping opportunities.

Contact the agencies listed here to request specific information and publications.

Bureau of Land Management
For camping information, write: Bureau of Land Management, 1849 C Street N.W., Room 5600, Washington, DC 20240.

National Park Service
For a "National Park Camping Guide" send $4 to the U.S. Government Printing Office, Superintendent of Documents, Washington, DC 20402-3925. Request #024-005-01080-7. For campground reservations call 1-800-452-1111.

U.S. Army Corps of Engineers
For camping information, write: Department of the Army, U.S.A.C.E., Regional Brochures, IM-MV-N, 3909 Halls Ferry Rd., Vicksburg, MS 39180-6199.

USDA Forest Service
For a free list of national forests, write: USDA Forest Service, Office of Information, P.O. Box 96090, Washington, DC 20090. For campground reservations call 1-800-283-CAMP.

38. Camping Clubs

Camping clubs let people share good times while exploring the country and enjoying a great way of life. National and brand-name camping clubs listed below sponsor fun-filled rallies and caravans, led by experienced "wagon-masters", who act as escorts and tour guides.

Clubs also offer travel services like mail forwarding and provide camping information through club magazines and newsletters (shown in italics). Club members are part of a network of friends who enjoy the camaraderie and social atmosphere at campgrounds and RV parks across the United States. For a list of Canadian RV clubs, contact a provincial RV dealers' association. Refer to item 33, Appendix A.

Escapee Club
100 Rainbow Dr.
Livingston, TX 77351
Tel: (409) 327-8873

Family Campers and RVers
4804 Transit Rd., Building 2
Depew, NY 14043
Tel: (716) 668-6242
Camping Today

Family Motor Coach Association
8291 Clough Pike
Cincinnati, OH 45244
Tel: (513) 474-3622
1-800-543-3622
Family Motor Coaching
(Motorhome owners only)

The Good Sam Club
P.O. Box 6060
Camarillo, CA 93011
Tel: (805) 389-0300
1-800-234-3450 (U.S. only)

**The International Family
Recreation Association**
P.O. Box 6279
Pensacola, FL 32503-0279
Tel: (904) 944-7864
The Recreation Advisor

Loners of America
Rt. 2, Box 85E
Ellsinore, MO 63937-9520
Tel: (314) 322-5548
Loners of America News

Loners on Wheels
P.O. Box 1355
Poplar Bluff, MO 63902
Fax: (314) 785-2420

The National RV Owners' Club
P.O. Drawer 17148
Pensacola, FL 32522-7148
Tel: (904) 944-7864

**North American Family Campers
Association Inc.**
P.O. Box 2701
Springfield, MA 01101
Tel: (413) 283-4742
Campfire Chatter

RV Elderhostel
75 Federal St.
Boston, MA 02110-1941
Tel: (617) 426-7788

RVing Women
21413 W. Lost Lake Rd.
Snohomish, WA 98290
1-800-333-9992, ext. 90050

39. Publications for RV Owners and Campers

There is a host of publications dedicated to RV travel and camping. Several cater exclusively to the RV lifestyle, offering destination tips, product reviews, and RV cooking recipes. They also include RV rally and show information so RVers can keep up with the latest news from their favourite brand-name or camping club. Write or phone the publications below and ask to be sent a complimentary copy. For a list of Canadian RV publications, contact a provincial RV dealers' association. Refer to item 33, Appendix A.

Campers Monthly
(Mid-Atlantic and Northeast editions)
P.O. Box 260
Quakertown, PA 18951
Tel: (215) 361-7255
(11 issues) $10/year

Camperways
Woodall Publishing Co.
28167 N. Keith Dr.
Lake Forest, IL 60045
Tel: (708) 362-6700
(monthly) $15/year

Camping and RV Magazine
P.O. Box 458
Washburn, WI 54891
Tel: (715) 373-5556
(monthly) $17.95/year

Camp-orama
Woodall Publishing Co.
28167 N. Keith Dr.
Lake Forest, IL 60045
Tel: (708) 362-6700
(monthly) $15/year

Chevy Outdoors
P.O. Box 2063
Warren, MI 48090
Tel: (313) 575-9400
(4 issues) $8/year

Disabled Outdoors
2052 W. 23rd St.
Chicago, IL 60608
Tel: (312) 358-4160
(4 issues) $10/year

Family Motor Coaching
8291 Clough Pike
Cincinnati, OH 45244
Tel: (513) 474-3622
1-800-543-3622
(monthly) $24/year

Go Camping America
P.O. Box 2669, Dept. 23
Reston, VA 22090
Free vacation planner on request. Lists many helpful sources of information.

Highways
TL Enterprises, Inc.
3601 Calle Tecate
Camarillo, CA 93012
Tel: (805) 389-0300
(monthly) $6/year

Midwest Outdoors
111 Shore Dr.
Hinsdale, IL 60521
Tel: (708) 887-7722
(monthly) $11.95

Motorhome
TL Enterprises, Inc.
3601 Calle Tecate
Camarillo, CA 93012
Tel: (805) 389-0300
(monthly) $24/year

Northeast Outdoors
70 Edwin Ave., Box 2180
Waterbury, CT 06722
Tel: (203) 755-0158
(monthly) $8/year

"Plan-It-Pack-It-Go" Camping Guide
Woodall Publishing Co.
28167 N. Keith Dr.
Lake Forest, IL 60045
Tel: (708) 362-6700
504 pages; $11.95 plus $2.75 postage

The Recreation Advisor
Recreation World Services, Inc.
P.O. Box 6279, Dept. 5N
Pensacola, FL 32503-0279
Tel: (904) 477-7992
(10 issues) $15/year

RV Lifestyle Publications Catalog
Recreation Vehicle Industry
Association
P.O. Box 2999, Dept. POF
Reston, VA 22090-0999
Free with self-addressed stamped
($.52 postage) long envelope.
(Lists many helpful RV/camping
publications that can be ordered by
mail.)

RV Times
Royal Productions Inc.
P.O. Box 6294
Richmond, VA 23230
Tel: (804) 288-5653
(11 issues) $15/year

RV Today
4005 - 20th Ave. W., Suite 110
Fisherman's Terminal
Seattle, WA 98199
Tel: (206) 282-7545
(monthly) $12/year

RV West
4133 Mohr Ave., Suite 1
Pleasanton, CA 94566
Tel: (510) 426-3200
(monthly) $12/year

Southern RV
Woodall Publishing Co.
28167 N. Keith Dr.
Lake Forest, IL 60045
Tel: (708) 362-6700
(monthly) $15/year

Trailer Life
TL Enterprises, Inc.
3601 Calle Tecate
Camarillo, CA 93012
Tel: (805) 389-0300
(monthly) $22/year

Trails-A-Way
Woodall Publishing Co.
28167 N. Keith Dr.
Lake Forest, IL 60045
Tel: (708) 362-6700
(monthly) $15/year

Western RV News
1350 S.W. Upland Dr., Suite B
Portland, OR 97221
Tel: (503) 222-1255
(monthly) $8/year

Workamper News
201 Hiram Rd., HCR 34, Box 125
Heber Springs, AR 72543
Tel: (501) 362-2637
(6 issues) $18/year

40. Membership and Ownership Type of RV Resorts

A unique form of travel option is available through several networks of membership and ownership camping and RV resorts across the United States. Fees and privileges vary, but all membership and ownership resorts allow members to stay at "home" campgrounds and affiliated member resorts. Free or nominal-cost stays are available for prospective members to try out the concept.

These properties are generally open only to members and owners, but some have rental sites, park trailers, and cabins available, making them an ideal vacation spot for those who don't own an RV. There are numerous amenities and activities, including golf, health clubs, and social events.

Contact the following companies for information on locations, membership, sales, and rental availability:

Coast to Coast Resorts
64 Inverness Dr. E.
Englewood, CO 80112
Tel: (303) 790-2267

Resort Parks International
P.O. Box 7738
Long Beach, CA 90807
1-800-635-8498

Leisure Systems, Inc.
Safari/Jellystone Parks
6201 Kellogg Avenue
Cincinnati, OH 45230
1-800-558-2954

Thousand Trails NACO West
12301 N.E. 10th Place
Bellevue, WA 98005
Tel: (206) 455-3155

Outdoor Resorts of America, Inc.
2400 Crestmoor Road
Nashville, TN 37215
Tel: (615) 244-5237

41. Selecting a Tow Vehicle

Matching the right tow vehicle with an appropriate RV is easier now than ever. Today's van conversions, 4 x 4s, light trucks, most full-size cars, and many mid-size cars come with engines that offer the horsepower and fuel economy to make them choice vehicles. For further information on which vehicles are suitable for RV towing, consult the auto manufacturers' towing guide available from the companies listed below, or visit your local auto dealer.

Ford Motor Company
300 Ren Cen, P.O. Box 43306
Detroit, MI 48243

GMC Truck
General Motors Corp.
Customer Service Division
31 Judson St.
Pontiac, MI 48058

Toyota Motor Sales U.S.A., Inc.
19001 S. Western Ave.
Torrance, CA 90509

Chevrolet vehicle information is available through their computerized system "Spec Manager" at local dealers.

The "Dodge Trailer Towing Guide" is also available through local dealers.

42. RV Retail Shows

Recreation vehicle retail shows, which are often sponsored by local dealerships, offer you the opportunity to see many makes and models of RVs in one location. This is helpful when comparison-shopping for a vehicle that will fit your travel plans and budget. Shows let you talk in person with RV industry experts who can assist you in finding the right RV.

There are annual RV shows in every region of Canada and the United States. Watch your local television stations and newspapers for notices about an RV show in your area, or contact your closest RV dealer. For a free list of shows in the United States, write to:

Recreational Vehicle Industry Association
P.O. Box 2999, Dept. SL
Reston, VA 22090-0999

43. Scenic Byways in the United States

If you are planning to travel in your RV or car, you probably wish to select scenic routes wherever possible. In addition to taking you off crowded highways, these networks of "Scenic Byways" offer views of mountains, forests, historical sights, and great waterways. For more information, write to:

Scenic Byways
The American Recreation Coalition
1331 Pennsylvania Ave. N.W., Suite 726
Washington, DC 20004

APPENDIX

B

Suggested Reading

Many excellent books and publications are available to enhance your retirement and Snowbird experience. Most are available at your local library or bookstore. Some booklets are free for the asking. Here is a selected listing of books on lifestyles and leisure time, where to retire, retirement planning and retirement, tax and money management, travel, senior travel, discount shopping, and running your own business.

1. Books on Lifestyles, Leisure Time, and Health

Gault, Jan. *Free Time: Making Your Leisure Count.* New York: John Wiley & Sons, 1991.

McCants, Louise, and Robert Cavett. *Retire to Fun and Freedom.* New York: Warner Books, 1990.

Michaels, Joseph. *Prime of Your Life: A Practical Guide to Your Mature Years.* New York: Little, Brown, 1991.

Shephard, Roy J., and Scott G. Thomas. *Fit after Fifty: Feel Better—Live Longer.* Vancouver: Self-Counsel Press, 1989.

Underwood, Richard D., and Brenda Breeden Underwood. *Wise and Healthy Living: A Comprehensive Approach to Aging Well.* Vancouver: Self-Counsel Press, 1989.

2. Books on Where to Retire

United States

Brooks, Mary Lucier. *Retirement Communities in Florida.* Sarasota: Pineapple Press, 1993.

Dickinson, Peter. *Sunbelt Retirement.* Washington, DC: Regnery Publishing, 1992.

Giese, Lester J., L. Anne Thornton, and William Kinnaman. *The 99 Best Residential and Recreational Communities in America.* New York: John Wiley & Sons, 1992.

Howells, John. *Where to Retire: Your Travel Guide to America's Best Places.* Oakland, CA: Gateway Books, 1991.

Rosenberg, Lee, and Saralee H. Rosenberg. *50 Fabulous Places to Retire in America.* Hawthorne, NJ: Career Press, 1991.

Savageau, David. *Retirement Places Rated: All You Need to Plan Your Retirement or Select Your Second Home.* New York: Prentice-Hall, 1990.

Warner, Diana. *How to Have a Great Retirement on a Limited Budget.* Cincinnati: Writer's Digest Books, 1992.

Outside Canada and the United States

Howells, John. *Choose Costa Rica: A Guide to Retirement and Investment.* Oakland, CA: Gateway Books, 1994.

Howells, John, and Don Merwin. *Choose Mexico: Live Well on $800 a Month.* Oakland, CA: Gateway Books, 1994.

Symons, Allane, and Jane Parker. *Adventures Abroad: Exploring the Travel/ Retirement Option.* Oakland, CA: Gateway Books, 1991.

3. Books on Retirement Planning and Retirement

Bolles, Richard N. *The Three Boxes of Life and How to Get out of Them.* Berkeley, CA: Ten Speed Press, 1978.

Danilov, Dan, and Howard David Deutsch. *Immigrating to the U.S.A.* Vancouver: Self-Counsel Press, 1993.

Fyock, Catherine Dorton, and Anne Marrs Dorton. *Unretirement: A Career Guide for the Retired, the Soon to Be Retired, and the Never Want to be Retired.* New York: AMACOM Publishing, 1994.

Gray, Douglas A., et al. *Risk-Free Retirement: A Complete Canadian Planning Guide.* Whitley, ON: McGraw-Hill Ryerson, 1993.

Howells, John. *Retirement on a Shoestring.* Oakland, CA: Gateway Books, 1992.

Hunnisett, Henry S. *Retirement Guide for Canadians.* Vancouver: Self-Counsel Press, 1991.

Wilson, Jim. *Housing Options for Older Canadians.* Vancouver: Self-Counsel Press, 1991.

Wyman, Jack. *Retired? Get Back in the Game: 37 Stories of Vibrant Men and Women Who Are Joyously Productive.* Scottsdale, AZ: Doer Publications, 1994.

Free Booklets and Pamphlets

- Published by the Canadian Bankers' Association:
  - *Steps to Retirement*
  Available through any bank.

- Published by the Canadian Life and Health Insurance Association:
  - *Planning for a Successful Retirement*
  - *Planning for Success: Taking Charge of Your Financial Future*
  - *Retirement: As You'd Like It*
  All available by phoning 1-800-268-8099.

- Published by the Royal Bank of Canada:
  - *Retirement*
  Available from any Royal Bank.

- Published by Canada Deposit Insurance Corporation:
  - *CDIC: We Have a Lot of Answers about Deposit Insurance*
  Available from any bank or credit union.

- Published by Canada Mortgage and Housing Corporation:
  - *Housing for Older Canadians: New Financial and Tenure Options*
  - *NHA Mortgage-Backed Securities: Your Questions Answered*
  Available by contacting your closest CMHC office.

4. Books on Tax and Money Management

Books on Canadian tax planning and tips, as well as tips, strategies, or issues to consider when living, investing, working, or operating a business in the United States are noted below. Some of these books may be free for the asking from major Canadian chartered accountancy firms. Check with them about other publications. Refer to the Yellow Pages under "Accountants— Chartered." Other books are available in your local library or bookstore.

Budd, John S. *Second Property Strategies* (2nd edition). Whitby, ON: McGraw-Hill Ryerson, 1995.

Budd, John S., et al. *Canadian Guide to Personal Financial Management.* Scarborough, ON: Prentice-Hall. Annual.

Cohen, Bruce. *The Money Adviser.* Toronto: Stoddart Publishing. Annual.

Deloitte and Touche. *How to Reduce the Tax You Pay.* Toronto: Key Porter Books. Annual.

Jacks, Evelyn. *Jacks on Tax Savings.* Whitby, ON: McGraw-Hill Ryerson. Annual.

Jacks, Evelyn. *Jacks' Tax Tips.* Whitby, ON: McGraw-Hill Ryerson. Annual.

McCarley, Bruce D. *Retirement Planning: A Guide for Canadians.* Toronto: Key Porter Books, 1994.

Publications Free from Accountancy Firms

Deloitte Touche Tohmatsu International
• *United States: International Tax and Business Guide*

Coopers and Lybrand
• *Foreign Nationals Working in the U.S.: Tax and Other Matters*
• *Tax Aspects of Doing Business in the U.S.: A Guide for Foreign Companies*
• *Tax Planning Checklist*
• *U.S. Expatriate Tax Planning: A Practical Approach*

5. Books on Travel

Many travel books can help maximize your travelling enjoyment and experience. Check with your local library, bookstore, travel companies, and auto clubs. Obtain the free tourist kits from each state (refer to item 18 in Appendix A). Pick up the various books available on travelling in the United States published by the AAA. Contact your local branch of the Canadian Automobile Association (CAA) (see item 27 in Appendix A). Also check the state and local editions of annually updated travel guides published by the following companies. They contain maps, details of interesting sites, history, and information about accommodation and restaurants.

• Berlitz
• Blue Guides
• Fodor
• Frommers
• Insight
• Michelin
• Thomas Cook

Bruns, Rebecca, et al. *Hidden Mexico: The Adventurer's Guide to Beaches and Coasts.* Berkeley, CA: Ulysses Press, 1994.
Delaney, John F. *Travelwise: A Guide to Safety, Security and Convenience When You Travel.* Vancouver: Self-Counsel Press, 1990.
Farewell, Susan, et al. *Hidden New England: The Adventurer's Guide.* Berkeley, CA: Ulysses Press, 1994.
Gleasner, Bill, and Diana Gleasner. *Florida off the Beaten Path: A Guide to Unique Places.* Old Saybrook, CT: Globe Pequot Press, 1994.
Leslie, Candace. *Hidden Florida Keys and Everglades: The Adventurer's Guide.* Berkeley, CA: Ulysses Press, 1994.

Pager, Sean. *Hawaii off the Beaten Path: A Guide to Unique Places.*
    Old Saybrook, CT: Globe Pequot Press, 1994.
Path, Jim, et al. *Hidden Pacific Northwest: The Adventurer's Guide.*
    Berkeley, CA: Ulysses Press, 1994.
Riegert, Ray. *Hidden Coast of California: The Adventurer's Guide.*
    Berkeley, CA: Ulysses Press, 1994.
Riegert, Ray. *Hidden Hawaii: The Adventurer's Guide.* Berkeley, CA:
    Ulysses Press, 1994.
Riegert, Ray. *Hidden San Francisco and Northern California.* Berkeley, CA:
    Ulysses Press, 1992.
Riegert, Ray. *Hidden Southern California.* Berkeley, CA: Ulysses Press,
    1994.
Ritz, Stacy, and Candace Leslie. *Hidden Florida: The Adventurer's Guide.*
    Berkeley, CA: Ulysses Press, 1994.
Rodriguez, June Nayler. *Texas off the Beaten Path: A Guide to Unique
    Places.* Old Saybrook, CT: Globe Pequot Press, 1994.
Scarborough, Carolyn, et al. *Hidden Southwest: The Adventurer's Guide.*
    Berkeley, CA: Ulysses Press, 1994.
Staats, Todd R. *New Mexico off the Beaten Path: A Guide to Unique Places.*
    Old Saybrook, CT: Globe Pequot Press, 1994.

6. Books on Senior Travel

Algar, Michael, and Pam Hobbs. *Free to Travel: The Canadian Guide for 50
    Plus Travelers.* Toronto: Doubleday, 1994.
Cannon, Shirley, and Robin Cannon. *50 Plus Globetrotting: The World of
    Senior Adult Travel.* Toronto: Prime Books, 1992.
Howells, John. *RV Travel in Mexico.* Oakland, CA: Gateway Books, 1989.
Malott, Gene, and Adela Malott. *Get up and Go: A Guide for the Mature
    Traveller.* Oakland, CA: Gateway Books, 1989.
Sullivan, Donald L. *A Senior's Guide to Healthy Travel.* Hawthorne, NJ:
    Career Press/Monarch Books, 1995.

7. Books on Discount Shopping

Ellis, Iris. *Fabulous Finds: The Sophisticated Shopper's Guide to Factory
    Outlet Centers.* Cincinnati: Writer's Digest Books, 1991.

8. Books on Running Your Own Business

Arkebauer, James B. *Golden Entrepreneuring: The Mature Person's Guide
    to Starting a Successful Business.* New York, NY: McGraw-Hill, 1995.
Cooke, Ronald J., and Marg Alice Daly. *Money-Making Ideas for Seniors.*
    Toronto, ON: Stoddart Publishing, 1989.

Gray, Douglas A. *Have You Got What It Takes? The Entrepreneur's Complete Self-Assessment Guide.* Vancouver: Self-Counsel Press, 1993.

Gray, Douglas A. *Start and Run a Profitable Consulting Business* (4th edition). Vancouver: Self-Counsel Press, 1995.

Gray, Douglas A., and Donald Cyr. *Marketing Your Product* (2nd edition). Vancouver: Self-Counsel Press, 1993.

Gray, Douglas A., and Norman Friend. *The Complete Canadian Franchise Guide.* Whitby, ON: McGraw-Hill Ryerson, 1994.

Gray, Douglas A., and Brian Nattress. *Raising Money: The Canadian Guide to Successful Business Financing.* Whitby, ON: McGraw-Hill Ryerson, 1993.

Gray, Douglas A., and Diana L. Gray. *The Complete Canadian Small Business Guide* (2nd edition). Whitby, ON: McGraw-Hill Ryerson, 1994.

Gray, Douglas A., and Diana L. Gray. *Home Inc.: The Canadian Home-Based Business Guide* (2nd edition). Whitby, ON: McGraw-Hill Ryerson, 1994.

May, Bess R. *Starting and Operating a Business after You Retire: What You Need to Know to Succeed.* Garden City Park, NY: Avery Publications, 1993.

Rogak, Lisa A. *100 Best Retirement Businesses.* Dover, NH: Upstart Publishing Group, 1994.

APPENDIX
C

Retirement, Financial, and Estate Planning Checklist

By completing this extensive checklist, you will focus on key points and issues as well as assemble information, all of which will assist you in developing a financial and estate plan. It will help clarify your wishes when you discuss your needs with your lawyer, tax accountant, financial planner, or financial institution. It will also enhance your peace of mind to know your affairs are in order when you head to the United States for an extended stay. This checklist should be dated, and reviewed and updated annually; a copy should be kept in your safety deposit box. Some items may not apply to everyone. Although this checklist highlights many key areas, your advisors can suggest additional issues for you to detail in your specific situation.

Index of Topic Headings

A. Personal Information
B. Current Financial Net Worth
C. Current and Projected Retirement or Snowbird Monthly Income and Expenses
D. Banking Information
E. Real Estate
F. Personal Property
G. Investment Portfolio
H. Tax Shelters
I. Investments/Ownerships in Businesses
J. Insurance
K. Projected/Potential Financial Needs
L. Where Your Retirement Income Will Come From
M. Retirement Life Values, Interests, and Preferences
N. Retirement Planning Goals

A. PERSONAL INFORMATION

		You	**Your Spouse**
1.	Name (full)	_____	_____
	Address (Canadian)	_____	_____
	City/Province	_____	_____
	Postal Code	_____	_____
	Phone Numbers: residence	_____	_____
	work	_____	_____
	Fax Numbers: residence	_____	_____
	work	_____	_____
	Address (U.S.)	_____	_____
	City/State	_____	_____
	Zip Code	_____	_____
	Phone Numbers: residence	_____	_____
	work	_____	_____
	Fax Numbers: residence	_____	_____
	work	_____	_____
	Date of Birth	_____	_____
	Place of Birth	_____	_____
	Citizenship	_____	_____
	Social Insurance Number	_____	_____
	Place of Marriage* (if applicable) (*Specify whether legal or common-law)	_____	_____
	Name of Doctor (Canada)	_____	_____
	Name of Doctor (U.S.)	_____	_____

2. **Children** (indicate if by previous marriage of you or your spouse, adopted, or born in a common-law relationship)

Name	Date of Birth	Married?	Telephone Number(s)	Dependent On You?

3. **Grandchildren**

Name	Date of Birth

4. **Other Dependents**

Name	Date of Birth	Telephone Number(s)	Relationship to You

5. Have you entered into a pre-marriage or other marriage contract with your spouse? If so, outline a summary of the contract's terms. Where is the document located?

6. If you or your spouse were previously married, describe any remaining financial obligations (e.g., child support, alimony).

Obligations	You	Your Spouse
Name of former spouse	_____	_____
Address	_____	_____
City/Province or State	_____	_____
Postal or Zip Code	_____	_____
Social Insurance Number	_____	_____
Phone Numbers: residence	_____	_____
work	_____	_____

7. If you or your spouse have any prospective inheritances, detail sources, approximate amounts, and possible dates of receipt.

8. Explain any present or potential special support needs (e.g., for a disabled child, spouse, or parent).

9. **Location of Documents and Other Information**

Item	Location
1) Birth certificates	_____
2) Marriage certificate	_____
3) Children's birth certificates	_____
4) Pre-marriage agreements or marriage contracts	_____
5) Maintenance, alimony, or custody orders	_____

6) Divorce decrees or separation
    agreements   _____

7) Husband's latest will and any codicils   _____

8) Wife's latest will and any codicils   _____

9) Husband's Power of Attorney   _____

10) Wife's Power of Attorney   _____

11) Wills of family members, if pertinent   _____

12) Passports   _____

13) Citizenship papers   _____

14) Cemetery deeds   _____

15) Directions regarding burial   _____

16) List of heirs   _____

17) Medical records   _____

18) Insurance policies   _____

      – Life   _____

      – Disability   _____

      – Out-of-country medical   _____

      – Property   _____

      – Automobile   _____

      – Home   _____

      – Other   _____

19) Stocks   _____

20) Bonds   _____

21) Term deposits   _____

22) Investment certificates   _____

23) Notes or mortgages receivable _____

24) Real estate documents _____

25) Leases _____

26) Inventory of assets of estate _____

27) Appraisals _____

28) Bank books _____

29) Financial records _____

30) Income tax returns _____
(personal and business)

31) Valuation day documents _____
(value of asset as of 1972, if applicable,
for taxation value base purposes)

32) If you own a business, balance sheets _____
and profit/loss statements for last 5 years

33) Business agreements _____

34) Employment contracts _____

35) Employee benefit plan documents _____

36) Buy-sell agreements if a shareholder _____
in a business

37) Partnership or shareholder agreements if _____
in a business

38) Trust agreements _____

39) Promissory notes (personal and business) _____

40) Loan documents (personal and business) _____

41) Automobile ownership documents _____
(personal and business)

42) RRSP/RRIF records _____

43) Pension plan documentation _____
(government and/or employer)

44) List of bank accounts _____

45) List of credit card/charge accounts _____

46) Miscellaneous documents _____

47) Other _____

10. **Advisors**

Lawyer   Name   _____

                   Address _____

                   Phone   _____

Accountant   Name   _____

                   Address _____

                   Phone   _____

Financial Planner Name   _____

                   Address _____

                   Phone   _____

Life and other Insurance Agents

                   Name   _____

                   Address _____

                   Phone   _____

Financial Institution

                   Name   _____

                   Address _____

                   Phone   _____

Banker   Name   _____

                   Address _____

                   Phone   _____

Investment Dealer

Name _____

Address _____

Phone _____

Other

Name _____

Address _____

Phone _____

B. CURRENT FINANCIAL NET WORTH

Liquid Assets (Can be relatively quickly converted into cash)	**You**	**Your Spouse**
Term deposits/GICs	$ _____	$ _____
Chequing accounts	_____	_____
Savings accounts	_____	_____
Stocks	_____	_____
Bonds	_____	_____
Term deposits (savings)	_____	_____
Pensions (government or employer)	_____	_____
Annuities	_____	_____
RRSPs/RRIFs/LIFs	_____	_____
Life insurance cash surrender value	_____	_____
Demand loans	_____	_____
– family	_____	_____
– other	_____	_____

Automobile _____ _____

Tax instalments made/withheld_____ _____

Other (specify) _____ _____

   Subtotal $_____ $_____

Non-Liquid Assets   **You**   **Your Spouse**
(Take longer to convert into
cash or to accrue total
financial benefit)

Business interests $_____ $_____

Long-term receivables, loans _____ _____

Deferred income plans _____ _____

Interest in trusts _____ _____

Tax shelters _____ _____

Principal residence _____ _____

Other real estate _____ _____
(e.g., second home, or
revenue or investment property)

U.S./foreign assets _____ _____
(e.g., Snowbird mobile home,
condo)

Personal property _____ _____

Valuable assets (e.g., art, _____ _____
antiques, jewellery)

Other (specify) _____ _____

   Subtotal $_____ $_____

Total Assets (A) $_____ $_____

Current Liabilities (Currently due within 1 year, or on demand)	**You**	**Your Spouse**
Bank loans (Currently due or on line of credit demand, or within 1 year)	$ _____	$ _____
Credit cards/charge accounts	_____	_____
Income tax owing	_____	_____
Alimony	_____	_____
Child support	_____	_____
Monthly rent	_____	_____
Other	_____	_____
Subtotal	$ _____	$ _____

Long-Term Liabilities (Generally not due for over 1 year)	**You**	**Your Spouse**
Term loan	$ _____	$ _____
Mortgages	_____	_____
– principal residence	_____	_____
– other property (investment, revenue, recreational, or commercial)	_____	_____
Other	_____	_____
Subtotal	$ _____	$ _____
Total Liabilities (B)	$ _____	$ _____
Net worth before tax (A minus B)	$ _____	$ _____
Tax cost if assets liquidated (if any)	$ _____	$ _____
Net worth after tax	$ _____	$ _____

C. CURRENT AND PROJECTED RETIREMENT OR SNOWBIRD MONTHLY INCOME AND EXPENSES

	Current	Projected at Retirement

I. **Income** (Average monthly income, actual or estimated)

	Current	Projected at Retirement
Salary, bonuses, and commissions	$ _____	$ _____
Dividends	$ _____	$ _____
Interest income	$ _____	$ _____
Pension income	$ _____	$ _____
Other	$ _____	$ _____
Total Monthly Income	_____ (A)	_____ (X)

II. **Expenses** (In Canada and the United States)

Regular monthly payments on:

	Current	Projected at Retirement
Rent or mortgage	$ _____	$ _____
Automobile(s)	$ _____	$ _____
Appliances/TV	$ _____	$ _____
Home improvement loan	$ _____	$ _____
Credit cards/charge accounts (not covered elsewhere)	$ _____	$ _____
Personal loans	$ _____	$ _____
Medical plan	$ _____	$ _____
Instalment and other loans	$ _____	$ _____
Life insurance premiums	$ _____	$ _____
House insurance premiums	$ _____	$ _____
Other insurance premiums (auto, extended out-of-country medical, etc.)	$ _____	$ _____

RRSP deductions $ _____ $ _____

Pension fund (employer) $ _____ $ _____

Investment plan(s) $ _____ $ _____

Miscellaneous $ _____ $ _____

Other $ _____ $ _____

                                             $ _____ $ _____
Total Regular Monthly Payments
                                             $ _____ $ _____
Household operating expenses:
                                             $ _____ $ _____
Telephone
                                             $ _____ $ _____
Gas and electricity
                                             $ _____ $ _____
Heat
                                             $ _____ $ _____
Water and garbage
                                             $ _____ $ _____
Other household expenses
(repairs, maintenance, etc.)
                                             $ _____ $ _____
Cable
                                             $ _____ $ _____
Other
                                             $ _____ $ _____
Total Household Operating
Expenses
                                             $ _____ $ _____
Food expenses:
                                             $ _____ $ _____
At home
                                             $ _____ $ _____
Away from home
                                             $ _____ $ _____
Total Food Expenses
                                             $ _____ $ _____
Personal expenses:
                                             $ _____ $ _____
Clothing, cleaning, laundry
                                             $ _____ $ _____
Drugs
                                             $ _____ $ _____
Transportation (other than auto)

Medical/dental	$ _____	$ _____
Day care	$ _____	$ _____
Education (self)	$ _____	$ _____
Education (children)	$ _____	$ _____
Dues (e.g., union or association)	$ _____	$ _____
Gifts, donations, and dues	$ _____	$ _____
Travel	$ _____	$ _____
Recreation	$ _____	$ _____
Newspapers, magazines, books	$ _____	$ _____
Automobile maintenance, gas, and parking	$ _____	$ _____
Spending money, allowances	$ _____	$ _____
Other	$ _____	$ _____
Total Personal Expenses	$ _____	$ _____

Tax expenses:

Federal and provincial income taxes	$ _____	$ _____
Home property taxes	$ _____	$ _____
Other	$ _____	$ _____
Total Tax Expenses	$ _____	$ _____

III. Summary of Expenses

Regular monthly payments	$ _____	$ _____
Household operating expenses	$ _____	$ _____
Food expenses	$ _____	$ _____
Personal expenses	$ _____	$ _____

Tax expenses $ _____ $ _____

Total Monthly Expenses $ _____ (B) $ _____ (Y)

Total Monthly Disposable Income Available
(subtract total monthly expenses from total monthly income) $ _____ (A–B) $ _____ (X–Y)

Total Annual Disposal Income Available
(multiply figures above by 12) $ _____ $ _____

D. BANKING INFORMATION

1) **Bank Accounts** (or accounts at trust company or credit union)

			Balance in Account		
Bank	Type and # of Acct.	You	Your Spouse	Joint	
1. _____	_____	$ _____	$ _____	$ _____	
2. _____	_____	$ _____	$ _____	$ _____	
3. _____	_____	$ _____	$ _____	$ _____	

2) Term Deposits

			Balance in Account		
Bank	Terms	You	Your Spouse	Joint	
1. _____	_____	$ _____	$ _____	$ _____	
2. _____	_____	$ _____	$ _____	$ _____	
3. _____	_____	$ _____	$ _____	$ _____	

3) Bank Loans

Bank	Use of Funds	Terms: Payments, Interest, Rate, Due Date	Security	You	Balance Owing by Your Spouse	Joint
1. _____	_____	_____	_____	$____	$____	$____
2. _____	_____	_____	_____	$____	$____	$____
3. _____	_____	_____	_____	$____	$____	$____

4) **Loan Guarantees**

Provide details of any guarantees you or your spouse have issued for the debts of other people or companies.

Nature of Debt	Relationship to Debtor	Degree of Risk	Amount of Guarantee	Person Who Signed Guarantee		
				You	Your Spouse	Joint
1. _____	_____	_____	$_____	$_____	$_____	$_____
2. _____	_____	_____	$_____	$_____	$_____	$_____
3. _____	_____	_____	$_____	$_____	$_____	$_____

E. REAL ESTATE

Property #1

Date Acquired: _____

Address: _____   Registered Owner(s):

_____   _____

_____   _____

Type of Property: House _____ Condo _____ Mobile Home _____

Co-op _____

Principal Residence: Snowbird Residence: Rental Property:

Yes___ No___   Yes___ No___   Yes___ No___

Insurance Company: _____

Policy Number: Amount of Coverage:

   Original cost $ _____

   Cost of additions $ _____

   Current value $ _____

   Less mortgages $ _____

   Equity $ _____

Has the property been appraised?   Yes ___ No ___

When _____ Value $ _____

Terms of mortgage(s): _____

_____

_____

Property #2

Date Acquired: _____

Address: Registered Owner(s):

_____   _____

_____   _____

Type of Property: House _____ Condo _____ Mobile Home _____

Co-op _____

Principal Residence: Snowbird Residence: Rental Property:

Yes ___ No ___   Yes ___ No ___   Yes ___ No ___

Insurance Company: _____

Policy Number: Amount of Coverage:

Original cost $ _____

Cost of additions $ _____

Current value $ _____

Less mortgages $ _____

Equity $ _____

Has the property been appraised?   Yes ___ No ___

When _____ Value $ _____

Terms of mortgage(s): _____

_____

F. PERSONAL PROPERTY

		Current Value	
	You	**Your Spouse**	**Joint**
a) Household furnishings	$ _____	$ _____	$ _____
b) Automobiles	$ _____	$ _____	$ _____
c) Trailers, RVs	$ _____	$ _____	$ _____
d) Jewellery	$ _____	$ _____	$ _____
e) Boats	$ _____	$ _____	$ _____
f) Coin collection	$ _____	$ _____	$ _____
g) Stamp collection	$ _____	$ _____	$ _____
h) Paintings, prints, sculptures	$ _____	$ _____	$ _____
i) Antiques	$ _____	$ _____	$ _____
j) Other	$ _____	$ _____	$ _____

G. INVESTMENT PORTFOLIO

Description	**V-day Value if Applicable**	**Cost**	**Current Value by Ownership**		
			You	**Your Spouse**	**Joint**
1. Stocks (list)					
_____	$ _____	$ _____	$ _____	$ _____	$ _____
_____	$ _____	$ _____	$ _____	$ _____	$ _____
_____	$ _____	$ _____	$ _____	$ _____	$ _____
_____	$ _____	$ _____	$ _____	$ _____	$ _____
_____	$ _____	$ _____	$ _____	$ _____	$ _____
_____	$ _____	$ _____	$ _____	$ _____	$ _____
Total			$ _____	$ _____	$ _____

Description	V-day Value if Applicable	Cost	Current Value by Ownership		
			You	Your Spouse	Joint

2. Bonds (list)

_____	$_____	$_____	$_____	$_____	$_____
_____	$_____	$_____	$_____	$_____	$_____
_____	$_____	$_____	$_____	$_____	$_____
_____	$_____	$_____	$_____	$_____	$_____
_____	$_____	$_____	$_____	$_____	$_____
Total			$_____	$_____	$_____
Total Stocks and Bonds			$_____	$_____	$_____

3. Mortgages and Loans Owing to You

Short-term

Borrower	Terms	Current Principal Outstanding to:		
		You	Your Spouse	Joint
_____	_____	$_____	$_____	$_____
_____	_____	$_____	$_____	$_____
_____	_____	$_____	$_____	$_____

Long-term

Borrower	Terms	Current Principal Outstanding to:		
		You	Your Spouse	Joint
_____		$_____	$_____	$_____
_____		$_____	$_____	$_____
_____		$_____	$_____	$_____
Total		$_____	$_____	$_____

H. TAX SHELTERS

	Current Market Value			Cost		
Brief Description	**You**	**Your Spouse**	**Joint**	**You**	**Your Spouse**	**Joint**
1. _____ _____	$_____	$_____	$_____	$_____	$_____	$_____
2. _____ _____	$_____	$_____	$_____	$_____	$_____	$_____
3. _____ _____	$_____	$_____	$_____	$_____	$_____	$_____
4. _____ _____	$_____	$_____	$_____	$_____	$_____	$_____
Total	$_____	$_____	$_____	$_____	$_____	$_____

I. INVESTMENTS/OWNERSHIPS IN BUSINESSES

	Business		
1. Where You Are the Investor	**1**	**2**	**Total**
Name of business	_____	_____	
Nature of business	_____	_____	
Your % equity interest in business	_____	_____	
Approximate fair market value of your business interest	$_____	$_____	
	$_____	$_____	$_____

	Business		
2. Where Your Spouse Is the Investor	**1**	**2**	**Total**
Name of business	_____	_____	
Nature of business	_____	_____	
Your % equity interest in business	_____	_____	
Approximate fair market value of your business interest	$_____	$_____	
	$_____	$_____	$_____

J. INSURANCE

1. Life Insurance Coverage

	Policies Where You Are the Insured			**Total**
	1	**2**	**3**	
Company	____	____	____	
Face value	$____	$____	$____	$____
Date of policy	____	____	____	
Type of policy	____	____	____	
Cash surrender value (if applicable)	$____	$____	$____	$____
Policy number	____	____	____	
Loan balances	$____	$____	$____	$____
Premium (annual)	____	____	____	$____
Beneficiary	____	____	____	

	Policies Where Your Spouse Is the Insured			**Total**
	1	**2**	**3**	
Company	____	____	____	
Face value	$____	$____	$____	$____
Date of policy	____	____	____	
Type of policy	____	____	____	
Cash surrender value (if applicable)	$____	$____	$____	$____
Policy number	____	____	____	
Loan balances	$____	$____	$____	$____
Premium (annual)	____	____	____	$____
Beneficiary	____	____	____	

2. Disability Insurance Coverage

Company	Policy Number	Annual Payment		Length of Coverage	Other Terms
		You	Your Spouse		
1. _____	_____	$ ____	$ ____	_____	_____
2. _____	_____	$ ____	$ ____	_____	_____
3. _____	_____	$ ____	$ ____	_____	_____
Total		$ ____	$ ____		

3. Personal Property, Home, or Vehicle Insurance

Company	Policy Number	Type of Coverage	Property Coverage	Amount of Coverage
1. _____	_____	_____	_____	$ _____
2. _____	_____	_____	_____	$ _____
3. _____	_____	_____	_____	$ _____
			Total	$ _____

4. When did you and your spouse last review and, if necessary, update your insurance coverage?

Type	Date	You	Your Spouse
Life	_____	_____	_____
Disability	_____	_____	_____
Personal Property	_____	_____	_____
Other	_____	_____	_____

K. PROJECTED/POTENTIAL FINANCIAL NEEDS

1. At what age do you plan to retire? _____

2. At what age does your spouse plan to retire? _____

3. Are you a citizen, or a resident, of another country? Yes _____ No _____
   If so, what country? _____

4. Do you and your spouse plan to become non-residents of Canada?
   Yes _____ No _____ If so, when? _____

5. Are you planning to reside or are currently residing 3 to 6 months a year in
   the United States? Yes _____ No _____ In another country?
   Yes _____ No _____ If so, which? _____

6. Have you thoroughly checked out the implications for your pension plan or
   health plan eligibility by being away an extended period?
   Yes _____ No _____

7. Do you or your spouse expect to receive any lump-sum retirement benefits?
   Yes _____ No _____   If so, how much?

	You	**Your Spouse**
	$ _____	$ _____

   From what source?_____

8. Do you or your spouse anticipate any employment after retirement (part-time
   or full-time) or income from part-time or full-time self-employment in a home-
   based or small business?

	You	**Your Spouse**
Estimated annual earnings	$ _____	$ _____

9. Do you or your spouse anticipate any major changes in your financial situation in the:
   – short term (less than 2 years)?   Yes _____ No _____
   – medium term (2 to 5 years)?   Yes _____ No _____
   – long term (more than 5 years)?   Yes _____ No _____

10. What combined level of income will you require in retirement (current year
    dollars)? _____

11. How many years of retirement have you projected? _____

12. If you or your spouse died or became disabled, what income would be
    required to maintain your family's current standard of living (current dollars)?

	You	**Your Spouse**
Until youngest child no longer financially dependent	$ _____	$ _____
Until age 60	$ _____	$ _____
Until age 65	$ _____	$ _____
Over age 65	$ _____	$ _____

13. What level of inflation do you anticipate will prevail during the time periods in
    #12? Have you factored that inflation factor into your projected future finan-
    cial needs? Yes _____ No _____

L. WHERE YOUR RETIREMENT INCOME WILL COME FROM

**Estimated Monthly
Retirement Income**

	You	**Your Spouse**
Employer's pension plan	$_____	$_____
Canada Pension Plan	$_____	$_____
Old Age Security	$_____	$_____
Guaranteed Income Supplement	$_____	$_____
RRSP/RRIF retirement income	$_____	$_____
LIF income	$_____	$_____
Annuity income	$_____	$_____
Profit-sharing fund payout	$_____	$_____
Salary expected from any earned income in retirement	$_____	$_____
Any other fees, payments for services	$_____	$_____
Disability insurance payments	$_____	$_____
Income expected from a business (part-time or full-time, home-based or small business)	$_____	$_____
Income expected from real estate investments or revenue property	$_____	$_____
Income from renting out part of the house (e.g., basement suite/boarders)	$_____	$_____
Savings account interest (credit union, bank, trust company, other)	$_____	$_____
Federal or provincial savings bonds interest, term deposit interest, guaranteed investment certificate interest, other	$_____	$_____

Other investments: stocks, bonds, mutual funds, etc.	$_____	$_____
Investment income from any expected inheritance	$_____	$_____
Income from other investments you expect to create income	$_____	$_____
Other income sources: alimony, social assistance, UIC, etc.	$_____	$_____
Total Expected Monthly Income:	$_____	$_____
Total Annual Income of you and your spouse (Multiply monthly incomes by 12)	$_____	$_____

M. RETIREMENT LIFE VALUES, INTERESTS, AND PREFERENCES

Read the following list of life values, interests, and preferences. Assign a value of importance to each on a scale of 1 to 5; 1 is least important and 5 is most important to you. Do you see a pattern to your answers? What steps are you taking to attain these objectives? How do your interests, values, and preferences rank with those of your spouse or partner? Are they compatible?

	You	Your Spouse
• Achievement (sense of accomplishment)	_____	_____
• Adventure (risks, excitement, exploration)	_____	_____
• Affection (giving and receiving love, warmth, caring)	_____	_____
• Emotional health (ability to handle internal and external conflict)	_____	_____
• Expertness (being good at something important to you)	_____	_____
• Family harmony (respect, affection, and sharing)	_____	_____

- Financial independence (sufficient money   _____   _____
  for things you need and want)

- Honesty and candor (being frank and   _____   _____
  genuinely yourself)

- Leadership (having influence and authority)   _____   _____

- Meaningful career   _____   _____
  (relevant and purposeful job)

- Personal freedom (independence,   _____   _____
  making your own choices)

- Physical health (feeling of well-being   _____   _____
  and vitality)

- Pleasure (satisfaction, enjoyment, fun)   _____   _____

- Recognition (respect, prestige, being   _____   _____
  well-known)

- Security (having a stable and secure future)   _____   _____

- Self-growth (continuing development,   _____   _____
  education, and exploration)

- Self-reliance (paying your own way)   _____   _____

- Service (contributing to others' needs)   _____   _____

- Spirituality (religious beliefs,   _____   _____
  meaning of life)

- Wisdom (insight, mature understanding)   _____   _____

- Other (Specify)   _____   _____

_____ _____   _____

_____ _____   _____

_____ _____   _____

_____ _____   _____

_____ _____   _____

N. RETIREMENT PLANNING GOALS

	You	Your Spouse

A. Financial Goal

- Have you determined when your children will finish their schooling?   _____   _____

- Have you determined when any other dependents you have will no longer require your financial support?   _____   _____

- Have you determined when your mortgage will be paid off?   _____   _____

- Have you checked up on the company pension you will receive in retirement, when it will be at the maximum, and when you are eligible to commence receiving benefits?   _____   _____

- Have you determined when you can get the maximum income from your RRSPs?   _____   _____

- Have you determined when you will become eligible for Canada Pension Plan and Old Age Security payments?   _____   _____

- Are you working towards supplementing your pension?   _____   _____

- Have you checked out discounts for seniors on transportation, entertainment, prescription drugs, banking services, etc. (in Canada and the U.S.)?   _____   _____

- Have you explored the kind of work you would like to do and where to find it?   _____   _____

- Are you investigating retirement income plans to convert your RRSP into (such as an RRIF or annuity)?   _____   _____

- Have you found out whether your hobby can earn extra cash for you?   _____   _____

- Are you checking out "tax breaks" for seniors ＿＿＿＿ ＿＿＿＿
and organizing your income to take
maximum advantage of them?

B. Residence Goal

- Have you decided whether to live with, or ＿＿＿＿ ＿＿＿＿
close to, your family?

- Have you decided where you want to live in ＿＿＿＿ ＿＿＿＿
retirement?

- Have you checked out the adequacy of ＿＿＿＿ ＿＿＿＿
transportation facilities?

- Have you checked out how to make your ＿＿＿＿ ＿＿＿＿
home safe from break-ins or accidents?

- Have you decided whether to sell your house ＿＿＿＿ ＿＿＿＿
or condominium and move to a smaller one,
rent an apartment, or live in a retirement
community or recreational vehicle park?

C. Activity/Recreational Goal

- Have you researched interesting voluntary ＿＿＿＿ ＿＿＿＿
work that you might do?

- Have you checked out travel, cruises, or ＿＿＿＿ ＿＿＿＿
other tours that you might enjoy?

- Have you found out how you can become ＿＿＿＿ ＿＿＿＿
more active in community affairs?

- Have you determined what you want to do in ＿＿＿＿ ＿＿＿＿
retirement?

- Have you checked out educational courses ＿＿＿＿ ＿＿＿＿
of interest to you?

- Have you assessed your skills, attributes, ＿＿＿＿ ＿＿＿＿
talents, interests, values, strengths,
and weaknesses?

- Have you checked out social activities for ＿＿＿＿ ＿＿＿＿
yourself and your partner?

D. Health Goal

- Are you doing everything possible to stay in _____ _____ good physical and mental condition?

- Have you investigated the medical facilities _____ _____ available in the community you intend to retire to?

- Have you researched the provincial medical _____ _____ coverage you obtain if you are travelling outside your province but within Canada, or travelling outside Canada (U.S. or elsewhere)?

- Are you working out a retirement plan with _____ _____ the active participation of your partner?

- Are you working at maintaining good _____ _____ relationships with family and friends?

- Have you obtained adequate travel medical _____ _____ insurance coverage to supplement your provincial coverage?

E. Estate Goal

- Have you recorded the location of your _____ _____ family assets (property, bank accounts, stocks, bonds, etc.), including documents and related information, and left one copy with your executor and another copy in your safety deposit box?

- Have you made or updated your will and _____ _____ power of attorney, and confirmed the availability, willingness, and suitability of the executor, trustee, and/or guardian?

- Have you checked out the tax implications of _____ _____ transferring specific personal or business assets to your beneficiaries?

- Have you told your family, a trusted friend, _____ _____ and your executor where your records are located?

- Have you consulted a lawyer, tax _____ _____ accountant, and financial advisor?

Reader Input, Educational Seminars, and Newsletter

If you have thoughts or suggestions that you believe would be helpful for future editions of this book, or if you are interested in having the author give a seminar or presentation to your group or association, anywhere in Canada or the United States, please write to the Canadian Retirement Planning Institute (see address below).

The institute offers a wide range of objective educational programs to the public and for organizations, associations, and companies throughout Canada and the United States on issues of particular interest to those over 40. Topics cover personal, retirement, and estate planning, money management, wills, powers of attorney, immigration, investment, taxes, real estate, and other topical, relevant subjects.

A newsletter designed specifically for Canadian Snowbirds who live part-time in the United States is also available. It is called *The Canadian Snowbird Advisor* and covers relevant and topical issues on such as matters as financial, retirement, and estate planning, tax and legal issues, immigration, real estate, investments, and money management. It is an indispensable source of objective and practical professional advice that will save you money, time, and stress. Ordering information can be obtained by contacting the Canadian Retirement Planning Institute.

Canadian Retirement Planning Institute Inc.
#300 - 3665 Kingsway
Vancouver, BC
V5R 5W2
Tel: (604) 436-3337
Fax: (604) 436-9155

About the Author

Douglas A. Gray, LL.B., is a lawyer, consultant, and businessman and Canada's most published author, with 17 best-selling business and personal finance books. He recently retired from his law practice at the age of 50 to concentrate on his educational interests of writing and public speaking.

He is an internationally recognized expert on financial and retirement planning and has given seminars to over 250,000 people nationally and internationally in his areas of expertise. He is a member of the National Speakers Association.

Mr. Gray is frequently interviewed as an authority on financial matters by publications such as the *Financial Post, Financial Times, Profit,* and the *Globe and Mail.* He is a regular guest expert on personal finance issues on CBC-TV *Newsworld.* He also writes a nationally syndicated weekly newspaper column on personal finance and real estate issues, with an estimated readership of over three million. In addition, he is a regular columnist for *Profit, Computer Paper, Opportunities Canada,* and *Canadian Moneysaver* magazines, as well as a periodic contributor to the *Globe and Mail* and *Maclean's.*

He is the president of the Canadian Retirement Planning Institute Inc. This organization offers objective educational programs nationally on a wide range of issues related to personal finance, tax, estate planning, and retirement planning that are of interest to Canadians and Snowbirds.

Mr. Gray lives in Vancouver, British Columbia.

Other Best-Selling Books

by Douglas A. Gray

☐ **Risk-Free Retirement: The Complete Canadian Planning Guide**
(with Tom Delaney, Graham Cunningham, Les Solomon and
Dr. Des Dwyer)
ISBN 0-07-551274-2

☐ **Condo Buying Made Easy: The Canadian Guide to Apartment and
Townhouse Condos, Co-ops and Timeshares (2nd edition)**
ISBN 0-07-551791-4

☐ **Home Inc.: The Canadian Home-Based Business Guide (2nd edition)**
(with Diana L. Gray)
ISBN 0-07-551558-X

☐ **The Complete Canadian Small Business Guide (2nd edition)**
(with Diana L. Gray)
ISBN 0-07-551661-6

☐ **Making Money in Real Estate: The Canadian Residential Investment
Guide**
ISBN 0-07-549596-1

☐ **Mortgages Made Easy: The Canadian Guide to Home Financing**
ISBN 0-07-551344-7

These books and others by Douglas A. Gray are
available at your local bookstore or by contacting:
McGraw-Hill Ryerson Limited
Consumer & Professional Books Division
300 Water Street, Whitby, Ontario L1N 9B6
Tel: 1-800-565-5758 / Fax: 1-800-463-5885 (orders only)